THE NATIONALIST

How A.M. Naik Overcame Great Odds to Transform Larsen & Toubro into a Global Powerhouse

Minhaz Merchant

1817

HARPER BUSINESS

First published in hardback in India in 2017 by Harper Business
An imprint of HarperCollins *Publishers*

HarperCollins Publishers India, Cyber City, Building 10-A, Gurugram,
Haryana-122002, India
www.harpercollins.co.in

2 4 6 8 10 9 7 5 3 1

P-ISBN: 978-93-5277-288-9
E-ISBN: 978-93-5277-289-6

Typeset in 11/15.7 Book Antiqua
By Saanvi Graphics Noida

Printed and bound at
MicroPrints India, New Delhi

MIX
Paper
FSC FSC™ C218906

This product is made of FSC®-certified and other controlled material.

HarperCollins Publishers, Macken House, 39/40 Mayor Street
Upper, Dublin 1, D01 C9W8, Ireland

For my wife Kahini
and children Suhail and Tehzeeb

Contents

Author's Note

WHAT BEGAN AS a biography of an extraordinary business leader morphed, during its writing, into a compelling story of triumph against the odds.

Anil Manibhai Naik was uprooted from a comfortable suburban life in Mumbai at the age of ten. His father, a senior teacher at a prestigious Mumbai school, was influenced by Mahatma Gandhi's call: 'India lives in its villages'. The Naik family moved lock, stock and barrel to rural south Gujarat. Young Anil spent the next several years sitting in a village school classroom on a *gobar* floor. It toughened him for the challenges that lay ahead.

Over the decades, with an engineering degree in hand, Naik would rise through the ranks at Larsen & Toubro (L&T) to become its chairman and managing director. L&T is not an ordinary company and Naik not an ordinary business leader. Outspoken in his views, Naik's candour and clear-headed assessment of the challenges that face the country and its economy mine a rich vein of insight.

L&T is involved in virtually every critical national project: India's first nuclear-powered submarine; strategic weapon and missile systems; space exploration, including maiden missions to the moon and Mars; global infrastructure; airports; metro rail systems; and almost all of India's nuclear power plants.

A highlight of Naik's fifty-three-year career is the successful demerger of L&T's cement business, UltraTech, and its sale to the Aditya Birla Group. Fiercely protective of L&T's professional character, Naik structured the historic demerger in such a way that it ringfenced L&T from hostile takeovers. He created the L&T Employees Welfare Foundation, which was enabled to acquire a 15 per cent shareholding in the company. A takeover target for both the Ambanis and Birlas, L&T's independence was preserved by Naik.

THIS IS a story of remarkable grit, ambition and entrepreneurial management on the part of a man who put in sixteen-hour workdays over more than half a century. As Naik says today: 'L&T is my temple.'

Work is Naik's worship. And it has been so from the time he joined as a junior engineer in March 1965 and up to the present day. At sixteen hours a day, he says, only half in jest, he has devoted 106 years to L&T: 'I will be a happy man when I retire from this wonderful company of ours.'

What emerges emphatically from Naik's storied career is his sense of nationalism. It permeates his thinking and informs his actions. Naik's nationalism is synonymous with advancing the national interest by building a strong and self-reliant India.

Naik has an intimidating presence but a soft core. Throughout his long career, he has demonstrated how uncompromising standards of excellence can blend seamlessly with a humane approach.

While growing L&T's revenue twenty-five times and market capitalization eighty times since becoming CEO and managing director in 1999, Naik has successfully fought battles with India's largest business groups, safeguarded L&T from future takeovers, made thousands of company employees millionaires through stock options, and transformed L&T into a global engineering and technology powerhouse. International operations today contribute 34 per cent to L&T's total group revenue.

L&T, under Naik's watch, has diversified into new-economy businesses, including high-end technology and engineering services, finance and global infrastructure. It has simultaneously strengthened its footprint in defence, manufacturing and complex turnkey projects. As Naik says, rhetorically: 'There is no company in the world – show me one – which can do what L&T does. In the US there is a shipyard that does only aircraft carriers, another shipyard that does only nuclear-powered submarines, but they don't do anything else. Here we do nuclear-powered submarines, aerospace, nuclear reactors, all kinds of things.'

Indeed, no other company worldwide comes close in comparison. The American engineering giant Bechtel, Japan's Daiwa House, South Korea's Doosan, China's CSCEC and Sweden's Skanska are roughly the same size as or smaller in cost-adjusted revenue than L&T – but they lack its breadth of operations, range of heavy engineering skills and the ability to design, develop and execute some of the world's most challenging infrastructure projects.

ABOVE ALL, Naik is a devoted family man and a generous philanthropist. He has already donated over 75 per cent of his income to a slew of charities through family trusts focused on healthcare, education and social transformation.

Naik's father, Manibhai, a teacher who devoted his life to serving the rural poor, is his role model. Manibhai taught his son to be fearless and honest. He said to him: *If you are in the right, you have nothing to fear.*

Naik has displayed courage and an inexhaustible reservoir of energy during his long career in L&T, dealing with violent union leaders as well as taking calculated risks in new businesses. With annual sales of Rs 1,20,000 crore and market capitalization of Rs 1,60,000 crore, L&T is today one of India's most valuable companies – and in market cap ahead of public sector giant National

Thermal Power Corporation (NTPC) and private sector telecom major Bharti Airtel.

This then is the story of a man who surmounted great odds to reach the pinnacle of success. It demonstrates more than anything else that honesty, the quality Naik prizes most, in the end pays the greatest dividend of all: the respect of your peers, the loyalty of your colleagues and the affection of your family.

Prologue

Making of a Global Leader

CHICAGO, 17 NOVEMBER 2001, 2.20 a.m. Anil Manibhai Naik, CEO and managing director of Larsen & Toubro (L&T), stretched his legs in his hotel room as he prepared to turn in for the night. It had been a cold, windy Chicago day and he was tired after an exhausting round of meetings with leading American CEOs keen to partner with L&T in a slew of technology projects.

Naik's mobile phone rang. He was surprised at receiving a call so late at night, but he immediately recognized the crackling voice at the other end: Mohan Karnani, president of L&T's cement business. 'Sir,' Karnani said without preamble, '*apna maalik badal gaya hai*. We have a new *maalik*.'

The new *maalik* was Kumar Mangalam Birla, chairman of the Aditya Birla Group.

Within minutes, Naik's phone rang again. It was Anil Ambani, managing director of Reliance Industries. Charming as ever, though unmindful of the ten-and-a-half-hour time difference between Mumbai (where it was early afternoon) and Chicago, Ambani said softly: 'Anilbhai, you never wanted us. So we are going. We have sold the entire shareholding of Reliance in Larsen & Toubro to Kumar Mangalam Birla.'

Naik absorbed the information calmly. His mind was whirring but he remained impassive. After exchanging pleasantries with Ambani, he tried to sleep.

At 7 a.m., Chicago time, Naik's phone rang again. This time it was Kumar Mangalam Birla. He was, as he always is, unfailingly polite. Apologizing for calling so early in the morning (in Mumbai it was already evening), Birla said quietly: 'You didn't come to us, Naikji. So we have come to you.'

With that the battle lines were drawn. The Aditya Birla Group's flagship company, Grasim, had acquired the Ambanis' shareholding in L&T in an all-cash deal. Now Kumar Mangalam Birla wanted more. L&T was an attractive target, so attractive that two of India's largest business families—first the Ambanis and now the Birlas—coveted it.

Smiling beatifically today, sixteen years later, Naik says: 'In the end we kept L&T independent. We ringfenced it from future takeover attempts by setting up the L&T Employees Welfare Foundation that eventually bought the Birla stake. And the Birlas got our demerged cement business that added to their cement production capacity. It relieved us of a non-core, asset-heavy business, making us an AAA-rated company by drastically cutting our debt-equity ratio. It was a win-win for all.'

The distinguished public activist and chartered accountant S. Gurumurthy, who played a key role in the negotiations, says today: 'The Birla episode proved that all's well that ends well. L&T and the Aditya Birla Group both gained. The Birlas got cement and L&T retained ownership of the rest of the company's businesses.'

Naik himself is sanguine: 'I would say, let us put all this behind us, both parties were happy with the arrangement. When Kumar Mangalam Birla shook hands with me after the deal was struck, he said to me: "Mr Naik, your name will go down in history because you have given ownership of L&T to the employees." It is a first in the annals of corporate India.'

It was. But between the phone calls on that chilly Chicago night in November 2001 and the final *denouement,* there would be financial engineering and fierce negotiations that lasted nearly three years and held corporate India in thrall.

MANY HAVE tried to capture the essence of Larsen & Toubro. The company is globally unique: it builds nuclear reactors, nuclear-powered submarines, systems for satellites and missiles, artillery guns, oil and gas platforms, airports and metros. Its activities do not end here. It also has a large footprint in infrastructure, infotech, finance, technology services and realty.

Describing L&T as an Indian multinational would be an understatement. It is, in fact, several Indian multinationals under one overarching corporate canopy. Complexity, though, can be a double-edged sword. L&T has grown so rapidly in the past fifteen years that it resembles a Korean *chaebol* – diverse, global, but bound together by one philosophy: engineering and technological excellence.

No other company worldwide comes close in comparison. The American engineering giant Bechtel, Japan's Daiwa House, South Korea's Doosan, China's CSCEC and Sweden's Skanska are roughly the same size as or smaller in cost-adjusted revenue than L&T, but they lack its breadth of operations, its range of heavy engineering skills and its ability to design, develop and execute some of the world's most challenging and complex infrastructure projects.

With an annual turnover of over $17 billion in 2016-17 and a market capitalization of nearly $25 billion, L&T is one of India's ten largest companies on both parameters. With just under 1,00,000 full-time employees and around 2,50,000 others employed on ongoing projects, it is among Asia's biggest employers. As much as 34 per cent of its annual revenue now comes from international projects.

A deeply felt sense of nationalism – a desire to build a strong, self-reliant India – drove Naik from the time he was a college student. L&T provided him an ideal platform from which to fulfil that lifelong mission; here he could leverage his engineering skills, tenacity and capacity for hard work. These would become legion, earning him the sobriquet 'Mr Infrastructure' from Deepak Parekh, chairman of one of India's most successful banks, HDFC.

INDIAN CEOs fall into three broad categories. The first consists of affable heirs who slide effortlessly into power by virtue of their family. To them the company is an heirloom. Younger inheritors, fresh out of Wharton Business School or Harvard University, go through the grind before occupying the corner office. That is *de rigeur* in modern business and gives the dynastic succession a patina of meritocracy.

The second category comprises professionals who have risen through the ranks over the years. Many head multinationals. Most are content to be professional CEOs for the rest of their careers under the watchful eye of the promoter-investor who recognizes the wisdom of separating management from ownership. The third category, newly minted, is defined by the VC-funded start-up entrepreneur. He is fearless, innovative and often a failure. Out of every ten start-ups that VCs and PEs fund, one turns out to be ten-bagger, four are moderately successful and the remaining five could go bankrupt any time.

Naik defies categorization. He did not inherit L&T. He is a professional, but cast in a completely different mould from career CEOs who run multinationals. And he is no wet-behind-the-ears VC-funded entrepreneur who treats success and failure as natural cousins.

Naik has ploughed a category of his own: the entrepreneurial professional who has risen through the ranks without patronage, who treats his employees like stakeholders, and has created a culture of innovation and technological excellence. The combination of toughness and a caring approach towards employees has made L&T one of India's most admired companies.

Naik became CEO and managing director of L&T at fifty-seven, an age when most highly paid professionals like him would be contemplating a comfortable retirement. Not Naik. Four years later, at sixty-one, he took over as chairman and managing director of L&T. Naik successfully demerged and sold the company's cement business to the Aditya Birla Group. He set up the L&T Employees Welfare Foundation. It made him an icon within L&T. Then came another extraordinary phase in his career: between 2003 and 2017, Naik transformed L&T from a blue-blooded but stodgy engineering company into a technology-driven global powerhouse with diverse interests in finance, infotech, global infrastructure, realty, shipbuilding, nuclear power and defence. Revenue and net profit rose exponentially. L&T's Hazira manufacturing complex, Vadodara's Knowledge City and the Kattupalli shipyard became symbols of world-class Indian engineering and technology.

As *Forbes India* noted in its 3 October 2014 issue: 'Naval analyst Commodore (Retd.) Ranjit Rai has been following L&T's progress over the years. He says, "It is India's equivalent of Bechtel, the US engineering multinational, and has excellent facilities. It is the only one that had the capability to work with titanium steel and build the nosecone and stern shafting for the *Arihant* nuclear-powered submarine."'

Some affectionately call Naik the 'bull terrier CEO' for his penchant to be a hands-on, hard-driving leader who expects from his colleagues nothing less than absolute commitment to L&T. Since joining L&T in 1965, Naik has led by personal example. He was among the first to arrive to work and among the last to leave office. His surprise night visits to the engineering workshops in Powai early in his career are now the stuff of legend and L&T lore.

But behind Naik's gruff exterior lies a softer side. He is a devoted family man. He spends time with the extended Naik family. And he never forgets the advice his father gave him when he was in college: be fearless.

Naik has seen the vicissitudes of life: dislocation from city to village at the age of ten, mid-career stagnation, and personal tragedy when his two-year-old granddaughter, Nirali, died of blood cancer in 2007. They have tempered him like fine steel, giving him an iron will. It is this will that has seen him through crises when legacy business groups tried to take over L&T or when he had to fight internal battles to make L&T the extraordinary company it has become under his leadership.

AT FIRST glance Dhirubhai Ambani and Anil Naik have little in common. The former battled controversies throughout his career even as he built Reliance Industries into India's largest private sector company. In contrast, Naik rose from the shopfloor to the boardroom, climbing rapidly up the executive ladder. Look closer though, and similarities surface. Both came from middle-class Gujarati backgrounds. Their fathers were both teachers. Dhirubhai, born a decade before Naik, went to Aden in 1949 at the age of seventeen as a petrol pump attendant, returned to India seven years later and worked for over two decades before launching Reliance Industries' initial public offering (IPO) against severe odds in 1977, months after the draconian Emergency had been revoked. He went on to become the most visionary industrialist India has produced.

Naik's ascent was equally hard-won. His early education was disrupted by his family's move to a south Gujarat village. He escaped the material deprivation young Dhirubhai had endured. But both learnt the hard lessons of life at a tender age.

Hazira is the lodestar that binds the two men. Dhirubhai Ambani built his empire with one of the world's largest and most advanced petrochemical plants in Hazira. It was built by L&T. As Naik rose steadily through the ranks of L&T in the 1980s, Hazira would lie at the centre of his strategy to put L&T on the world map as a technologically sophisticated engineering company with global clients. L&T needed to ship large cutting-edge equipment directly from a jetty, bypassing congested road and rail transport. Hazira, on the banks of the Tapti river leading into the Arabian Sea, fitted the bill.

Gujarat was again the *leit motif* for both Dhirubhai Ambani and Naik. While the Ambanis built their vertically integrated business around Hazira and Jamnagar, Naik created a world-class research, design and technology knowledge centre in Vadodara a few hundred miles away. The synergy between L&T's Hazira complex and Vadodara's Knowledge City is evident: a perfect match between strong fabrication capabilities and innovative engineering design.

Throughout his career, Naik has been driven by a fierce pride in India and a strong self-belief. Dhirubhai Ambani too was driven by the conviction that anything the world could do, India could do better. Like Naik, Dhirubhai was warm, approachable and empathetic. One of my publications ran a poll to select the 'Business Leader of the 20th Century'. Dhirubhai topped the poll by some distance. In poor health at the turn of the millennium, Dhirubhai attended office for only a few hours every day and preferred to lead a quiet life. When I sent a request for an exclusive interview, Dhirubhai replied that he hadn't given one in years but that he would make a special exception if I gave him a written questionnaire. I did and, true to his word, he replied to every question with the straightforwardness and confidence that marked his work and life.

Naik was an admirer of Dhirubhai's drive and vision. He said once: 'Dhirubhai thought far ahead of his time. In 1989, he visited L&T's heavy engineering division. The workshop was fairly large, but Dhirubhai made a very perceptive observation. He said that when the Indian economy grows exponentially, this workshop would become inadequate. This shows the tremendous faith he had in the country and its economy. He encouraged us to expand our capacities. What is more, he never took no for an answer. His belief and conviction made impossible things possible. That is how he was able to take Reliance to such great heights and put India on the global map.'

Naik's own work ethic is exceptional. 'I am the greatest disciplinarian because discipline is what demonstrates your seriousness for what you do,' he says. 'It's not for show. Everyone should aspire to become a role model in that sense, and discipline is one of the key factors. Initially, in the 1990s, when we had to submit bids to ONGC, we had people who would work through the night and then straightaway in the morning go to submit the tenders. I used to sit up with them up to 2 a.m. I would then go home and return before they finally left the office in the morning to submit the tenders. I didn't have to do it. But my being there would give them strength. If the boss is doing so much, they would think, then so can we.'

Naik's self-assurance has helped him weld a strongly entrepreneurial culture with impeccable professional management in L&T. By making employees the beneficiaries of the company's prosperity through the L&T Employees Welfare Foundation, Naik cemented his reputation as a corporate leader possessing both heart and vision.

NAIK IS ceaselessly on the move. At L&T's Mumbai headquarters he cuts through paperwork with speed and clinical efficiency. He is gifted with a memory that enables him to remember telephone numbers of colleagues, even ten-digit mobile numbers. Naik speaks in staccato sentences, yet he is an excellent raconteur. Of course, he is a man unafraid to speak his mind, rarely mincing words. He carries his nationalism on his sleeve—literally. The Indian tricolour and the L&T monogram are pinned to his jacket lapel. His views on patriotism are clear-cut. Shortly after India's surgical strike on terror launch pads in Pakistan in September 2016, he wrote a personal letter of congratulations to Prime Minister Narendra Modi:

> At the outset, I wish to congratulate you on the government's effective and widely welcomed response to cross-border terrorism. Further, your intense personal efforts towards aligning international opinion in favour of India have transformed global perceptions about the subcontinent.
>
> I am proud to say that L&T has, in its own way, been contributing to strengthening India's defence. As you are probably aware, L&T is the only company in the world capable of indigenously manufacturing nuclear-powered submarines, nuclear reactors of all kinds, critical missile and weapon systems and aerospace launch systems. While there are other companies which manufacture one or the other of the above programmes, L&T is unique in that it manufactures all the above under one institution.

Naik shares some key traits with the prime minister too. Both endured hardships in childhood. Modi, of course, experienced poverty first-hand in the small town of Vadnagar in Gujarat where he was born. Naik's family was relatively well-to-do and educated. His father, Manibhai, was a teacher at the prestigious Hansraj Morarji Public School in Bombay. Five years after Independence, heeding Mahatma Gandhi's stirring call, Manibhai moved to Endhal village in south Gujarat, his father Nichchhabhai's birthplace, to teach at a small school. From a comfortable life in a metropolitan city and a modern school, young Anil was transported in 1952 to an unfamiliar village where he sat with other children in the school's rudimentary classroom on a cow-dung floor.

Modi acquired his own toughness and resilience during his teenage years, helping his father at his tea stall and attending RSS *shakhas* in the morning. He washed the clothes of other *swayamsevaks,* cleaned their rooms and lived a frugal life. As British author Andy Marino wrote in *Narendra Modi: A Political Biography*: 'It was in early

1972, just after the Bangladesh war ended, that Vakil sahib stepped in and took Narendra formally into the RSS fold. His new home was quite basic, but it was the grandest residence Narendra had lived in, and he shared it with another dozen young RSS recruits. Thus began the long apprenticeship that would lay the deep foundations of Modi's organizational expertise. He began at the very bottom. "My daily routine was as follows," said Modi: "Waking up at 5.00 a.m., fetching milk, waking everybody up, participating in morning prayers, making tea and serving everyone. It was followed by cleaning utensils, going to the *shakha*, returning and making snacks for everyone. Then I served breakfast from 8.30 a.m. to 9.00 a.m., after which I had to clean up the entire building, consisting of eight to nine rooms. I swept and mopped the whole place, and washed both Vakil sahib's and my clothes. For lunch, I used to go to a different *swayamsevak's* house by rotation. After returning to Hedgewar Bhavan, I again got to work and made tea for everyone. This was my routine for at least a year, and this was the time when I met many people."'

Naik too was toughened by his experiences in the south Gujarat village of Endhal. He became grounded, acquiring a discipline that would stay with him throughout his emblematic career. It also infused in him a lifelong passion for giving back to the underprivileged. That sense of purpose drove him to contribute to charity even before he became CEO of L&T.

Modi's rise in the RSS through the 1970s and 1980s was slow but steady. Naik too, meanwhile, rose at a glacial pace through the ranks at L&T. Under the company's Danish founders, merit had been quickly rewarded. Naik, within five years of joining L&T, was sent to Britain in 1970. He was twenty-eight. But as new Indian managers took charge in the mid-1970s, seniority assumed greater importance. Merit counted less. Naik's ascent stalled. He rose to deputy general manager and eventually, at forty-four, was appointed general manager after twenty-one years in the company.

Unforeseen events altered his trajectory at L&T. Just as Modi had been catapulted to the chief ministership of Gujarat after a period of wilderness in the Bharatiya Janata Party (BJP), Naik showed his mettle when L&T came under threat of takeover in the late-1980s. In the eighteen years from 1999 to 2017, with Naik in charge, L&T established itself as an engineering and technology multinational with few peers.

This is the story of what Naik himself likes to call a journey from 'a village to the world'. L&T today builds India's nuclear reactors, nuclear-powered submarines, systems for weapons and missiles, ships, metro networks, airports, railway freight corridors, smart cities, refineries and space satellite systems. Its operations cut a broad swathe of geographies. More than all this, L&T is a company that is a strongly nationalistic enterprise. Naik has devoted over half a century to help build a strong L&T in the service of India. That is his enduring legacy.

1

Early Life Lessons

1942. INDIA WAS in ferment. Mahatma Gandhi had launched the Quit India movement from Bombay's famous August Kranti Maidan. A few hundred miles away, in a quiet corner of Surat, then a part of Bombay state, a child was born on 9 June 1942 to Manibhai and Maniba Naik. His name: Anil.

The Naiks are Anavil Brahmins. The community has produced luminaries like Morarji Desai, a former prime minister, and the lawyer Bhulabhai Desai. It attaches great importance to education and public service. Naik's father, Manibhai, was a senior teacher in Bombay's respected Hansraj Morarji Public School. Sitting in his tastefully furnished office, Naik's stern expression softens as he recalls his lineage: 'My grandfather Nichchhabhai's first job was in a *gurukul*. He served villagers for sixty years and died at the age of ninety-seven in 1971. My grandmother, Kashibaa, died at ninety-eight, some fifteen years later.' Longevity is embedded in the Naik genes. His father, Manibhai, and mother, Maniba, both lived to eighty-seven.

His grandfather, Nichchhabhai Ratanji Naik, was born in 1874, five years after Mahatma Gandhi. His family was steeped in Indian values and in the incipient freedom movement. The Naiks laid great stress on education. 'My father held MSc. and MEd. degrees,' says

Naik. His own children are highly qualified professionals: his son, Jignesh, is an electronics engineer and works for Google in Silicon Valley; and his daughter, Pratiksha, is a doctor with a successful practice in the United States.

People would come from faraway places to his grandfather's village to watch Nichchhabai, famed for his mathematical abilities, solve complex numerical problems. As headmaster of the *gurukul*, his simplicity, principled conduct and intellect left a deep impact on son Manibhai and grandson Anil.

'My grandfather was born in our village, Endhal,' says Naik. Leaning back in his chair, Naik reflects on a past studded with struggle, success and an extraordinary family tradition: 'We used to be known as Master *kutumb* – teacher's family. My grandfather was the first graduate in the area. In those days that meant a school graduate. That (passing out of school) was called the graduation ceremony. He was a gold medallist. He had an incredible ability to calculate numerals – mentally multiplying seven-digit numbers in a few seconds. He went to Baroda to receive his gold medal. It made him very proud to have won the medal in those days.'

Naik's voice breaks with emotion as he says: 'My grandfather was the first principal in the entire geography of nearly 50 sq. km of *gurukul* schools. He served the poor and the villagers in Gujarat for more than sixty years. Then my father returned to rural India in 1952. He served for over forty-five years. He worked in urban areas as well. So between my father and grandfather, they worked in south Gujarat for more than 100 years. That in essence inspired me. I asked myself, how will I do a fraction of what they have done? I am an engineer. I couldn't be a teacher like them. My father was the principal of a high school and my grandfather was the principal of a *gurukul* – a primary school, there were no higher secondary schools 100 years ago.'

Endhal is a largely tribal village, says Naik. 'People are mostly from scheduled castes and backward classes. All the upper caste people have gone to the big towns seeking what they think is a better life. But from a beautiful house in the village they end up in a one-room-kitchen flat in the city. They are willing to (make this) sacrifice so that the next generation can build a better future.'

The Naik family has for generations remained firmly bound to education. As Naik says with his customary ebullience, 'My father was very enthusiastic about education. My grandfather encouraged him; and my father encouraged his sister to become a doctor. At the time Bombay state was large, it stretched all the way to Karachi and right down to Goa plus a part of Madhya Pradesh. It was a huge state—as good as a country!'

Manibhai was deeply influenced by Mahatma Gandhi. The Mahatma's clarion call—'India lives in its villages'—resonated with Manibhai. When he was invited to be the founder-principal of a new school in a south Gujarat village, he accepted the offer. Says Naik, 'My father got an opportunity to come back to the village which is the root of our family. We came back in 1952. From then on, his whole life was spent in serving the poor.'

MANIBHAI MARRIED at twenty. His wife stayed with her parents while Manibhai continued his studies. After he completed his MSc. degree she came to stay with the extended Naik family. Manibhai then went to Surat to prepare for his MEd. degree. Anil was born there. As destiny would have it, the city, fifty years later, would be the crowning jewel in Naik's career, as Larsen & Toubro's Hazira manufacturing complex, Naik's brainchild, took shape on the outskirts of Surat.

'My parents told me, my mother particularly, that they were eagerly looking forward to a son because my first two siblings were girls,' says Naik. 'One of them passed away four years ago, at seventy-seven. My elder sister is now eighty-six years old and my brother-in-law is ninety-one.' When Anil was born there was jubilation, as his parents had been praying for a boy.

In an interview with the Gujarati publication *Ujas,* Naik looked back on his early years with a tinge of nostalgia. As the interviewer observed:

'In those days it was firmly believed in the Anavil Brahmin community that every family should have at least one son. It was believed that the son carries forward the family lineage. Anil was born to his mother after his two elder sisters, Urmilaben (Bachuben) and Pushpaben. Thus Anil's arrival was a matter of great joy for everyone in the family. Naturally, Anil became a darling of the family. The Anavils, in the early days, were supposed to be a community of agriculturists. Most of them engaged in farming, and agriculture was believed to be their main source of income. The status of a family in a village would be measured on the basis of its landholding. How large and big was the family's house was another parameter that defined its status. The bigger the landholding and the larger the house, the more respectability it meant in the community. In matters of matrimonial relations too it was expected that a daughter of a well-to-do family would be married into the family of similar status.

However, Anilbhai's family had different ideas in this matter. Education was given more importance. It had been so from the time of even Manibhai's grandfather. Thus, education for Urmilaben and Pushpaben was a top priority for Manibhai. Before that Manibhai had also enabled his younger sister, Lalitaben, to complete her education in medicine and become a doctor. At that time though, Manibhai did face resistance within the family, because it was felt that it would be difficult to find a suitable match from the community for a doctor-girl. Notwithstanding any such arguments, Manibhai encouraged his sister to become the first doctor in the Anavil community. Thus the Naik family had recognized the value of education many decades ago and accorded it utmost importance.'

ANIL WAS one and a half years old when his parents relocated from Surat to Mumbai. Manibhai had received, and accepted, an offer to be a senior teacher at Hansraj Morarji Public School in Mumbai. Indian Independence was around the corner as the freedom movement entered its decisive phase in 1944.

Recalls Naik: 'Hansraj Morarji Public School was set up under the aegis of the K.M. Munshi trust. There was a college of arts, science and commerce, and an engineering college, the Sardar Patel College of Engineering. It was built in a big compound. The area has become congested today but it was beautiful in the old days. There was a huge maidan where you could play cricket and football. I grew up in the Hansraj Morarji campus, living there for nearly eight years: three years in Worli and five years in Andheri. Then my father decided to go back to the village.' Here, his father would become principal of the primary school which Naik joined.

Like the rest of rural south Gujarat, Endhal village is dry, hot and dusty. Young Anil, not quite ten, moved along with his parents and siblings to their modest home. It was a world apart from their comfortable suburban flat in the bustling city of Bombay they had left behind. For the next several years, Anil would get used to the rough and tumble of village life, studying on a cow-dung floor, playing games with the village boys, many of them tribals, Adivasis and Dalits. It steeled him for the challenges that lay ahead. He developed his fearlessness and resilience during that defining decade when a newly independent India too was finding its feet in a complex world. He would be sixteen, in 1958, when he would again taste urban life in Anand, where studies and movies would compete robustly for his attention. His eyes twinkling, Naik says today: 'The college where I studied engineering, Birla Vishwakarma Mahavidyalaya in Vallabh Vidyanagar, has a building named after the founder, Mr Birla, and another building named after A.M. Naik.'

Naik's mind wanders back to his school days in rural Gujarat. 'I joined the village primary school in Endhal called Parthamik Shala in March 1952 in the sixth standard,' says Naik. 'I got a double promotion and jumped one class. My father had become the principal of the school in 1952.' In June 1953, eleven-year-old Anil was enrolled at K.V.S. High School in the nearby village of Kharel. He would study there for the next five years. The sudden shift from a posh city school to a rudimentary village school must have been a wrench for young Anil. Recalls Naik: 'The moment I went to the village I was on the floor—*gobar* floor, not even tiled. And that's where I studied in the seventh standard, then the eighth, ninth, tenth and eleventh. Then I went to study engineering in Vallabh Vidyanagar, 6 km from the town of Anand.'

KHAREL VILLAGE is at the centre of about twenty smaller villages. A brand new high school was a novelty. Manibhai was the founder-principal. Five years later, in 1958, Anil would stand first in the SSC Board examination in the entire Kharel centre. 'An advocate named Dayalji had built the school and requested my father to join as the principal,' recalls Naik. 'There were many teachers in Mumbai from our area, so he got Maganbhai from one village, Dhanubhai from another, and Dahyabhai from a third village. There were villages scattered around this school. I was too young to understand the huge change that was taking place in my life. Little did I realize then that I could later have been deprived of my Larsen & Toubro job because they wanted only IITians—and because my father would later send me to V.P. Science College in Vallabh Mahavidyalaya, Anand, to prepare for my engineering entrance exams for admission to Birla Vishwakarma Mahavidyalaya!'

The dislocation from an upscale Mumbai school to a village school had its own subterranean impact. Village life taught Naik the virtues of being grounded. Local-level school politics, moreover, meant that Manibhai, a man of unshakable principle, changed schools often. It was a semi-nomadic life and it toughened Naik for the challenges that lay ahead. 'My father soon went to a new school in another village, Bardoli,' he recalls. 'Near Bardoli there is a place called Sarabhon. He served there for two years and then he went to a very backward area in Dholikuva (Dighendranagar) and served there for another seven years.'

Though an itinerant life, it was filled with the excitement of change. 'We had to go from our village to school, first by bus to the nearest railway station, which was 4–5 km away,' says Naik. 'Then we would take a toy train of narrow gauge which used to go all the way up to Unnai forest. On the way is Dholikuva. My father spent the longest time in the school there – seven years.'

By the time Manibhai left the school in Dholikuva, Anil had already gone on to college. 'In fact, by then I had graduated and had started working in L&T,' he says. 'Then my father moved again to teach at a fourth school, Ambica High School, for another six years. It was located in Gadat village in Gandevi taluka. He retired from there in 1973. In 1971, my grandfather Nichchhabhai died, so my father anyway had to come back to the village to look after all our land. We had 38 *bighas* and he used to grow rice, wheat, jowar, many varieties of grain. He was sixty-two then. The school was 7 km from our village and the journey by bicycle was cumbersome. Finally, he could not do it every day. He continued cycling though, right up to the age of seventy-five.'

Naik was a good student. 'I always stood in the top five in my class,' he smiles. 'I was an all-rounder. My father made me an all-rounder. He is my role model. Even in school he would tell me, "You are going to be the prefect – not selected, but elected; there will be elections, let me see how popular you are among the students." And I did become the prefect.'

Confesses Naik: 'After joining the village school, I just followed whatever my father said. He asked me to study higher math instead of lower math. In the SSC exam, he asked me to take eleven subjects instead of seven. My father was a principled teacher and committed to his profession. Devoted to education, he would work eighteen hours a day. No leave for him even on Saturday or Sunday. He was deeply concerned about the poor people of the village, who had to walk long distances to reach a doctor. He always said that something must be done to provide healthcare and education to the poor. I am happy that I have been able to do something in that direction. The day I contributed to the village hospital, his eyes were filled with tears.'

IT WAS a typical warm day in rural Gujarat. The students in the school were in revolt. They had called for a strike, boycotting classes to highlight their grievances. As principal, Manibhai Naik decided to confine his rebellious son, Anil, the students' charismatic leader, to a room, fearing he would end up leading the planned demonstration against the school authorities.

'My father confided in me that this was his last year in the school and so I should not do anything for which he would face a problem,' recalls Naik of those often tumultuous days. But Anil, at fifteen, was already showing an iconoclastic streak that would mark him out through his career. Undeterred, he went up to the room window, clambered onto the ledge and leapt to the ground to lead the students' demonstration against the school.

Manibhai was aghast. The school's management trust committee, meanwhile, summoned the feisty Anil. 'They were senior to my father,' recalls Naik. 'One committee member asked me if I was bigger than my own father. He was a lawyer and wanted to trap me. I was only fifteen. I told him that my father is much taller than me and has accomplished much more, but in this case he is doing his job and I am doing mine. The committee member asked me what my complaint was. I told him that all students should get a good education but we found that the teaching quality in the school had gone down, particularly in English. There was a teacher, Gulabbhai, who had retired. The new teacher was very slow. He would take ten times more sessions than Gulabbhai to complete a lesson. The syllabus would just not get over!'

Anil had by now developed a well-earned reputation as a fiery student leader. The school authorities were wary of his influence over other students. He was already displaying three traits that would define his later work and life: a fierce independence of spirit; an ability to lead from the front that would, fifty years later, help ringfence L&T from predators and make several thousands of its employees millionaires through share options; and a commitment to nation-building which, as yet embryonic, would manifest time and again in a career bedrocked on a sense of national pride.

Anil displayed early signs of leadership as a student. He was easily the best orator in the school and would often speak up for fellow students.

Now the young firebrand was at the forefront of the ongoing protests. By now the students' agitation had reached a high level of intensity. 'The next day my father, as usual, went to school by a longer route,' recalls Naik. 'I used to run down the shorter route and reach one minute before he did. There was a lot of effort by teachers from different villages to motivate their own village boys and girls to break the students' strike. I heard one of the boys, a friend of mine, saying that he wanted to enter the school. We were all at the gate. His name was Suresh. He still lives in Surat. I told him not to try to enter the school as he would be hammered so badly that he would have to take a bullock cart to go home.'

Naik chortles at the memory. 'Since this was an SSC school, we had to get exam admission forms which the school would not provide, only the university would. So I went to another school in Amalsad, some 10 km away. I arranged for them to give us the forms so that we could appear for the exam. After that I told the students that it was my father's last year. Being his son I did not want to embroil him in a bigger mess than I had already. I made it clear I had nothing to do with the students' decision to agitate.'

All the changes Anil and the students wanted were eventually instituted by the managing committee, including withdrawing the new teacher. 'Retired Gulabbhai was called back to our class,' smiles Naik. 'My father, however, submitted his resignation as principal—not because of this case or the students' agitation but because he wanted to leave anyway. Politics had come in the way. Dayalji's nephew had gone to England to study. What we heard was that he had actually not got any degree from the UK at all. But he was brought in as a teacher as he was England-returned! Gradually he was promoted to the position of vice-principal and then principal. Maganbhai was already vice-principal but he quietly decided to work as his junior.'

By resigning, Manibhai Naik had once again acted on a matter of principle. 'A brand new school was constructed,' remembers Naik. 'We did not construct the school with our money, a trust put in the money but it was done under my father's supervision.'

The bond between father and son was extraordinarily strong. Not only did the relationship give young Anil a great deal of self-confidence, it inculcated in him the values of humility, generosity and public service. They were enduring values. The boy who was never seen in class began his *tapasya* with the determination of *Matsya Vedh* – a reference to the Mahabharata in which Arjuna pierces the eye of a fish revolving overhead by looking at its reflection in the water below and wins Draupadi's hand in marriage.

ANIL'S SSC school exams were rapidly approaching. He had to relocate temporarily to a nearby city as the exam centre was 10 km away. Naik stayed with a distant relative whom his father knew well. 'He was the vice-principal of a Tata school and an examiner in the SSC exams,' says Naik. 'There in Bilimora I spotted two cinema theatres. The exams started the next day, 11 a.m. to 2 p.m. and from 3. p.m. to 6 p.m. My father's relative had a baby daughter who was six months old. Her name was Vibha. I used to play with her till 9.30 a.m. and then go for my exam. No reading, no preparation, nothing. I thought to myself, what I have studied will come to my mind while writing the exam, no use mugging at the last minute.

'So I appeared, from 11 a.m. to 2 p.m. and then from 3 p.m. to 6 p.m. They would not allow any student to leave early. At ten minutes to 6 p.m., a warning bell would ring, before which no student could leave. I would submit my paper two or three minutes before the warning bell and go off to be in time for the 6 p.m. movie show. The relative in whose house I was staying would get worried as I would come home by only 10 p.m. He sent an SOS to my parents. He said he did not know what would happen with my exam results as every morning I would play with his baby daughter and come home by 10 p.m. and then go to sleep, and this pattern was continuing day after day. Two days went by, and we saw two more movies. So two theatres were done, and we took a state transport bus to a nearby taluka and saw a third movie there.'

Anil was a brilliant but unpredictable student. He recalls: 'My mother would often tell my father that there are complaints from school: Anil is throwing stones here and there. But my father smiled and told her that only naughty children would achieve something in life. You need intelligence to be naughty too, as long as no serious damage is done to anyone. My mother used to anxiously ask my father about the exam results two or three days ahead of the results. He would tell her, let him get the results in class. Though, as the school's principal, he already knew what my marks were, he wouldn't, as a matter of principle, reveal my results even to my mother. My father was a super-principal. He was good in math. But he gave me 99 marks out of 100 in math. I did not understand why he cut one mark for me. He would give my classmate 100 out of 100. I asked him why. He replied, "The day you get 100 per cent you will stop improving. Next year's paper could be very tough and you may not get 100 out of 100." For cutting one mark from my paper he would give me the official excuse of a spelling mistake on my part. But this sort of discipline has stood me in good stead.'

During school vacations Anil's cousin used to come over to his house. 'He was about the same age as me,' remembers Naik. 'We played together and fought with each other too. There was a coconut tree nearby. He would bring the coconuts down with a stick and I would try to catch them. One day one of the elders shouted at me so I ran towards the back of the house near a well. I threw a huge stone into the well. Hearing the sound of a big splash the elders thought I had jumped into the well. They came out running while I hid behind the well.'

Anil was a prankster. But above all else was Anil's love for movies. It was insatiable. 'My father once sent my mother to fetch me from a movie,' he recalls. 'My friends and I were in the movie theatre. She came in and shouted out for me. I was in the first row. The seats in the cinema hall fortunately cost only 5 annas in those days. We anyway did not have much money to spend. We left the movie halfway. Then came my exam results. My father had full confidence in me. And I stood first in the centre! The relative at whose house I had stayed was flabbergasted. I had not studied much but still stood first.'

IN JUNE 1958, when he turned sixteen, Naik enrolled at V.P. Science College in Vallabh Vidyanagar, where he would prepare for a year for admission to an engineering college. His father had decided to send him to Vallabh Vidyanagar for a special reason. As Naik says today with a smile, 'After hearing all the horror stories about my going for movie after movie, he sent me to a university town. But he did not realize that on one side of that town was Baroda and on the other side, Ahmedabad! Anand itself had two theatres. I was notorious as I hardly attended classes. My absence was marked every now and then by the teachers and my name appeared on the notice board with a warning that I may not get permission to sit for the exam as my attendance is not satisfactory. So in the last two months I went to all the classes and made up for my absence.'

As he had in school, Naik got rapidly involved in college student politics too. While in his first year in the science stream, he contested elections. The local Patels dominated college elections. 'They were tough guys,' recalls Naik. 'Five were fighting for one post. So the Patel boys came over and told me to withdraw. I asked them why. They said they were locals and I had to withdraw. I told them that since they had threatened me I would definitely not withdraw. I lost the election but so did the Patel candidate. This was the beginning. After that I won all the elections, and in my last year I was the leader of 25,000 to 30,000 students. I could handle the union very well in L&T as I had been a student leader. My leadership was inborn.'

The geometry teacher in college was very close to Naik's father. He was, like Naik, an Anavil Brahmin. The teacher would look pointedly at Anil and say cryptically that those who had done well in their SSC school exams may not necessarily do well in college. By now Anil's reputation for skipping classes was firmly established.

'My chemistry teacher, Professor Dave, would be upset with me and ask me a question from elementary chemistry,' says Naik, his eyes crinkling at the memory, 'which I would answer quite easily. Then there was Professor Virkar in the geology department. I did not attend his classes at all, nor did I attend any tutorials on the subject. After three months of college I finally went for the tutorials. Professor Virkar asked me whose geology book I liked. I did not know Professor Virkar was himself an author of a book on geology. So I said, "Professor Chauhan," who was another writer and teacher. Professor Virkar got upset. I did not attend his classes again. After another three months I decided to show all the professors who thought I would fail that I wasn't that bad and prepared hard for the trigonometry and chemistry papers. I got first rank in both subjects. The complaints from my professors stopped.'

MEANWHILE, ANIL'S chemistry professor called for him. He said he too had been mischievous as a student, had taken part in extra-curricular activities and had hardly studied. 'I thought to myself, so there is someone else like me too!' says Naik. 'After that he always had a word of appreciation for me whenever he saw me.'

Then came the preliminary monthly exams. Anil did well but failed in the zoology practicals. 'Professor Virkar failed me,' says Naik. 'There were twenty-nine days left after the preliminary exams for the finals. I was determined to do well. I told my roommate to go and study with his friends. I asked him to lock me in the room in the hostel. My room was the first one in the corridor. The other students used to see a locked room and thought I was roaming about in Ahmedabad watching movies. But I was studying silently inside the room for twenty-nine days. I prepared for nine questions out of twelve. My friend used to open the room door at 12.30 p.m. I would freshen up, eat and have him lock me up again at 1 p.m. He would open the room at 7 p.m. I would have a wash, dinner, and then study together with him.'

In his first six months in college, Naik had a roommate called Suresh. 'His father was a *khadidhari* and lived near our village,' says Naik. 'He was a doctor and closely known to my father. He used to come for a surprise check, arriving by the 4.30 a.m. train. By 5.30-6 a.m., he would be in our room. He once caught his son having tea instead of milk. He would stay till late evening, even till 9 p.m., to check the "environment" in our room. At 9 p.m. he would ask his son, "Where is your friend Anil?" Suresh would say I had gone to the railway station and would come home by 9.30 p.m. I was actually watching the 6–9 p.m. movie. When I returned to my room, Suresh's father would ask me where I had been roaming around. I told him we friends walk about in town and discuss various subjects on our way to the railway station. Finally he came to know that I had actually gone to see a film. He then went all the way to my village and complained to my father that I had not been studying and that he was going to remove his son from my room.'

'Six months later, after mid-term, he actually removed his son and put him in another hostel,' says Naik, chuckling. 'When the exam results came, I stood seventh in the university out of a total of 1,200 students. I was going back to the hostel that day, walking through the main avenue where you meet many people. I ran into

Professor Virkar. He asked me why I was still here. He had assumed I had failed! I told him that I had come to appear for the engineering entrance exam. He inquired about my percentage. I asked him whether he had seen my name on the board and that I had stood seventh in the university. He shook hands with me and said that he had made a mistake in judging me and that I was brilliant!'

—

WHEN NAIK was in his first year in V.P. Science College, Anand had two theatres. Nearby Baroda had several. 'You could come out of one and enter a second, come out from the second and enter the third,' grins Naik impishly today. 'Once we saw three consecutive shows, from 3 p.m. to 6 p.m., 6 p.m. to 9 p.m., and 9 p.m. to 12 a.m.! That was just once. But two shows, one after the other, we did many times. We used to take the 1.45 a.m. train, reach the hostel at 3-3.30 a.m. and go to sleep. The next day, no class! And if it was Saturday, no class on Saturday either! We would happily bunk!'

Movie-mad sixteen-year-old Anil had a favourite actor: Dilip Kumar. Naik retains his fondness for movies, and his favourite actor even today is Dilip Kumar. His face lights up as he says: 'I saw 105 movies in my first year in science college in 1958. I saw Bimal Roy's *Madhumati* seven times!'

The college was strict. 'At the end of the day,' Naik says, 'the principal would call all my friends and tell them to dissociate from me. He would say, "When Anil studies, he ranks in the top five and you all fail." There were fourteen of us. Thirteen failed the engineering entrance exam in the first year. I was the only one who passed with a first class.'

Sports—especially badminton and cricket—engaged much of Naik's time in college. He represented the college in badminton and table-tennis and was elected the sports secretary. His college activities made for a well-rounded personality and would serve Naik well in his career that would soon unfold.

—

ONE MONTH before the final engineering entrance exams, Anil's father wrote him a letter. It left a deep impression on him. The four-page letter, written in Gujarati, advised Anil to be fearless. If you are honest, you will have the courage to do the right thing, Manibhai wrote. It is advice Naik has followed throughout his life. Naik recalls: 'In his letter, my father wrote how important my student years were and how important study itself was. The last line of the letter said he had confidence in me and that I would not forget the main purpose of my life. That is what stuck in my head and that is partly what helped me achieve such a high rank in the exams.'

When the results were announced, Anil was ranked sixteenth in the all-India engineering test. Naik's father had told Anil to be an all-rounder but not at the cost of his studies. All the others who had complained about the rebellious Anil—that his extra-curricular activities were harming his studies—didn't do well in the entrance exam for the engineering degree course. His roommate in the second term stood 168th. His other twelve friends all passed one year later than he did. All later went to the United States for higher studies. 'One actually passed two years after me,' recalls Naik. 'Today they all are in America, repenting having gone there. One reason is that they are still trying to accept the new reality of life in the US. Their children have married American boys and girls. In the 1960s there were not many Indians there. Today, of course, no one is bothered, all are marrying different communities, castes and nationalities, and all parents are okay with that. But things were different then.'

After the engineering entrance exam, and just before the results were declared, Anil's father had told him to go to Chikhli to meet Gulabbhai, who had had his son Suresh moved out of Anil's room, fearing his son may be distracted from his studies. Naik recalls: 'He had a *jhula* in his verandah and always used to sit there. He welcomed me when I arrived. He asked me what percentage I was expecting in the exams. I told him 74-75 per cent as I was not sure about one mark. I used to go through my own exam paper thoroughly and assess my own marks. He told me not to bluff, as his very studious son was expecting similar marks. How could I get the same score? When the results came, I got 74.8 per cent. His son got 38 per cent.'

The saga with Suresh's family didn't end there. Several years after graduation as a mechanical engineer and having joined Larsen & Toubro in 1965, Naik decided to pay Suresh's father a visit. It was 1968. 'I went to the village in a new Ambassador car which L&T had given me,' Naik says. 'I had told my father, let's go to Chikhli and meet Gulabbhai. I stopped the car right in front of his house. Before we could climb up to his verandah, he came down, looked at the car and asked me where I had got it from. I told him that my company, L&T, has given it to me for four years after which it would be mine and that they would replace this with a new car. It's surprising, he said, that I now owned a car and his son was still studying.'

At the engineering college, Birla Vishwakarma Mahavidyalaya in Vallabh Vidyanagar, the years passed swiftly. Naik took his studies seriously. He graduated in 1964 with a degree in mechanical engineering. Naik, now twenty-one, had matured into a serious young man. He retained his *joi de vivre* and love for movies, but a taxing study schedule left little time for extra-curricular activities. The early 1960s were a challenging period for the Indian republic, still just over a decade old. The future promised much, but America too loomed large in most young Indian engineers' minds.

Armed with his degree in mechanical engineering, Anil too wanted to go to the US for further studies before returning to India to fulfil his ambitions. Several engineers from south Gujarat had already done so. However, his parents, especially his mother, Maniba, disapproved. In an interview with *Ujas,* Maniba said she 'did not like the idea of her only son going to a far-off land, and perhaps even settling there later.' Respecting Maniba's intense disapproval of his going so far away, Anil gave up the lure of

America. He decided to take up a suitable job and share his father's financial responsibilities. However, in view of his mother, Maniba, not allowing him to go to the US and thus preventing him from earning a lot of money, he often lovingly taunted her, saying, 'Maniba, it is because of you that I had to stay back in India and struggle hard to earn money, and since I do not earn enough money I have to make do with whatever little I get here. Had I gone to America I would have earned in crores and billions.'

2

Beginning of a Corporate Journey

COLLEGE OVER, ENGINEERING degree in hand, it was time for Naik to get down to work. Naik's sister, Pushpa, worked in a Mumbai suburb as a teacher. She had become the third generation to follow the teaching profession in the Naik family, after Nichchhabhai and Manibhai. Anil's father now asked him to go to Mumbai and stay with Pushpa and find a job.

'Even when I first went to the science college at the age of fifteen, my father had not come along to drop me,' says Naik. 'He had told me to take a particular bus, go to Bilimora, take a train, go to Anand, take a bus again to Vallabh Vidyanagar, find the admission office and get admitted. Nobody came with me. That's how he made me strong. I had to struggle for everything. But he made me struggle in order to improve myself. That is why he is my role model.'

Naik now applied to over fifty companies for a job. One of them was Nestor Boilers. At around the same time, coincidentally, Manibhai gave his son a personal note addressed to Viren Shah, who was the chairman and managing director of Mukand Iron and Steel Ltd and would later be Governor of West Bengal. Shah had been a student of Manibhai's in Hansraj Morarji Public School. He met Anil and sent him to the company's personnel manager.

Naik recalls the meeting as if it had happened yesterday: 'The manager, one Mr Shukla, gave me an employment form to fill up. My English was very weak as I had studied in Gujarati. Even when you go to engineering college in Gujarat, people talk in Gujarati. When Shukla saw my form, he told me, "Don't you think your English could be better? You will have to improve your English." I felt bad as I knew I was getting the job only because of a request from my father to his former student, Virenbhai Shah. Nonetheless, I submitted the form at their office in Kurla. On the way to Kurla station, I began thinking, there is no hurry to join Mukand, so I should try other places. If I can get a job on my own ... and then I got Nestor Boilers! That is how I got my first job at Nestor, for Rs 350 per month. Virenbhai's Mukand had offered me Rs 400, but I declined that offer and took up Nestor's as I was getting it on my own merit.'

Nestor had Parsi management. 'They were very nice people,' says Naik. 'I did very well, and after six months they gave me a Rs 150 raise. So I was now earning Rs 500 a month. After another six months came the annual increment. I was in a small workshop comprising fifty people. I looked after the union and everything. The boiler was the main workshop. Then the management changed and the company was taken over by Gujaratis from East Africa. The first set of Gujaratis went away in three months. The second set of Gujaratis, also from East Africa, came and held on. The elderly owner was a very nice man, but his thirty-five-year-old son was a problem. By then I was in charge of the workshop. The Parsi manager who was overall in charge had stopped coming because he had had a nervous breakdown. So overnight I was made burner-in-charge as well as boiler-in-charge.'

Then the Poonawalla incident happened. Naik overheard the owner's son shouting at Poonawalla, another elderly Parsi manager, in an insulting way. It upset Naik deeply. He started looking for a job again. 'I would never have left Nestor,' he says. 'I was works manager at the age of twenty-two. But it was a matter of principle, of working with people who had values.'

The episode left a bitter taste in his mouth. Says Naik: 'Poonawalla felt very bad when he was told by Shirish that his job could be done by a Rs 200-man and they were paying him Rs 750. That is the day I felt this is an issue about value systems. My father would never agree with such values. My father is my role model. I kept thinking, will he agree, will he not agree, to this particular situation?' Naik made up his mind. He would resign.

Naik was about to get a raise and a monthly salary of Rs 850 at Nestor. 'I was also about to be sent to the UK as the burner guys and the boiler guys were both in the UK. On 2 January 1965 I was set to leave.' Naik was firm in his intention to quit. There was no way he could continue at Nestor. He began to explore other options.

Says Naik: 'There were only three companies I wanted to join at that time: the Tatas, Voltas and Larsen & Toubro. In our college campus everyone had talked about only these three. Tisco, in any case, was a steel company in Jamshedpur. Voltas and L&T were in Mumbai. Voltas was a trading company, I was not interested in trading. I was interested in manufacturing. So I said I would go to L&T to do manufacturing, and then started researching how to go about applying. At that time there was nothing India was making indigenously except products for import substitution—what nobody did L&T was willing to do! The entire orientation in me was very deeply towards building a strong India. You get a platform, then how you use the platform is up to you. L&T had those ingredients—and a platform.'

In November 1964, Naik appeared for an interview at L&T. He recalls: 'I had got a call for a job similar to fabrication of a workshop boiler. I was interviewed by an Englishman named Tim Baker. He spoke Cockney English! My English being weak, I had started practising it. I bought audio cassettes, stood in front of a mirror, and with facial expressions, gestures and the right pronunciation, it eventually took me four years to speak fluently. The Englishman at L&T asked me if I knew how to design a boiler. I asked him if he wanted to design a boiler using the thick cylinder formula or thin cylinder formula. There itself he was clean bowled! He himself had, I learnt later, studied only up to seventh standard. He was a welder—a copper welder. From there he had moved up to be a supervisor, charge-hand, foreman, and then works manager.'

At the interview Baker told Naik to describe how he would design a boiler using the thin cylinder formula. Naik recalls: 'But I asked what efficiency—70 per cent? So Baker called S.S. Rao, chief of design. He asked him to understand what I was saying. Rao asked me: if you want to bring down an agitated vessel from 1440 rpm to 12 rpm, what kind of gear train would you use to slow it down to 300 rpm, then maybe after one more step, and the fourth or fifth step, bring it down to 12 rpm? So I replied: in that case the gear box and its paraphernalia will be so big that it can't sit on top of the vessel. We would have to go for a worm mill solution. Rao said I had given him the most exhaustive reply about the gear train.'

Naik smiles at the memory: 'After approval from Baker I had to meet his boss, Gunnar Hansen. We went to his office room. Hansen asked me how many people reported to me at Nestor. I told him about 350. He said that was a lot. It would be a long time before I could get such responsibility in L&T. Since my English was poor, I used to convert the Gujarat words in my mind into English before speaking. I thought to myself, how can he say this even before trying me out? So I told Hansen, "Who knows, time will tell." He thought I was cocky. He told me to leave.'

Much drama was to follow. Naik chuckles as he describes what happened next. 'Baker came out two minutes later, grumbling. He met P.J. Thomas, who was in charge of estimates. He told Thomas that the old man (Hansen) would not let him do what he wanted. Baker then took me to his room and said, "Hansen thinks you are overconfident. I had told you before your going to the old man your pay would be Rs 760, but he is saying Rs 670. I had told you your designation would be assistant engineer, but he is saying it will be junior engineer. I had said supervisory category, but he has said to take you in the unionized category." '

Unfazed, twenty-two-year-old Naik told Baker not to worry. His ambition and dream throughout college had been to join Larsen & Toubro. He says today: 'My father and grandfather served the poor, my father devoted his life to the poor. I did not know how to be a teacher, my sister did that job, but as an engineer I should select a platform that builds India. L&T was the only company that came to my mind. But I was not from IIT, and L&T was only interviewing IIT graduates. So I told Baker that I am accepting your job offer anyway. Baker felt relieved that I did not argue about salary or designation. I accepted the offer the way it was. I joined L&T on 15 March 1965, four months after my interview with Baker and Hansen, as soon as Nestor Boiler's boss, Mr Shah, relieved me.'

Getting into L&T was a dream come true for Naik. But even he didn't know at the time what an eventful journey he was about to embark on. First, though, he had to circumvent the bureaucracy that pervaded corporate India in the mid-1960s. 'I was chasing L&T House for my appointment letter,' Naik says. 'The administration manager was to deliver the letter. So I went to L&T House, but did not get the letter for nearly two months. Finally, I got the letter on the spot by hand from one Mr Governor, a Parsi gentleman. Very nice people … they were all Parsis at that time. Meanwhile, Nestor Boilers was not relieving me, putting all kinds of pressure on me. They did not pay my salary for my last twenty-seven days there. It was due to me, but they said you are resigning, you are going on your own. It was not right, but that was how the owner's son was as a person.'

Naik's commitment to L&T was to prove unshakable. 'From 1974 to 1985, in eleven years, I got only one promotion,' he says. 'Anybody else would have left, not I. I loved L&T. I was devoted to L&T. It was my temple. So I said, in this life I will not leave L&T.' It was the first step in Naik's lifelong mission: to be part of an organization that would help build a strong, progressive India.

FEW COULD have imagined eighty years ago that L&T would become one of the world's most technologically advanced engineering conglomerates. Two Danish engineers laid the foundation in 1938. Søren Kristian Toubro, a twenty-eight-year-old civil engineer, and his schoolmate, Henning Holck-Larsen, a chemical engineer, were hardly archetypical entrepreneurs. Toubro had arrived in India in 1934 on an assignment for Copenhagen-based F.L. Smidth & Co. A/S. A year later, the Danish firm sent Holck-Larsen, then twenty-seven, to India. Holck-Larsen was tasked with analysing the company's cement business in India.

India, still a British colony, presented a challenge to the two young Danes. The Great Depression had swirled through the United States in the 1930s, creating mass unemployment and distress. Europe was not immune. British India too had felt the tremors of the Depression.

And yet Holck-Larsen and Toubro saw in India what others did not: the vast potential of a soon-to-be-free nation. Mahatma Gandhi, Jawaharlal Nehru and Sardar Vallabhbhai Patel were the future, not the British. Industry in India was rudimentary: the British had ensured that the benefits of industrialization passed India by. But Holck-Larsen and Toubro knew that when independence came—as it inevitably would, in a decade or less—indigenous industry would present entrepreneurs the opportunity of a lifetime.

Both engineers decided to resign from F.L. Smidth & Co. A/S in 1938. The saga of Larsen and Toubro was set to begin. Their first tiny office in Mumbai was in Ballard Estate, a district that years later would host L&T House, the company's stately headquarters, before operations shifted northwards to the Mumbai suburbs.

When the Second World War broke out in 1939, the two Danish entrepreneurs had to dig deep into their reservoirs of innovation. Denmark was soon occupied by Germany. L&T, formed as a partnership in 1938, suddenly lost a large chunk of its business. Displaying the enterprise that would characterize L&T in the succeeding decades, the two partners turned adversity into opportunity. The travails of war added a steely determination to the two young men, who began manufacturing some of the dairy machinery and products they had earlier imported.

L&T grew rapidly. But capital was needed. The two partners and associates put in Rs 10,000 each. Engineering Construction Corporation (ECC) was registered on 27 April 1944. A year before Independence, on 7 February 1946, L&T morphed from a partnership into a private limited company. Four years later, in 1950, it became a public limited company with a paid-up capital of Rs 20 lakh. The early shareholders, Mangaldas Desai and his son, Narottam (Nicky), served on the board. Their relationship with the two Danes would remain cordial and professional through the decades.

THE IDEA of forging a partnership named Larsen and Toubro (L&T) was conceived in Matheran, a small, picturesque hill-station near Bombay, during an Easter vacation in 1937. When his boss at F.L. Smidth asked him why he wanted to leave the established Danish firm, Holck-Larsen is said to have replied, 'I wish to have greater freedom and be independent.'

'You will find it is an illusion,' he was told.

Undaunted, young Holck-Larsen and Toubro stuck to their decision. Their willingness to make sacrifices, forego comforts and commit themselves to hard work, despite the odds against them, cemented their relationship. Those qualities would continue to define L&T's work ethic even eight decades later.

What was the trigger that made two Danes with secure, well-paid jobs in Europe give up those jobs and stay on in a foreign country with an uncertain future? Toubro was reassured by Mahatma Gandhi's statement, which he had read in *Bombay Chronicle* almost as soon as he landed in India. '(I am) not leading a movement to rid India of its white colonial masters in order to substitute them with brown ones,' Gandhi had declared. It assuaged any doubts Toubro might have had about the new India that was set to emerge.

In 1939, L&T made a small profit of Rs 1,000. But with war flaring up in Europe, India began to feel the headwinds. Realizing that imports were soon likely to be in short supply, Holck-Larsen and Toubro, inventive as ever, decided to set up a small workshop in Bombay for fabrication and service facilities.

In April 1940, after Denmark fell to Hitler's blitzkrieg, the import of Danish machinery stopped completely. L&T was now on its own. To circumvent wartime shortages and the limited quantity of machinery in stock, the partners decided to dismantle them and make wooden moulds of the components. They then gave these moulds to metal workers in Bombay's Kumbharwada (now part of the sprawling Dharavi slum) to recreate. The castings were meticulously inspected and assembled. L&T was now, in effect, manufacturing rudimentary machinery. The die had been cast.

The partners soon expanded their range for ice factories and refrigeration plants. Holck-Larsen and Toubro now needed a full floor of office space, followed by a second, in JK Building, opposite what eventually became L&T House. The Victoria Jubilee Technical Institute (VJTI) in Bombay was the company's main source for technical staff, in a country still under the yoke of British colonialism. When the Royal Navy approached L&T for ship repair, the British brought a captured Italian vessel, *Hilda,* towed it all the way from the Persian Gulf, anchored it outside Bombay harbour and turned it into a workshop. Using it as a base, L&T workers would clamber onto vessels lined up on either side to do the repair work. The Royal Navy suggested that they could help in degaussing[1] ships. While work was in full swing, disaster struck. On 14 April 1944, a ship berthed in Bombay harbour with a cargo of raw cotton loaded on top of explosives blew up. The surrounding area was devastated. Toubro, degaussing a ship nearby, was lucky to escape unhurt.

[1] Degaussing – To neutralize the magnetic field of a ship by encircling it with a conductor carrying electric currents. This was used extensively in World War II by the Allies to protect their ships against the magnetic mines deployed by the Germans.

WITH A growing reputation for reliability, the two engineers found themselves being offered other fabrication opportunities—machine-gun nests, protection of ships' bridges and gun stiffening. L&T put up sheds at Mallet Bunder for vital spare parts, a carpentry shop and overhauling facilities. Another workshop for fabrication was set up in Falkland Road. The internment during the Second World War of German engineers who were building a soda ash plant for the Tatas gave L&T an opportunity to install manufacturing plants. The legendary Sir Homi Mody persuaded the Tata board to give the contract for erecting the plant to the young Danes. Although Europeans usually travelled only first class on Indian Railways, Holck-Larsen and Toubro travelled third class to conserve their scarce resources. But they were equally intent on creating a good impression. So in the dead of night, they got down at a dusty, windswept railway station and had their tickets upgraded for the final lap of the journey. Early the following morning, they stepped out at Mithapur, fresh and 'first class'.

They quickly set to work and erected the equipment for the plant five months ahead of schedule. It was a trend that would distinguish L&T from its peers in the future.

Indian Independence lay just over a year away. But opportunities in post-War, post-colonial India, though nascent, were already visible. Narottam (Nicky) Desai, who retired as L&T chairman in 1989, remembers his father, with his 'long experience of people and instinct about them', sharing his assessment of Holck-Larsen: 'I think this is a good man, a man we can trust.' Sitting in his south Mumbai apartment today, Desai, now ninety-three, says Holck-Larsen had 'this uncanny ability to inspire trust and confidence'.

Although L&T's balance sheet was not robust—certainly not robust enough to justify the investment Desai agreed to make on behalf of himself and his friends—Mangaldas Desai's decision to buy a stake in L&T was based on intuition and faith. Desai and his networked friends gave L&T the visibility it needed in Bombay's clubby commercial fraternity. In the past, the Danes would turn to the city's Multani moneylenders to raise capital whenever needed. Now L&T could approach the banks. For instance, funds needed for the purchase of Caterpillar equipment lying with US military authorities in India were loaned by Chartered Bank.

In 1948, the company acquired 55 acres of marsh, swamp and jungle land in Powai to accommodate its growing businesses. Years later, Holck-Larsen would describe this as the 'turning point' in the company's history. The Caterpillar service station was shifted to Powai in 1950. In December that year, L&T became publicly listed. Holck-Larsen did not believe ownership required a substantial stake in the company. At one time he held a marginal stake—about 1.5 per cent—but still felt the company was his and ran it entirely professionally. It is a philosophy L&T has retained seventy years later, though now imbued with an entrepreneurial vision that Naik assiduously cultivated.

The two sanguine Danes were always clear-headed about their mission: L&T would erect, install and manufacture the machines that produced the commodities people bought. From the very beginning, L&T did whatever it chose to do with an unerring eye on quality. The company's motto was: 'In Service Lies Success'. Both partners knew that customer confidence needed to be built through systematic, conscious effort. Little did they imagine at the time how that *modus operandi* would be honed to perfection decades later by an Indian, yet unborn: Anil Manibhai Naik.

L&T's philosophy was to choose the right man for the right job, train him in the culture and values of the company, give him headroom to perform, and freedom to meet targets and produce results. Outcomes were the key. The accent on merit would be institutionalized by Naik when he took charge as CEO and managing director.

THE 1950s was a heady decade in newly independent India. It was a difficult time, though, for the Indian economy. The British had left India with little industry and, as Holck-Larsen often bemoaned, virtually no engineering expertise. L&T was a curious amalgam of an engineering company founded by two north Europeans, financed initially by a respected family of Gujarati lawyers (the Desais), and run professionally with an accent on technological innovation largely unknown in the India of the 1950s. India at Independence was beset by seemingly intractable problems.

Industry gained traction as India embarked on a new developmental path. Companies like L&T played a key role as a modern Indian state emerged from two centuries of colonial depredation. The Indian economy had been battered not only by colonialism but by the disruption of Partition. Dependence on imports was high and poverty rampant. India's political leadership adopted the model of planned economic development to counter the problems plaguing the country. India evolved a mixed economic system, combining features of paternalistic capitalism and Fabian socialism. The public and private sectors co-existed, and no curbs were to be placed on individual enterprise and private ownership. That was the theory. In practice, things were vastly different.

The government announced the Industrial Policy Resolution (IPR) on 6 April 1948. The resolution outlined its approach to industrial growth and development. It emphasized the importance to the economy of securing a continuous increase in production and ensuring its equitable distribution. The policy segregated industries into four broad categories. The central government would have absolute monopoly over three industries – arms and ammunitions, atomic energy and railway transport. Six other industries, including coal, shipbuilding, and iron and steel, were deemed basic industries. Only the government could set up new units in these six sectors. The third category comprised eighteen industries, including sugar, cement, salt and electricity. These industries would remain in the private sector, but their overall control would be in the hands of the government. The private sector was free to operate in other domains, but the government retained the right to supervise those industries.

Thus was India's early socialist, command economy model born. On 15 March 1950, the Planning Commission was established to initiate planned economic growth. It would take another sixty-four years and the advent of Prime Minister Narendra Modi to dismantle the Commission and create NITI Aayog with an entirely different mandate.

Holck-Larsen, though, had words of praise for post-Independence India's planned economy: 'L&T never made (much) money. But we made profits as there was considerable scope provided by India's five-year development plans for L&T's products and services. The company's growth was due to its participation in this larger adventure.'

THE FIRST of India's five-year plans was launched in 1951. Based on the Harrod-Domar model, the plan focused chiefly on agricultural development and price control. The total proposed expenditure for the plan was Rs 2,069 crore, later raised to Rs 2,378 crore. Of the overall outlay, 27.2 per cent was allocated to irrigation and energy and 17.4 per cent to agriculture and community development. The balance was allocated to transport and communications (24 per cent), industry (8.4 per cent), social services (16.64 per cent), land rehabilitation (4.1 per cent), and other sectors and services (2.5 per cent).

This demonstrates just how small India's economy was in the early 1950s when the Naik family moved to Endhal village in south Gujarat from a comfortable life in Bombay. During this period several Indian Institutes of Technology (IITs) were set up, beginning with Kharagpur in 1951, followed by Bombay (in Powai, in 1958, serendipitously near L&T's works complex), Kanpur (1959) and Madras (also 1959). The Delhi IIT was established in 1961.

They would play an increasingly vital role in L&T's rise as an engineering and technological behemoth. The company became one of the biggest recruiters from the IITs in the 1960s. During the same period, L&T recorded significant growth. India's economy too was undergoing a gradual change. The government's attention was shifting from agriculture to industry. The second five-year plan, announced in 1956, focused on the country's industrial sector, especially heavy industries in the public sector, which Prime Minister Jawaharlal Nehru called the new temples of industry. Between 1956 and 1961, industry recorded rapid growth. Production of machinery for cement and paper began. Power generation capacity was augmented. New hydroelectric power projects and fertilizer plants were set up. Three major steel plants—in Bhilai, Durgapur and Rourkela—were established. Infrastructure development received an impetus.

L&T was still a stripling company, but as India's economy expanded in the 1950s, so did L&T's ambitions and horizons. In 1957, the company received its first large engineering and construction order. It was asked to erect three blast furnaces, a pig iron casting machine and, later, a rolling-mill building for the Rourkela Steel Plant. With the completion of the project in 1959, L&T had earned the title of the largest erection contractor in India.

L&T's flagship department in the early-1950s was its dairy division, representing some of the leading manufacturers of dairy equipment in Denmark, the United Kingdom and Switzerland. They introduced the latest technologies to India. One of the division's major contracts at the time was building the Amul dairy in Anand, Gujarat. Unknown to anybody, Anand would become a signpost in young Anil Naik's journey from the portals of college to the workshops of L&T.

The Amul plant was dedicated to the nation by Nehru on 2 October 1955. On the day of the ceremony, in typical fashion, Toubro was busy testing some of L&T's equipment and could only be introduced to the prime minister at the reception that followed. It was a work ethic that would define L&T in the future as well: quiet, methodical and reliable. The emphasis on enhancing shareholder value would add an important layer. But for that the company would have to await the arrival of Naik who, in the mid-1950s, was still a thirteen-year-old lad studying in a village school in south Gujarat, far away from L&T's Powai headquarters where he would begin work as a junior engineer exactly a decade later.

Another of L&T's early manufacturing lines in the 1950s was bottles and caps. It was the largest supplier of seals for soft drink bottles, breweries, distilleries, processed foods and pharmaceuticals in India as well as south Asia, west Asia, Africa and the Far East. The business was sold in 2003 as part of a restructuring under Naik's leadership. But it was an early sign of what might lie ahead for L&T: global projects. In the 1950s L&T also entered the switchgear business. Representatives of Lauritz Knudsen, a Danish company, arrived in India to assess the switchgear market. In L&T they found a firm not only interested in their products but willing to work with their company to set up a manufacturing facility in the country, initially for low-tension switchgear. In time, L&T began to manufacture a full range of switchgear.

As business grew, the Powai facility expanded too. A new building came up almost every year. When the government started to restrict the issue of import licences to encourage indigenous manufacturing, L&T's Powai plant began manufacturing food processing and dairy equipment. Gradually, more complex machinery was added to the manufacturing range. Following the launch of Operation Flood by the National Dairy Development Board (NDDB), L&T received substantial orders for its complete range of machinery.

Within a few short years though, in 1965, L&T would become deeply involved with India's nuclear programme, changing its profile dramatically—and irrevocably—as a builder to a rapidly modernizing nation. At the centre of L&T's transformation would be a young engineer who had just joined the company at the start of an extraordinary career.

3

Rising above the Rest

THE DECISION TO leave Nestor Boilers, his first job, when he was just twenty-two, changed Naik's destiny. Larsen & Toubro had long been his dream company. It gave him a platform to gain, as Naik says thoughtfully today, 'the kind of satisfaction two generations before me gained serving people, the satisfaction of working for the nation, of *building* the nation. It is on a broader canvas than being a school teacher, however noble that is. It took me four-and-a-half months, however, to join L&T because, as I said, Nestor was not prepared to release me. They were ready to give me anything that I wanted, but once I make up my mind, particularly on principles, on a value system, money does not matter. It has not been an issue in my life ever. Even now, what I earn I give away. So money has never attracted me to a point where I will stick around just for money. I will stay for a value system and for what I am contributing to the nation, whether it is in line with what my grandfather did in helping poor people, or what my father did. Those things are primary.'

Young Naik encountered a medley of characters in his first week at L&T. One was a man called Panchal who was carpentry-in-charge—in effect the foreman of the carpentry shop. Another was the engineer-in-charge, named Ahuja. 'Panchal was so powerful that he did not report to Ahuja,' recalls Naik. 'He reported directly to Baker. In my first week I was supposed to meet Ahuja. So I went to him. Ahuja asked me, "Whom do you report to?"

'I said I reported to Baker. "Do you know the risk involved in reporting to Baker?" he asked. "Someone has to bail you out every time. Do you know Pai (stores-in-charge)? Do you know Sundaram (dispatch-in-charge)? Do you know Keshwani (warehouse-in-charge)? These are the three musketeers. As planning-in-charge, if you don't know how to deal with these three and how to get the material out from the stores in time for manufacturing, everything gets delayed. And these three are unmanageable. You need me to help you out." Then he said, "Go around, meet the other foreman." So I now went to Chandran. He was in charge of training 400 trainees/apprentices who reported to him. He was a king in his own way. The organization was such that everyone was a king in his own domain.'

They were small kingdoms, though. 'Chandran's domain was a training kingdom where there were only Keralites or Tamilians, nobody else,' says Naik. 'Balasaheb Thackeray had telephoned Holck-Larsen more than once on why there was no local man being employed in L&T. Holck-Larsen told Gunnar Hansen, please find out why nobody is coming locally. Hansen asked Tim Baker the same question. None of them could figure out the reason. As foreigners they had no idea what was happening in our local politics. So Chandran was called by them one day and asked, what do you think of hiring locals. Chandran said I have presented you many locals but you are not selecting them. But Chandran had a clever tactic: seven out of the ten candidates he would call for interviews were south Indians and three were locals. And he would select the worst of the locals. Chandran himself was Tamilian. He would present the weakest local candidate to Baker who invariably would reject him.'

Naik is animated as the memories of those early days come flooding back: 'So Baker would say, the locals are useless. Hansen keeps telling me to take them but how can we hire them, the fellows can't even talk and south Indians will at least speak some broken English, these guys can't speak even one word. There was no practical test at that time, but there were lots of technical questions during the interviews. And because they were only trainees, they were coming to learn. They had not done any welding themselves, they were eleventh standard pass.'

One day Hansen got another call from Holck-Larsen. There is some degree of concern, Holck-Larsen told Hansen. Balasaheb had called again. He repeated his complaint that nobody is being employed from among the locals. Baker immediately called K.J. Pherwani. He told him to sort out the problem. 'He himself could not figure out the problem,' says Naik. 'It was deep-rooted, and many people were involved. I needed time to study it and find a solution.'

MORE DRAMA followed. 'I was sent to D'Costa, the terror!' Naik grins. 'He was the general foreman. All other foremen reported to him except the machine shop and carpentry, which were independent. D'Costa wore a half-sleeved white shirt and white shorts. That was his everyday work wear. I went to meet D'Costa in my normal clothes. Without a tie. He said to me, "I wish you all the best." Anybody else would have been scared of his reputation for terrorizing other employees, but I was enjoying myself.'

Naik remembered his father's advice: be fearless if you are in the right. 'They were all *dadas*, super *dadas*,' chuckles Naik. 'They saw me as a young boy of twenty-two. "What do you want to do?" D'Costa asked me. I said I am in charge of planning. Now, D'Costa had several assistant foremen. I said I wanted to go around the workshop. He asked me if I wanted to get introduced to all the assistant foremen. I nodded. Okay, he said. "I won't call them into my cabin because I don't want to disturb them, so I will take you around but only for the first and last time in my life. So you must absorb everything that I show you. This is your orientation." '

Naik's orientation continued apace. 'I was then sent to Balakrishnan. He was more of a gentleman, relatively softer, so he got along with many people, and with me too he was kind,' recalls Naik. 'Next I went to Pherwani, he was also among the more congenial of the lot. He gave me a feeling of comfort. So I figured out that Pherwani was the man I had to be friends with if I had to crack the system.'

Naik's first week at L&T passed by in a flash. Baker sat in a glass cabin so he could see what the employees were doing. K.M. Gopalkrishnan (KMG), Baker's secretary, kept watch outside. One day Baker called KMG and said, 'I never see this guy Naik sitting there on his chair, what is he doing? Whenever I look, he is not there.'

KMG replied gravely, 'Sir, he believes in being on the workshop floor, he does not believe in sitting in an air-conditioned office.' Baker was pleased, nodding, 'Good boy!'

Says Naik: 'KMG could have finished me off by saying that I was roaming around.' There were other niggling problems, though. Naik explains: 'The practice at the time was that even technical assistants put papers in an out-tray and the peon would come once every few hours to take them away. He would take them to the mail room, and another peon would pick them up once in a while and then finally distribute the papers. So if I put the papers in the mail room, the foreman would get them the next day. What I therefore did was to gather up the papers, walk down to the foreman, open the drawings and explain what was to be done, hand them over to him, go to stores, tell them I wanted this material delivered and come back afterwards to check whether the material had been taken out and transported to the workshop. When Baker learnt of all this, he said, "Fantastic, very good. This is exactly what is required to be done. Carry everything physically. Only then can you see with your own eyes that it has reached. Even after that, how do you know if the foreman has understood what is to be done? You are doing all this very well, good!" '

Naik soon became one of Baker's favourites. The Englishman saw in him the potential that would manifest itself in the future with ever-greater certitude. Says Naik: 'On the first day that I joined L&T, in the very first hour, Baker had said to me, "I have recruited forty-one engineers since 1958. In the past seven years I have sacked thirty-eight. Only three have survived. One was S.S. Rao, another was Ahuja, and there was one more. I don't want you to be the thirty-ninth to be sacked." It took just a few months for him to develop a positive opinion of me. Pherwani was also one of my greatest supporters during those early days in L&T.'

But the all-powerful carpentry foreman, Panchal, continued to resist reporting to anyone, including Naik. One day Baker got up from his seat. Panchal was sitting next to him. Baker told Panchal that Naik was going to be sitting here, in his (Baker's) seat one day, and pointed to his own chair. ' "You better realize," Baker told Panchal, "he is going to be sitting here in my chair," ' recalls Naik with relish. 'This was not related to me by Baker. Panchal himself told me that Baker had said this.' Adds Naik: 'Panchal, after that meeting with Baker, came to my room and said he wanted talk to me. He said he had lost and I had won. He would now report to me in all sincerity and honesty. That was the turning point for me at L&T.'

MEANWHILE, THE problem of having to hire local employees persisted. No newspaper advertisements were placed for apprentices, Naik discovered. 'So I placed an advertisement,' says Naik. 'More local applications came in. That itself shook up Chandran and the labour officer. Hansen's secretary, R.S. Mani, was Tamilian. His administration-in-charge, T.S. Parmeshwaran, was a Keralite.'

In the 1960s, the Dravidian movement in the south had created a parochial clannishness that would reduce with time. In L&T, though, 'All applications at the time were coming to the mail room and going only to a particular office boy, Menon,' says Naik. 'And Menon was passing them on to Chandran. So I said, henceforth—and I had full authority from Baker to override whatever Chandran said—all applications will be received by another peon named Kadam, a Maharashtrian, and all applications will come directly to my office and not to Chandran's. My office had a man called Pallav. Kadam would give all the applications to Pallav, who would go through them and show me whom we should call and whom we should not call. This was in 1966. Soon, good local applications came pouring in.'

It was at that time that Baker went off to England. 'All the new graduate engineer trainees (GETs) joined while he was away,' says Naik. 'In the absence of Baker, M.H. Pherwani was in charge. That's the time I met him more frequently. He put me in charge of eight or nine GETs, which was a big number as only twelve GETs used to join the company every year. He told me I have to make up for the last three years as Baker had not employed a single GET. In 1964 he did not take any, in 1963 he did not take any, in 1962 he did not take any, and now in 1965 he had not taken any. There was a big backlog. I was appointed engineer-in-charge when Baker finally came back from England. And then, for the first time in the history of L&T, an examination was conducted for apprentices based on an eleventh standard SSC paper.'

Internal rivalries in L&T gave Naik an early insight into solving tricky personnel issues with a firm but fair hand. The hardened D'Costa had befriended Naik by now. Ahuja was making life miserable for D'Costa by transferring him to a project site in Valsad in Gujarat, forbidding him even weekends off with his family in Bombay. With Naik's reputation now established as a problem solver and a young man who had Baker's ear, D'Costa turned to Naik to intervene. Naik told him to deal directly with Baker. D'Costa put down his grievances against Ahuja in a letter to Baker. The end result: Ahuja, widely disliked by the blue-collar workers at L&T, was transferred to the cattle-feed plant. It was a punishment posting.

'Happy with my work and for sorting out the apprentice problem, Baker had promoted me to engineer-in-charge within just twelve-and-a-half months of my joining L&T in March 1965,' recalls Naik, with customary precision. 'In eastern India, meanwhile, we had a joint venture to build the Rourkela Steel Plant. The Germans were supposed to build it. They took us on as a local partner. Eight Germans lived there for three years on contract. They were to leave in 1967. Holck-Larsen was worried about who would run the workshop in eastern India after the Germans left. He called Hansen and told him to go there. He asked Baker to go there too. Then he called Pherwani and told him to take over from Baker. This is how these two Europeans, Hansen and Baker, left Mumbai's Powai plant. But by that time Pherwani was already having reservations about me. He thought that at twenty-four I was too young to take on major responsibilities. He forgot that he himself, at thirty-two or thirty-three, was too young for the position he was holding! But we got along fine.'

IN FEBRUARY 1967 Baker officially informed Naik that he was leaving for L&T's workshop in Kansbahal near Rourkela. Pherwani would now be Naik's boss. Naik's salary had increased to Rs 1,325 a month, a considerable figure in the 1960s. Pherwani was impressed with Naik. 'His only reservation,' says Naik, chuckling, 'was that I used to work eighteen hours a day and he nine. He depended on me for workshop load implementation and handling union workers, which was not his cup of tea at all. He was a sophisticated man.'

Baker had left behind a note that Naik should be promoted to supervisory A grade, with his monthly salary going up from Rs 1,325 to Rs 1,500. 'Pherwani did not object,' recalls Naik. 'He said I deserved it and I had done a wonderful job.' Naik rattles off the milestones: 'Rs 760 on confirmation, then Rs 1,025 on 1 April 1966, then Rs 1,325 in 1967 when Baker was going to Kansbahal. In 1968,

I was appointed assistant manager within three years and fifteen days of joining. That remains a record in L&T.'

On the fast track, Naik was promoted to production manager in 1970. It was the year too that Naik went abroad for the first time. He was twenty-eight and rising rapidly through the ranks. He toured Britain, Germany, Canada and the United States on his first foreign trip. It wouldn't be his last.

Several episodes during these years shed light on Naik's character and strong work ethic. They would define his career. Naik recalls that, despite warnings, discipline remained a chronic problem at L&T's workshop. Workers would go fishing in Powai lake. Naik himself was told to stay away from Powai after 7 p.m. But gutsy as ever, Naik would turn up at the factory at midnight and stand at the attendance punching machine to see when workers in the shift left. Until then, workers would sign out for the 12 a.m. shift at 11 p.m. Initial opposition from the workers to Naik's tough stand gave way to affection as they realized that he took pains to know each worker personally—their family, their difficulties, where they came from and everything about them. He even remembered their six-digit pay slip numbers.

Union problems at L&T's Powai workshop, though, were endemic. Naik recalls one incident vividly: 'Chandran was shaking with fear as he rushed into my cabin, cowering behind the desk. He refused to meet the angry and violent union leaders.' Naik calmed him down and stepped out of his room. He spoke to the gathered mob in quiet but firm tones. Within a few minutes the situation was defused. The workers respected Naik—an engineer, but nonetheless one who worked alongside them and saw himself as one of them.

Naik would often get onto his Vespa scooter and go to the Powai workshop after midnight to check whether workers in the third shift were moonlighting. Soon enough, word got around. The purr of this scooter alerted the workers. The moment they heard it they would quickly resume work. So Naik began to park his Vespa a short distance from the workshop and walk silently the rest of the way to check on the workers. Productivity improved rapidly.

BY 1973, Naik had been promoted to works manager. A year later he was designated deputy general manager when the works manager designation was discarded and replaced by the title deputy general manager. Naik's stagnation phase now began. He recalls: 'That's the day it started. On the one hand it appeared that I had been promoted but on the other hand it would be several years before I moved up. In contrast, in my first decade at L&T I had received six promotions.'

Naik had risen to become the youngest production manager and the youngest deputy general manager at L&T. By 1974, however, there was a management change at the top. L&T's European managers began to retire. Senior Indian managers were appointed directors on the basis of their seniority. For someone who, from 1965 to 1974, had risen up the hierarchy the fastest in L&T's history, with six promotions in nine years, Naik now found himself stagnating during the eleven years from 1974 to 1985. Though he had opportunities to leave L&T, he refused to even go for the interviews. As he told Sucheta Dalal, editor of *Moneylife*: 'It may sound strange, but at L&T I got the best opportunity to exploit my skills as an engineer and also work for what is good for the country. I don't think there was any other company which could provide me that kind of a platform.'

Naik today asks, rhetorically: 'If these challenges and freedom of work, action and empowerment were not there in L&T, would I have stayed? Possibly not. L&T provides tremendous freedom. We do make mistakes but we learn from them. This company gives you the feeling of ownership. I never felt that this company did not belong to me, although our salary got frozen during the socialistic regime for years together. And when the caps were finally removed, our children had started earning more than us, especially in the IT industry. In 1989, I became a director on the board and, in 1999, I became the CEO. But if I look back at what made me stick on, it was great excitement, the feeling of owning the company, empowerment and the environment.'

After 1974, even as Naik's career stalled, he hunkered down, working as hard as ever, spending over sixteen hours a day in the office and on the workshop floor. The Licence Raj remained an impediment to industrial growth. Gradually, as a palliative in what was still a socialist-driven economy with high taxes and stifling regulations, several new items were added to the Open General License (OGL) list. The number of items on OGL, which had been re-introduced in 1976, increased from 79 during the year to 1,339 by 1990. The share of canalized imports—imports over which the government had a monopoly—reduced. The government introduced numerous export incentives and relaxed industrial controls. The tax system finally began to see reforms, however tentative and faint-hearted. L&T had to rely on hard-to-get licences for offshore platforms, despite its stellar work since the 1960s in nuclear power reactors and, later, on nuclear-powered submarine prototypes.

IN 1965, L&T had been chosen as a partner for building nuclear reactors. Dr Homi Bhabha, then chairman of the Atomic Energy Commission (AEC), had in fact first approached L&T in the 1950s to fabricate critical components for atomic reactors. He convinced Holck-Larsen, a friend with whom he shared an interest in the arts, that the company could do it, indeed must do it. L&T has since contributed significantly to the Indian nuclear programme and specifically to nuclear power plants at Tarapur, Kota, Narora and Kalpakkam. Holck-Larsen was once asked by a junior engineer why L&T should get into building nuclear plants when companies in the US and Germany were losing money on nuclear jobs. He replied, 'Young man, India has to build nuclear power plants. If not L&T, who will do it?'

Naik is animated as he traces L&T's nuclear lineage: 'In 1965 we became a nuclear fabricator. That is where the story started. When I joined L&T in 1965, the initial nuclear agreement had just been signed. A new workshop was being created in Powai. We were manufacturing and dispatching the fabricated material to the Tarapur nuclear plant. Even before Tarapur, the Rajasthan atomic nuclear project is from where we got the first order in 1965. I joined when the nuclear shop was set up to manufacture nuclear equipment for the Rajasthan atomic power project. The first one in Rajasthan was called RAPP-1. It was imported from Canada. RAPP-2 was ordered from L&T. The next nuclear plant was in Madras. The contract for that too was given to L&T. And so was MAPP-2. BHEL then came into the picture. But they could not make reactors. So all reactors were with us, all steam generators too. So far, virtually all of India's nuclear reactors have been made by L&T.'

During the 1970s L&T was contracted to work with Indian Space & Research Organization (ISRO). Its then chairman, Vikram Sarabhai, chose L&T as manufacturing partner. In 1972, when India launched its space programme, L&T was invited to participate. Naik was responsible for taking the programme forward as manager-in-charge of the manufacturing process. 'Of the 104 satellites that were launched from a single rocket in February 2017, the central portion was made by us,' points out Naik. 'The launching station was also made by us.'

In 1985 L&T entered into a partnership with Defence Research and Development Organization (DRDO). L&T was not yet allowed by the government to manufacture defence equipment but was permitted to participate in design and development programmes with DRDO. After the design and development was done, L&T had to hand over all the drawings to DRDO. The government would then assign the production work to a public sector defence unit or ordnance factory for manufacture. After a series of successes and positive policy initiatives, L&T today makes a range of weapon and missile systems, command and control systems, engineering systems and submarines through DRDO.

Says Naik: 'There were three main groups in L&T—Group I, II and III. I was in charge of everything in Group II—nuclear power plants, defence systems and space launch vehicles through DRDO, DAE, ISRO, and industrial equipment for chemical, fertilizer, cement and dairy plants. The nuclear-powered submarine programme was conceptualized and cleared by the government in the 1980s. We were involved in equipment design, realization and qualification since 1986, engaged in the hull technology development from 1990, and in full-fledged manufacture a few years later. After the opening up of the sector in 2001-02, other large business houses sought involvement in defence projects. The Tatas and L&T, both veterans in the sector, are not crossing swords because the Tatas are more into electronics, vehicles and, recently, aviation. There are hardly any areas of common interest except military communication, where we have partnered as co-developers. That leaves a few launcher systems, but here L&T has a far deeper presence. The Mahindras want to be in air force projects, both aircraft and helicopters, because they and the Tatas are the majors in the automobile sector and globally, auto and aero go together.'

Apart from the three main groups, there were several smaller groups too at L&T. While Group I looked after earthmoving equipment, Group II was responsible for heavy engineering, hydrocarbon and a slew of other businesses. Group III handled switchgear and electrical equipment. Group IV comprised all the marketing groups. Group V was into cement manufacturing. Group VI made equipment. Group VII looked after shipping. 'At one stage,' says Naik, 'there were eleven groups. But then they were reorganized. Construction was a group by itself, called ECC.'

L&T had bid for a large project in Abu Dhabi in 1976. ECC's balance sheet, however, did not meet the bid's financial qualification requirement. So it was merged into L&T. ECC was eventually rechristened L&T Construction and now accounts for the largest slice of the group's annual revenue. Till the 1980s, L&T was principally a fabrication company. It was in the late-1980s, when

Naik became vice-president, that the company began to execute turnkey projects. A new era had begun. And Hazira would soon occupy centre stage.

BEFORE THAT, though, India's economy was plunged into turmoil. Trouble had been was brewing in India's balance of payments through the 1980s. Multiple oil crises had pushed up the cost of imports. Meanwhile, exports had been impacted by the global economic slowdown in the late-1980s. This had led to a burgeoning current account deficit. India's foreign exchange reserves plunged. The country was forced to rely on external sources to finance the deficit, leading to escalating debt.

L&T needed huge investments to prepare itself for a fresh phase of growth. Naik had been meticulously developing the Hazira manufacturing complex since the mid-1980s. The platform for L&T's surging future growth had been laid. It would take another decade for that growth to manifest and catapult L&T into the elite league of Indian multinationals.

Naik leans back in his chair in L&T's boardroom as he reflects on a career that has had its share of crests and troughs. 'There was a time when, in spite of being the most hardworking, dedicated and passionate manager, my career had stalled. That didn't dampen my spirit and I didn't let it come in the way of my work. I worked even harder during that phase and let no one know my personal lows. I did this because to me L&T and my work at L&T were sacrosanct. Many job offers came my way at that time but I was never tempted to take them as I had already dedicated my life to L&T. Today people get restless if they are not promoted once every three years, and here I was with one promotion in twelve years! I finally became a director when I was forty-seven. The short point is: if you are truly dedicated to your organization and committed to its cause, you will not let personal lows come in the way of achieving excellence at work.

'To me L&T is like a temple and I consider myself its keeper. If anyone tries to take over L&T, I'm like a wounded tiger. I will do everything within my power to ensure that L&T stays independent and adheres to the highest standards of governance. In fact, it was a takeover attempt that allowed me to unlock L&T's value by demerging the cement business and creating the L&T Employees Welfare Foundation. While the cement demerger created a more focused L&T, it also yielded great value to the employees. They became stakeholders in a true sense and began to see the need to increase the value of the company. The welfare foundation ensured that the company was protected from further takeover bids.'

He continues softly: 'So only my destiny brought me to L&T. There is no company in the world – show me one – which can do what L&T does. In the US there is a shipyard that does only aircraft carriers, another shipyard that does only nuclear-powered submarines, but they don't do anything else. Here we do nuclear-powered submarines, aerospace, nuclear reactors, all kinds of things. I am a start-up man in the corporate world. But an executor as well as a deliverer. My administration is very strong. That is my legacy and my challenge: to continue to grow technologically and execute to perfection.'

The biggest challenge – and triumph – of his career now loomed on the horizon: Hazira.

4

Hazira: Jewel in the Crown

THE JAMMU TAWI Express chugged into Surat railway station at 9 p.m. It was a warm, humid night in August 1983. Anil Naik, then joint general manager of Group II in L&T, stepped quickly out of the train. Without wasting time, he drove to a marshy piece of land that the company had acquired. He had put on large gumboots to negotiate the wet, swampy terrain. Accompanying him were senior executives from L&T. As he walked kilometre after kilometre along the marsh, the high tide suddenly came in. Water gushed around him. He quickly retreated to higher ground. It was Naik's first visit to this plot of waterlogged marshland. Within years it would be the site of one of the world's most technologically advanced manufacturing complexes.

GREEN. DISCIPLINED. Tranquil. Those are the first thoughts that skip through your mind as you enter L&T's 755-acre Hazira manufacturing facility on the outskirts of Surat, coincidentally the city in which Naik was born. Hazira is now widely regarded as among the most sophisticated, high-technology manufacturing complexes in the world. Naik's eye for detail is evident everywhere: in the sculpture reflecting L&T's soaring spirit near the entrance which was built entirely in-house; in the lush green landscaping everywhere that has Naik's imprimatur; and in the quietly disciplined workforce. Everything moves like clockwork. The workmen fabricating nuclear reactors, offshore platforms and nuclear-powered submarines go about their work with silent precision.

The ever-bustling head of the process plant and nuclear business at Hazira, senior vice-president Yogesh Trivedi, is an irrepressible bundle of energy. He greets us as we thread our way through Surat's traffic on the way to Hazira. 'In the late-1970s and early-1980s, Mr Naik was the boss for heavy engineering,' he says. 'He was planning everything. Even in those days we were doing great things. For example, we were involved in building nuclear reactors of 220-235 MW. Out of the total of twenty-two nuclear reactors in India, L&T has played a role in eighteen.'

Trivedi is proud of the company's extraordinary bandwidth across technologies and product segments. He says, with characteristic ebullience: 'We started fertilizer projects, refinery projects, petrochemical projects, satellite launchers. Our lifting capacity was a maximum of 100 tonnes then but we used to lift 180 tonnes. We were engineering people so we were essentially solving problems "on the fly", which came naturally to the whole team. We did all kinds of innovation. We did not have much money but tremendous creativity in engineering, and Mr Naik was right there in the trenches!'

Trivedi rewinds to the early-1980s, when Naik was coming into his own after a period of relative quiescence in L&T. Naik looked at the future and thought (out aloud), as Trivedi recalls, that 'a 150-tonne unit will some day be 1,000 tonnes, what is 10-15 feet in diameter will some day be 35 feet or even 50 feet in diameter. What is 100 feet long may become 400-500 feet long, what is a 220 MW nuclear reactor can become a 1,000 MW nuclear reactor, what is a two-inch thick plate may become a one-foot thick plate. None of us ever imagined all this. We were then based in land-locked Powai.'

As he rose through the ranks in L&T, Naik had started thinking of creating a brand new site on the coast from where L&T could ship the heavy equipment it manufactured to anywhere in the world. There was a full order book in India, but Naik realized that it would not be enough in the future. L&T would have to go global. 'In the late-1970s and early-1980s, to think like that when India was still a closed economy was remarkable,' says Trivedi.

A number of locations for the new facility were shortlisted. 'Mr Naik zeroed in on Hazira,' says Trivedi. 'It's virtually on the shores of the Arabian Sea. So he put it to the board of directors and it got sanctioned, though with some difficulty. He said we will make the world's best here—nuclear reactors and nuclear-powered submarines will be made here too. At that time we did not have a licence for offshore platforms. He fought tooth and nail for a licence. It was the era of the Licence Raj. The government would not give us a licence for offshore platforms, it was a protected sector. But Mr Naik managed a very interesting strategy by calling the proposal a helicopter-landing platform. After that we just took off, and by the mid-1990s anyway, the Licence Raj had gone.'

The first 200 acres of Hazira were bought from the government. 'In hindsight, that was a masterpiece of strategic thinking,' says Trivedi, as he takes us around the large complex in a convoy of buggies. 'We took care not to take any private land, only government land, so that we don't waste energy in futile battles. We surveyed it. It was on the waterfront, and I was the fortunate soul to take possession of the land from the Collector in October 1983. It was a very interesting piece of land. It was right next to Tapti river, touching the Arabian Sea. It is a peak delta. We had 1.4 km of waterfront—a strip really, like a funnel—and 1.7 km of road boundary. It was a triangular piece, or trapezoidal, as we say in engineering jargon.'

In 1983 Hazira was marshland. Within four years it would be transformed into a high-technology manufacturing facility ranked among the top five of its kind in the world. Visualized by Naik at a time when India's economy was still encased in a socialist straitjacket and Indian politics was torn asunder by the Punjab insurgency, his foresight today, over three decades later, appears near-prophetic.

IN THE initial years, Naik would return to Hazira week after week, from Thursday to Saturday (an off-day at the Powai works), so that he could be back at the Mumbai workshop on Sunday. From a swamp covering several hundred acres, the transformation of Hazira into a manufacturing complex that builds equipment for nuclear-powered submarines, nuclear reactors, fast interceptor vessels and offshore oil and gas platforms is one of the most extraordinary stories in Indian corporate history. Hazira is a miracle built on marsh. During high tide, 50 per cent of Hazira's land would go under several feet of water. 'There was no land, it was all sea!' exclaims Trivedi. 'We were still new to this place. We called Mr Naik. He came immediately. It was already night. And remember, the water was not plain water, it was churning sea water and contained sea snakes and all kinds of muck.'

Naik surveyed the scene with the Hazira team. What the L&T engineers had thought was a perfect piece of land now clearly required to be filled up to make the project workable. Says Trivedi, 'If you fill up the whole thing with concrete, then it will cost you a fortune. Mr Naik made it a weekly routine to come here by the Jammu Tawi train on Thursday evening. He would reach here at around 9 p.m. Our meetings would start on Thursday night itself. The meetings would go on up to two in the night. The next morning we would be back at the site.'

Naik recalls those heady, adrenaline-filled days: 'We built the Hazira complex in thirty months. We had not realized that the entire land was very porous and marshy. We had to put concrete columns – piles. The whole structure is standing on piles 43 feet in depth. When I went around the land I used to walk several kilometres. When we went there in the monsoon we couldn't even see the land. Only the black strip of road was visible. There was water on this side and on that side. Both sides were full of water in high tide. Only in low tide could you see the land. I used to visit the land during high tide and think to myself that there is no way we can build anything here, there is only water. You dare not walk there because you could land in the river if you walk too close to it. You simply don't know where the river starts.'

The dangers were stark but Naik and his team remained undaunted. 'In low tide you could see the land, so you go in, but it was all *kichad*,' says Naik. 'I used to wear gumboots and walked 4-5 km. We then did a navigation study based on the Khadakvasla model. There is a model of the Tapti river in Khadakvasla. We identified where the river is getting eroded, where the depth is more … we studied all that. Plus how much land we would have to fill up because the difference between high tide and low tide was four metres! So we would have to fill up two metres before we could use 40 metres of piling. The initial project cost was Rs 30 crore. Around Rs 11-12 crore went into restoring the land alone.'

These were the enabling works needed just to get the land ready. 'The complex cost us a total of Rs 42 crore more than thirty years ago,' says Naik. 'Now it is worth about Rs 8,000-10,000 crore because we have built many more structures there. Of the 755 acres, 550 acres is filled up. We have kept the balance 205 acres for future defence work that will start from next year. By 2021 it will be a beautiful defence manufacturing plant. So there is defence, there is power, there is oil and gas, there is heavy equipment, there is nuclear—it's the pride of India.'

Naik's voice cracks with emotion as he speaks about Hazira. But back in the early-1980s, L&T's board of directors needed much coaxing to approve the Hazira project. Naik was then still a joint general manager, though clearly destined for higher things. 'When I set up Hazira I had to go three times to the board because we were then not used to spending Rs 30 crore on such projects,' he says. 'This was a mega project thirty years ago. No one was willing to take responsibility for it. What if it does not work out? I put a lot of force behind it—convinced the board that it will work. Please let me do it, I said. So we went ahead, but we overshot the budget. Today Narottam (Nicky) Desai, who was then the chairman of the board, says: "Anil, if you had not been in L&T at that time, L&T would not have been what it is now."'

There is only a handful of manufacturing complexes like Hazira in the world. Says Naik: 'In India there is nothing comparable. It took three-four years of losses in Hazira before it achieved break-even around 1992. It then made excellent profits until four years ago. Heavy investments were made all over the world for nuclear manufacturing, but then came the tsunami in Japan. Everything collapsed. The whole world stopped putting up nuclear plants. So now there is huge surplus capacity worldwide. Hazira's profitability is not that good but it is not loss-making. It still makes a profit of about Rs 200 crore a year. It should actually have grown to Rs 500 crore in profitability but for the nuclear slowdown, though that is now gradually easing.'

As the salience of Powai declines, Hazira has picked up the slack.

THE ENGINEERING difficulties in building a high-technology manufacturing facility on marshland posed a huge challenge. Ingenuity was needed. 'In the villages of Mora and Damka, we discovered there was a particular kind of sand known as *panna* sand,' says Trivedi. '*Panna* is a little coarse. It could strengthen and stabilize the swampy land base. But how to remove that sand and take it away? The villagers had their own problems. We took permission from the Collector but the villagers were unhappy. They created a ruckus. One day when we were transporting the sand, the women from the village lay down in front of our trucks, obstructing all movement.'

Naik plunged into action. He met the Collector, the taluka chief and the district development officer. He then went to the villages and spoke to the protestors. Speaking to them in colloquial Gujarati,

Naik allayed their fears. He told them that the Hazira complex would create new jobs for them and bring all-round development to the area: roads, power, water, sanitation. Says Trivedi today: 'Naik convinced them. Who else could have faced the villagers; they would beat you up! But Mr Naik explained to them in Surti language, very genuinely, about the job opportunities and prosperity that Hazira would bring. So we finally got the *panna* sand.'

Simultaneously, however, another problem was brewing. The shop's concrete columns would have to support loads of 400 tonnes to 500 tonnes, using EOT cranes. To ensure that they did not sink into the swampy land, the columns needed a solid load-bearing base. Trivedi recounts the ordeal: 'Now this is a river silt basin. We went on digging, up to 45 metres—but there was no stone, only slush. After another few metres we encountered sea water. Then we drove piles into the ground, capped them with a concrete base and placed rafters on top of the columns. The columns could literally dance as there was no stone below the ground to hold them steady. So we locked the rafters. It was an engineering challenge. We adopted an innovative technique—we did what is known as friction piling. If you keep on driving piles into the ground, you will meet some resistance. At one point you will gain sufficient resistance by displacing the earth and creating friction. So, finally, *panna* sand plus friction piling plus heavy engineering did the trick in this marshy swampland in Hazira!'

Naik and his team of engineers had more challenges in store. Trivedi, who was in the thick of the action, recalls some of them: 'The workshop was in place, but what to do about getting people? In our business, when you build nuclear reactors it's assumed that you put up a workshop, get people, and start making reactors. But it's not like that. It requires a tremendous amount of training. So Mr Naik identified 500 schools around Surat and all over Gujarat. We were told to first go to the top five schools in each taluka we visited, pick up the first five rankers from among the tenth standard pass students, interview them and select from among them.

Mr Naik personally interviewed the first three batches. The kind of engineering work we were doing required depth of knowledge in mathematics, geometry and trigonometry. To measure angles you should be able to decipher drawings, understand instructions in English and apply the procedures, codes and specifications.

'In 1984-85, even before the first workshop in Hazira was created, we had started a training centre in Udhna, a suburb of Surat. We set up a small workshop and began training. Look at Mr Naik's vision! The Hazira workshop is going to come up two-three years down the line, but Mr Naik already knows he will need people so he decides to train them in advance! Simultaneously, the project is going on, finances are being managed, engineering challenges met, and we were still looking after the Powai workshop. However, Mr Naik's philosophy was that while you must work hard, once in a while you must also relax. So even as we were working on Hazira day and night, he would take us to Kwality restaurant in Surat for dinner, followed by his favourite dessert: ice-cream!'

APART FROM Naik, several other executives were involved in the Hazira project: K. Venkataramanan, V.K. Magapu, M.V. Kotwal and V.C. Bedi, among others. Recalls Venkataramanan, an IIT Delhi alumnus who worked alongside Naik for five decades: 'Hazira was Naik's vision. For the growth of heavy engineering, we needed to scout for land with a waterfront. Powai could not have ever handled large, oversized equipment. We also had a dream at that time to enter offshore, for which we required a waterfront. L&T was quite small at that time. India had a licensing regime. We had lots of problems in getting a licence for Hazira to manufacture what we wanted to manufacture. Plus, we had no experience of building waterfront facilities, knowledge of tides and currents. Therefore it was a fabulous experience and journey. At that time, the whole area used to be inundated by sea water during high tide. We had to wear gumboots. And my size being twelve, I had a tough time getting the gumboots off my feet after use!'

A former managing director and CEO of L&T, Venkataramanan has a strong background in R&D. He played a significant role in sorting out the technical challenges Hazira posed. 'After land acquisition, the next important activity was piling,' he says. 'This was also the first initiation in a big way for ECC in piling and building a quay wall. The peculiarity of Hazira is the absence of any rock to build piles on. That is why a lot of people used to ask whether such heavy workshops can be built with piles which do not really rest on rock. I come from an R&D background – civil engineering was not my discipline. But as project manager of Hazira, I had to go into the details about piles and learn about pre-cast and pre-stressed concrete. Those were great days. Every week Mr Naik used to come to Hazira by train. He was fully involved in the selection of workmen trainees, planning and guiding the construction of the facility and at the same time helping secure work for the facility, whether it was for hydrocrackers or offshore platforms.'

Vijay Kumar Magapu, the articulate IIT Madras alumnus and an old L&T hand, was at the time living in Canada with his family. He was persuaded by Naik to return to India to take charge at Hazira. 'My children were in state-of-the-art schools in Canada,' Magapu recalls. 'I pulled them out and brought them to a malaria-infested Surat. Back then, however, we were the bad boys of the boardroom. We started off with a small allotted budget for the Hazira project. This was enhanced later, but we were going to overshoot even that. We were very apprehensive about how Mr Desai, who was then chairman, would react. I had earlier been working in Powai. There I followed the rules and made others do so. But at Hazira, in everything we did we were conscious that we were setting the agenda for the next 100 years. It is the jewel in the crown of the engineering division. I was there till 1994. We raised an impressive facility out of mud on a river bank. We built the roads and put in the tables and chairs, we recruited the people. But how do you fuse all this into a business? That's the tough part. I believe there are four steps to this:

1. Be visible, and see that each part of the machinery is driving towards one objective;
2. All parts must be fully willing and engaged to take on the challenge. Observe the psychology;
3. Establish good practices—transparent policy, merit-based recognition; no politics, an open door policy that doesn't suffocate and frustrate employees;
4. Build the itch of adventure and technology. When we were setting up Hazira, we were told it's too big an ambition, and you can't do it. We set about proving that we could. We were the guys in the garage, working in the back of beyond. Doing our thing. No baggage to carry. No paradigm to follow.'

M.V. Kotwal, who also headed operations at Hazira for a number of years, adds: 'As far as people are concerned we had an advantage and a disadvantage. The advantage was that we started with a clean slate. We had learnings from Powai, we also knew which of our practices we should change. But here we did some unlearning of the past and learning of new things. I remember the first day Magapu and I walked through the workshops wearing boiler suits. It was not a done thing in those days. So people were looking at us thinking, what are these strange apparitions walking about ... but then gradually the culture seeped in. We wanted to be people who lead the change rather than observe the change.'

The early going was tough. Kotwal recalls a particularly unnerving incident: 'In October 1986, when there are yearly high tides, we (Trivedi, I and a few others) decided to visit the land during high tide which was at 2 a.m. that night. We were walking near the land edge with torches and lanterns as there was no power then. Near the south end of the plot, there was a small *nullah* through which water used to enter the plot. We suddenly realized that the high tide had gushed in. We were practically at the mouth of the *nullah*, and we would have been sucked in by the gushing waters. We ran to safety in the muddy water, came out of the plot and sat on the culvert till dawn set in. To our surprise we noticed that more than 50 per cent of the plot was under water in the morning. From then onwards our approach to handling the project underwent a sea change. After a lot of detailed studies it was decided to raise the plot plinth level by 1.4 metres so that one could be safe there. This required additional monetary provisions and cutting down of costs elsewhere.'

NAIK AND his team boldly decided, first up, to build a workshop much larger than what would have been considered necessary.

A 220 MW nuclear reactor was being upgraded to 500 MW. 'There is a little story here,' smiles Trivedi. 'India originally got a Canadian natural uranium reactor. These are pressurized heavy water reactors. They came from Canada and then we started learning the technology. In 1974, Indira Gandhi's government tested a nuclear device at Pokhran. This had immediate repercussions. The Americans pulled out of Tarapur, and soon the Canadians walked away too. Mrs Gandhi was a tough leader. She was supported by Nuclear Power Corporation of India Ltd (NPCIL) and L&T. We said: don't go to anybody, we will build our own nuclear reactors. Typically India would have gone to the French or Russians saying, give us a new reactor. We did not do that. We said we will develop it in-house. So the first thing that NPCIL and L&T did together, and Mr Naik was fully involved in this, was to convert a Canadian design of a nuclear reactor into a completely Indian design. Everything was done in-house.'

By 1987, even as the Hazira facilities were getting ready, the team had a small workshop constructed by its own workmen. The trainees from Udhna were transferred here and they started working on small engineering jobs, practising for bigger jobs. L&T, meanwhile, built a hostel for the workers, who were from all over Gujarat. Slowly, orders began coming in. The Hazira complex was still new; few knew its capabilities. 'If you want to make a nuclear reactor, you have to prove yourself,' says Trivedi. 'The investments and the risks are huge.'

Naik was clear-headed about what he wanted to do in Hazira and meticulous in the way he went about it. He made the team of engineers list more than a hundred mistakes they had made in Powai. Everyone ate the same canteen food as everyone else. Workers had to change into their work clothes at the gate, then punch in their cards inside the shops so that they were ready for work without wasting a minute. During working hours, no tea breaks were allowed. Discipline was sacrosanct.

The maiden assignment at Hazira was building pylons for the new Howrah Bridge. Much more challenging was the Reliance Industries refinery, with a capacity of 600,000 barrels per day, which L&T helped to build. 'L&T's other breakthrough came with Indian Oil's refinery in Gujarat,' says Trivedi. 'They were looking to build the first hydrocracker for their cracking unit. In those days the best crude would be bought, refined and put into the market. Then came the era of heavy crude. Heavy crude was cheaper but required very complicated, high-temperature processing. So a process known as hydrocracking was developed. L&T, meanwhile, had tied up with Japan Steel Works (JSW) for technology transfer. Mr Naik convinced Chevron that our capability matched their requirement, and we got the first two orders of 435-tonne hydrocrackers, capable of withstanding temperatures up to 450 degrees centigrade. We had successfully graduated from 100-150 tonnes to 435 tonnes. We also graduated from a two-inch to a nine-inch thick wall. We went from low-temperature steel to high-temperature steel. In engineering terms, the outer layer provides the strength while the stainless steel inside deals with the corrosion. We delivered the first two hydrocrackers in 1991.'

Walking around the Hazira complex, we pass a big tree planted by founder Holck-Larsen. All the trees, placed in neat rows, have been planted by well-known personalities visiting the complex. Naik has planted forty trees. National Security Advisor (NSA), Ajit Doval, on a visit to Hazira planted one too. 'The place where you are standing is so beautifully green,' smiles Trivedi. 'It is difficult to imagine that this used to have a few feet of seawater in high tide! Mr Naik is very passionate about greenery. He won't allow any facility to be commissioned unless the landscaping is up to his standard. You see this green cover? It is actually sweetened soil, which was saline. This is a functional requirement. We do a lot of work where the assemblies require a dust-free environment. Once the reactor or nuclear steam generator goes inside the reactor vault, access for maintenance is limited. So this greenery also helps us to lower dust levels in Hazira.'

Explaining the way the workshops are laid out, Trivedi says: 'The orientation of the workshops is in a 'T'-shaped grid. The small feeder assemblies go to the big workshop and the big workshops send out the manufactured equipment to the sea through a roll-on, roll-off jetty.' He adds: 'We adopted this special layout shape because we wanted to have access to the Tapti river for the heavy loading of equipment. This first workshop was essentially meant for building nuclear reactors. We then did three more workshops here and went on adding to them. There is a super-heavy workshop too. If you have a 2,000-tonne job, you can simply send it via the sea from here. In 1981 we were very happy doing 100-, 200- and 300-tonne jobs in our Powai facility. But Mr Naik imagined that some day we will do 2,000-tonne jobs too. Today we are actually doing reactors of that size. He foresaw this over thirty-five years ago.'

Hazira is a Class 1 defence manufacturing establishment and has a very specific requirement of a 13-foot security wall. 'There are workshops inside which only cleared personnel can access,' says Trivedi. 'These are off limits for any outsider. Non-Indian citizens have to take very special sanction to visit.'

We walk with safety helmets into workshops that make nuclear reactors, submarine hulls, defence equipment and hydrocrackers. Further away in the sprawling complex is a yard for manufacturing offshore platforms. Small ships, fast boats and coast guard vessels are built here. A large offshore platform in front of us is nearing completion. It will be shipped through the Tapti to an ONGC oil and gas complex in the Arabian Sea.

Trivedi points to L&T's transition into supercritical thermal power plants. 'The world uses 535-degree-Celsius boilers but lately it realized that when you go from 535 degrees to 600, 625, 650 degrees, you extract 4 to 5 per cent extra efficiency. That means if you put up a 1,000 MW plant, in effect a 50 MW plant comes free! That's what we did. Mr Naik and the team at the time went to the best possible manufacturers and technology providers worldwide and put up manufacturing facilities for supercritical boilers and turbines here. We entered into a joint venture with Mitsubishi for these supercritical boilers in 2007-08. It is now known as Mitsubishi Hitachi Power Systems (MHPS). This became one of the best supercritical boiler plants in India. To match a supercritical boiler you need a turbine which will have 565/593 degree Celsius capacity and a matching generator. So we have two joint ventures, one with Mitsubishi (MHPS) for boilers and the other for turbines and generators, again with MHPS. Mitsubishi has two different technologies, so both joint ventures are with MHPS.'

The next big facility we see at Hazira is almost a kilometre in length. India did not earlier have the capability to produce its own nuclear forgings with such a facility. 'Nuclear reactors require very critical nuclear forgings,' points out Trivedi. 'India's nuclear technology was dependent on Canada and other countries. The dependence applied to nuclear forgings too.'

The challenge was to become self-sufficient as quickly as possible. In 2009-10, the government deliberated over which among several private sector companies should form a joint venture with Nuclear Power Corporation (NPCIL). L&T was selected. It became an equity partner with NPCIL. L&T holds a 74 per cent stake and NPCIL a 26 per cent stake in the joint venture.

Over 2,000 engineers and technologists work in the Hazira complex. The campus has between 12,000 and 16,000 people in all. Around 5,000 are L&T employees. To ensure a congenial work–life balance, L&T has built a residential colony for engineers in nearby Surat. Magdala housing is the first platinum-rated Indian green building council society in Gujarat. 'The initial problem lay in hiring the best people and training them for nuclear-level, defence-level work,' says Trivedi. 'The second challenge was to retain them. So we created several facilities, and Mr Naik ensured acquisition of land in Magdala. There is a training centre and a state-of-the-art safety school too at Hazira, because for us safety is not something you just talk about.'

HAZIRA WAS up and running by 1987. Naik's ascent at L&T now gathered pace. He was appointed vice-president and a member of the board in 1989, and president in 1995. Within four years, in 1999, Naik had become L&T's CEO and managing director. The journey from GM to CEO had taken just thirteen years.

'Even earlier, as joint GM, I was looking after a lot of new activities which were really not under the purview of my designation,' says the feisty Naik, taking stock of an action-packed, transformative three decades. 'But I was very curious to do something new.' Naik confesses that he is a start-up man in a corporate setting. 'That's how nearly 80 per cent of L&T has been created,' he says. 'I have started 30-40 businesses. In Hazira, in the mid-1980s, I arranged for 200 acres near Surat, which was unheard of at the time. What was I going to do with 200 acres, everybody was asking. I said some day it will be filled and we will need more. Now we have not 200 acres, but 755 acres. We had to buy another 555 acres.'

L&T began heavy engineering in Hazira because it wanted a waterway to the world. 'Big equipment cannot be carried from

Powai to the port,' says Naik. 'So we took the sea route from Hazira. We continue to make small and medium equipment in Powai. But even equipment that is a little more than medium-sized is becoming difficult to transport, what with the current population and traffic density. Moreover, the port has gone to the other side of the city (Mumbai) at Nhava Sheva (JNPT) so the distances have increased significantly. Heavy engineering has to move to the coastline at Hazira. It could also move to our Kattupalli shipyard and facility near Chennai when Hazira gets full. So we'll have one facility on the east coast, one on the west coast.'

Hazira is in every sense of the word Naik's brainchild. His pride in it is unmistakable. How did he pick the location? Looking back, Naik recalls that a three-member team had surveyed many locations in Gujarat, Maharashtra and Mangalore. 'I ruled out Kerala as we can't cope with the political changes,' says Naik. 'Mangalore was heavily unionized. Maharashtra lacked infrastructure. We went to Saurashtra, but again there was no infrastructure. So Surat was finally chosen. It is now one of the biggest industrial towns in Gujarat after Jamnagar. There is a big Reliance petrochemical complex, L&T's engineering complex, Essar's plant, NTPC's power plant, ONGC's base station, IOCL … everybody is in Hazira today.'

When L&T finally began making offshore platforms in the early 1990s, Naik invited L&T's board of directors to Hazira. During his speech to the directors, he had tears in his eyes. He said his Hazira budget estimate had gone up to Rs 42 crore, overshooting the original estimate. The whole board was unhappy with him, he said, and yet, with a single order of Rs 372 crore for an offshore platform from ONGC the investment has been recouped. 'This was a monumental fightback, because in those days of the Licence Raj nobody gave you a licence for offshore platforms,' says Trivedi. 'He got this one done and we have never looked back.'

Trivedi adds context to Hazira's growing technological sophistication: 'Instead of ordinary equipment with alloy steel we bought a rolling machine to roll steel up to ten-inch thickness in hot condition. In Hazira we took it up to eight-inch thickness and then about ten years back we built reactors up to one-foot thickness. So the entire range in heavy engineering was covered. We graduated every year, added one-foot thick hydrocracking reactors and eventually came to a point where almost everything the world wants can be made at Hazira. We make ammonia converters, urea reactors, nuclear reactors, everything. Some equipment, of course, are still made in Powai, but they are small in diameter. There will come a time when they will be made only in Hazira. Vadodara is a specialized manufacturing facility for exotic materials requiring clean conditions for process plant internals, sonar domes and defence composites.'

WHEN HE took office as CEO in 1999, Naik injected a dose of entrepreneurship into what was a respected but slow-moving company. L&T's turnover rose twenty-five-fold in the next eighteen years, and market capitalization increased eighty-fold. Hazira was emblematic of Naik's entrepreneurial drive. An entrepreneurial approach was evident in the company's other projects too. L&T built a prototype for the first nuclear-powered submarine in India. A nuclear-powered submarine is around 100 metres long. It has a nuclear reactor section and is outfitted with several pieces of high-tech equipment. The company made one section for Indian Navy's defence group. Once the establishment was satisfied, it gave L&T the order for *Arihant*.

'*Arihant* is the single biggest achievement of the heavy engineering industry in India,' says Trivedi. 'By building a complete nuclear-powered submarine we absorbed the technology. In fact, we improved the processes of the Russians beyond what they could imagine.' President A.P.J. Abdul Kalam and Defence Minister George Fernandes visited Hazira to formally flag off the manufacturing process. Says Trivedi: 'All the processes were developed in-house at Hazira. Existing basic processes were suitably modified. One by one, the technologies were developed, and then *Arihant*'s hull was ready. The hull of a nuclear-powered submarine is the real challenge.'

Having built nuclear reactors and nuclear-powered submarines, the third phase for Hazira began in 1999-2001. Indian orders had slowed. Hazira was working at only 70 per cent capacity. Mr Naik was restless. Recalls Trivedi: 'I was a techie, a hard-core engineering and manufacturing guy, and then he says, "Now all should do marketing." So I was sent off to the US to do marketing for Hazira! We got the first Rs 54 crore order from ExxonMobil. From that day, Hazira has never looked back. Today we export the most complicated chemical reactors all over the world. If you fill up gasoline anywhere in the US, there is an 80 per cent chance that the gasoline has passed through an L&T chemical reactor built in Hazira. And if you do that in Canada, then there is a 90 per cent chance the gasoline has passed through L&T's chemical reactors.'

In 2008, L&T received a $421 million order for twenty-two chemical reactors from Chevron. 'We completed the order in two-and-a-half years,' says Trivedi. 'It is a record for the biggest ever single order in the history of reactors in the world.'

After successfully setting up Hazira, L&T focused on big work and large orders. 'The vision Mr Naik has created will be a winner for the next fifty years; Hazira is among the finest manufacturing facilities in the world,' says Trivedi, as we walk into a pristine, clean workshop making the hull for a classified defence project. 'Every Indian can be proud of it, of the amount of value addition L&T has done for Indian infrastructure. It's a blessing. Nuclear submarines, nuclear reactors, hydrocarbon reactors, offshore platforms, fast interceptor boats, turbines, supercritical boilers, nuclear forgings—all these are now made in Hazira's 755 acres. We have land available for expansion and we have big plans for defence.'

Those plans are critical to India's long-term defence needs. In 1974, following the first Pokhran nuclear test, global companies, led by the US, put India under military and economic sanctions.

In 1998, after Pokhran-2, India was again placed under sanctions. L&T had the dubious distinction of being on the sanctions list because it made sensitive military equipment. No technology was allowed to come in. 'As a result,' says Trivedi, 'we are always worried that nuclear forgings could become a bottleneck. Tomorrow if Japan or France refuses to give them to us, what happens to our nuclear power plants? So we developed the technology in-house. If you look at this from a national perspective, it's like a lifeline. With the nuclear forging facility, Mr Naik has created a unit because of which the world cannot blackmail India.'

HAZIRA WAS the staging ground for L&T's close and continuing engagement with Reliance's refinery at Jamnagar. The world's largest FCC (Fluidized Catalytic Cracker) regenerators and the largest CCR (Continuous Catalytic Reforming) were some of the many precedent-setting equipment built at Hazira and shipped up the coast to Jamnagar. The third phase of the refinery is ongoing. Dubbed J3, it is a mega project even by the standards of Reliance and has over Rs 1.2 lakh crore invested in it. L&T has contributed significantly to J3 in terms of critical equipment as well as through construction and project services.

Meanwhile, six APRs (Advanced Pressure Reactors) of Westinghouse design are at the planning stage. Says Trivedi: 'They are 65 metres in height, and built to withstand an aircraft crash. Take an Airbus A-380 or any other aircraft, crash it on that reactor but still nothing will happen to it. It is one of the world's safest nuclear reactors.' L&T is Westinghouse's strategic partner. The six reactors will eventually be set up in Andhra Pradesh.

After the Fukushima nuclear disaster in March 2011, the nuclear reactor industry came to a standstill. That situation is gradually changing. Britain and the United States are building new reactors. China is building over twelve new reactors. Finland is putting up a reactor. Two nuclear reactors are coming up in the Middle East.

A young Anil Naik peers keenly at the camera. Behind him are his father Manibhai Naik, mother Maniba and sisters Pushpaben (left) and Urmilaben.

Naik married Geetaben on 14 May 1964.

Above: Naik when he joined L&T in March 1965.

Left: Naik's dedication to his work would not have been possible without the strength and support of his wife.

The Naiks brought up their children in a typical middle-class environment in suburban Mumbai.

Naik prevailed upon his ageing parents to leave their native village and settle in his Mumbai home.

From left: daughter Dr Pratiksha and her husband Dr Mukulbhai Shah, Mr and Mrs Naik, son Jignesh and wife Rucha Naik, and granddaughters Sharini and Riya.

In traditional finery, Mr and Mrs Naik celebrate their 50th wedding anniversary in 2014 in Mumbai.

At home with unfailing companions Frooti, Hema, Moti and Baddi.

In the early years of his marriage, Naik's work schedule did not allow even a day off. Much later, the couple managed the customary trip to Agra.

Receiving the Padma Bhushan from the President of India Pratibha Patil on 31 March 2009. Characteristically he dedicated the award to L&T's employees.

The Ambassador of Denmark presents Naik the Danish Knighthood – Order of the Dannebrog Knight First Class in 2015.

In 2009, Naik received the 'Gujarat Garima' – the highest state award – from then Chief Minister Narendra Modi.

Doctorate of Letters awarded by the Sardar Patel University of Vallabh Vidya Nagar is presented to Naik by the Governor of Gujarat, Dr Kamla Beniwal, in 2011.

Doctorate of Letters from the Veer Narmad South Gujarat University is presented by the Governor of Gujarat, Om Prakash Kohli, in February 2016.

Naik receives a Doctorate in Science from the Maharaja Sayajirao University of Baroda in December 2016.

Former President Dr A.P.J. Abdul Kalam presents Naik the 'L&T Ratna', commemorating his record of 50 years of service, at a function in Mumbai on 23 March 2015.

The Economic Times Business Leader Award – 2008 is presented to Naik by then Prime Minister Dr Manmohan Singh.

Doctorate of Philosophy from the Gujarat Technological University is presented by the Governor of Gujarat Dr Kamla Beniwal in 2013.

Spelling out strategic initiatives in an interaction with the company's co-founder, Henning Holck-Larsen.

Henning Holck-Larsen presents a memento to Naik.

A historic moment as three of L&T's chairmen from different eras,
(L to R) A.M. Naik, Henning Holck-Larsen and N.M. Desai, share a stage.

Naik presents a memento to Ole Toubro, the son of Søren Kristian Toubro, one of the company's co-founders, on 23 March 2015.

With L&T's first Indian Chairman & President, N.M. Desai, who led the company from 1977 to 1989.

With Narendra Modi when he was Chief Minister of Gujarat.

Naik says he makes it a point to call on political leaders even after they have stepped off the *gaddi*. Here, with former Prime Minister Dr Manmohan Singh.

A commentator once said, 'In Mr Naik's case, even his dreams are touched by the India colours.'

In 1999, Naik took over as CEO of L&T.

At the L&T complex in Hazira, near Surat, which Naik transformed from acres of marsh into a world-class engineering facility. Oil platforms, reactors and vessels meeting international benchmarks are manufactured at this complex.

Under Naik, L&T's internationalization efforts stepped up a gear.

Left: Naik's high-octane leadership of L&T has been the subject of many business magazine cover stories.

Below: In his entry in the Visitor's Book at L&T's Hazira campus, National Security Advisor Ajit Doval describes L&T-ites as a team with 'vision, talent and resolve'.

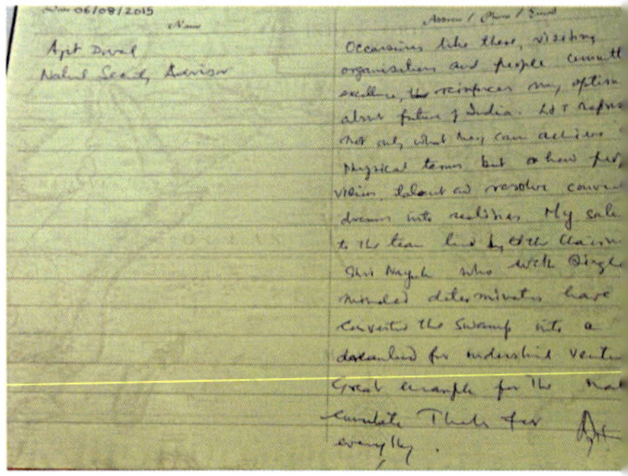

06/08/2015

Ajit Doval
National Security Advisor

Occasions like these, visiting organisations and people committed to excellence, reinforces my optimism about future of India. L&T represents not only what they can achieve in physical terms but how their vision, talent and resolve convert dreams into realities. My salute to the team led by their Chairman Shri Naik who with single minded determination have converted the swamp into a dreamland for industrial venture. Great example for the nation to emulate. Thanks for everything.

Flanked by Shankar Raman (left) and S.N. Subrahmanyan, Naik discusses the performance of the company with the country's leading financial analysts.

In India, there hasn't been a single accident in its cumulative operating experience of 400 years in nuclear reactors since the 1960s.

With the slowdown in nuclear reactors worldwide after Fukushima clearly abating, good news for Hazira's nuclear reactor building capacity came in May 2017 from the Indian government. A news report said:

> The Union Cabinet has cleared the building of 10 new nuclear power plants to add 7,000 MW to India's nuclear power generation capacity. These will be indigenous 700 MW pressurised heavy water reactors. While India has been ramping up its nuclear power capacity, the significance of the decision lies in the scale of the project which will make it easier for domestic industry to raise supply capacities and lower costs. The new reactors would be in addition to the ones that are expected to come onstream by 2021-22 which will add 5,300 MW in addition to the current capacity of 6,780 MW from 22 reactors. The reactors are under construction at Kudankulam, Kakrapar and Rajasthan Atomic Power Plant (RAPP). The government said the new reactors would come up in 'fleet mode as a fully homegrown initiative'. It would be one of the flagship Make in India projects in this sector. 'With likely manufacturing orders of close to Rs 70,000 crore to domestic industry, the project will help transform the Indian nuclear industry by linking our goal of a strong nuclear power sector with our indigenous industrial capacities in high-end technologies,' the government said.[1]

Adds Trivedi: 'Even after the tsunami our reactors were fine. So far so good. We have also built a 50 MW fast breeder reactor – among the first in the world. Now a 500 MW fast breeder reactor is about to be completed in Kalpakkam, south of Chennai. A heavy water reactor uses heavy water to take the heat away. The heavy water is pressurized to such an extent that even at 350 degrees Celsius it remains water, not steam. When it goes to the steam generator it expands, giving away its heat. But in the case of fast breeder

---

[1] *The Times of India*, 18 May 2017.

reactors, liquid sodium is used as a heat exchanging medium. If liquid sodium is put in the air, it will explode: it immediately reacts with oxygen.'

AS WE walk through Hazira's impressive facilities, Trivedi points out the key parts of a 500 MW Cryostat for a thermonuclear reactor being built for the ITER (formerly known as International Thermonuclear Experimental Reactor) project in southern France. Thirty-five nations are collaborating to build the world's largest tokamak, a magnetic fusion device that has been designed to prove the feasibility of fusion as a large-scale and carbon-free source of energy based on the same principle that powers our sun and stars. The experimental campaign that will be carried out at ITER is crucial to advancing fusion science and to prepare the way for the fusion power plants of tomorrow.

Thousands of engineers and scientists have contributed to the design of the ITER project since the idea for an international joint experiment in fusion was first launched in 1985. The ITER members—China, the European Union, India, Japan, South Korea, Russia and the United States—are now engaged in a thirty-five-year collaboration to build and operate the ITER experimental device, and together bring fusion to the point where a demonstration fusion reactor can be designed.

'It's a first-of-its-kind project in India,' says Trivedi. 'We are supplying critical parts for the Cryostat. They are going to France in 52 sections from Hazira. It's one of L&T's most prestigious projects. Hyundai and Bechtel are also part of the project. We are supplying the high-vacuum pressure vessel of the thermonuclear reactor. It is 29 metres in diameter, 29 metres tall. The beauty is that the special steel was made on the west side of the Hazira plant and the Cryostat parts are being built on the east side of the Hazira plant. So all the steel was made in Hazira.'

He shows us the sections being put together in what is a

landmark global collaborative project. Thermonuclear reactors show great future promise. We saw another highly classified project for defence being built in the Hazira complex, but the details cannot be revealed. The project's final cost is likely to be over Rs 25,000 crore.

L&T's Heavy Engineering Independent Company (HEIC) manufactures and supplies custom-designed and engineered critical equipment and systems to core sector industries such as refineries, petrochemicals, fertilizers and power, as well as nuclear, defence and aerospace. Its state-of-the-art manufacturing facilities are located at Hazira, Powai, Ranoli (Vadodara), Coimbatore, Talegaon and Sohar (Oman).

Trivedi, an inexhaustible bundle of energy, constantly refers to the nuclear forgings, submarine hulls and chemical reactors in Hazira's workshops as 'beautiful monsters'. His enthusiasm is contagious. 'In many ways,' says Trivedi, 'the Hazira manufacturing complex represents the aspirations, capabilities, genius and destination of modern India. Everything that we aspire to as Indians today is built into this beautiful campus. We have delivered nuclear reactors, submarines, hydrocracker reactors and many other benchmark products all over the world. The creative restlessness which is built into the genes of L&T resurfaced in 2007, and for the next three years we expanded the Hazira complex to incorporate joint ventures and new facilities: a supercritical boiler, turbines, generators piping up to 1,000 MW and a joint venture with NPCIL for a forge shop.'

Hazira was a defining moment in Naik's career. It made L&T the company it is and Naik the man he is. 'In the initial months,' he says, 'I would spend three days a week in Hazira and then later, two days a week. I did that for two-three years. And then, one day a week for another five years. You can't create a complex like that sitting in a room.'

Hazira was a triumph against the odds—of nature, resources and technology. Says Naik: 'We made 700 MW nuclear reactors in Hazira. We still do it. Nowhere else can it be done unless you are on a waterway. And then we started thinking what we can do in defence. We were already making nuclear reactors, chemical reactors, petrochemicals, refineries, offshore platforms. We progressed step by step to make the most complex equipment. Today we make equipment of the highest level of complexity.'

AVANI VANSIA is deputy manager (TQM & organizational excellence) in Hazira. She retells the evocative story of how a marshy patch of land was transformed into a world-class manufacturing complex. She points to a photograph. 'See these big columns? This was the first heavy workshop. Today what you see is a different world.' As we walk down Hazira's quiet green pathways, other staff recall the early days when the complex was still under construction in the most challenging terrain. 'Mr Naik used to be in Hazira on Friday night, then the whole of Saturday, no holidays for him,' says Avani. 'And Sundays too he was working, so he would go back in the night and start work in Powai again on Monday morning. He would save literally every minute of his time.'

L&T bought the land at Hazira for just Re 1 per sq. metre, reveals Avani. The total investment in what was a saltwater wasteland was Rs 8 lakh. 'No one wanted to come here,' says Atik Desai, Hazira's chief administrative officer. 'L&T was among the very first.' It has turned out to be among its best investments. 'Dhirubhai Ambani, his sons Mukesh and Anil, Nita Ambani, Kokilaben, all visited our Hazira facility,' recalls Avani. 'Mr Naik took them around. This was when we were doing the hydrocracker reactors for Reliance Industries' Gujarat refinery.'

As we sit around the conference table in an elegantly furnished boardroom in Hazira, Trivedi laughs infectiously: 'At the end of the day, Mr Naik and all of us are hard-core engineers. Somewhere in our genes the embedded software is engineering.' Later, while walking to the jetty by the Tapti river, Trivedi exclaims: 'See this monster,' pointing to a huge offshore platform under construction.

'Equally monstrous was the FCC regenerator we supplied to Reliance. It was like a 13-storey building being rolled out. Roll-on, roll-off! It went into the sea and then sailed to Jamnagar.' He waves his arms theatrically. Everywhere you go in L&T's Hazira complex, one quality abounds: unfettered enthusiasm. And a sense of mission.

Naik, while a workaholic, encourages his staff to let their hair down too, says Avani. 'On 29 January 2017,' she says, 'some 350 L&T families, including wives and children, organized a three-hour programme. Mr Naik attended. There were 7,000 people in the audience. It was an absolutely top-class programme in Surat. Mr Naik gave Rs 3 lakh to the team from his personal funds and Rs 2 lakh to L&T's ladies' club, which runs an NGO, Swayam, that supports AIDS-affected women, most of whom have been abandoned by their families. This organization adopts them, arranges for their medicine, gives them work and allows them to live a peaceful life. The ladies' club NGO is very close to Mr Naik's heart.'

L&T's DEFENCE seeds were sown in 1986 working with DRDO. 'That was the only thing allowed by the government,' says Naik. 'The government was not giving a licence to the private sector to produce, but allowed us to work with DRDO to make the prototype of the first Indian nuclear-powered submarine. We were also entrusted with the Integrated Guided Missile Programme for design and prototyping of missile launchers. The drawings for these had to be handed over to DRDO for the government to then give it to a defence PSU or an ordnance factory for manufacture, after the prototype succeeded in user trials.'

Defence manufacturing is increasingly a priority for L&T. Today almost the entire range of missile launchers, rocket launchers and torpedo launchers are delivered from L&T's Talegaon complex, the first weapon systems production unit in the private sector dedicated to India's defence, set up a decade back. The Akash and BrahMos missile airframes and propulsion subsystems are made partly in

L&T's Coimbatore facility and partly in Ranoli near Vadodara, which specializes in advanced composites and also produces heat shields and deck plates for mounting and protecting payloads (satellites) in India's space launch vehicles. The satellite solar array deployment devices as well as launch vehicle boosters are delivered from Powai.

Through meticulous planning, L&T has over the years built an integrated, interlocking network of synergistic facilities and capabilities across India. For instance, L&T's Coimbatore facility does the precision manufacturing of metallics, Ranoli makes the composites, and Powai assembles the solar array devices for satellites and launch boosters for ISRO. For submarines, Powai undertakes detailed design of jigs, fixtures, toolings and sequences through a virtual reality centre co-located with the design centre. Hazira produces the hull, and the integration is done at a classified government facility. For the weapons and engineering systems, factories at Powai and Talegaon design, engineer, produce, and fully integrate complex systems, complete with application-specific software.

Submarines have an acoustically transparent titanium shield around their sonars—their eyes and ears to sense all that is present in all six directions in 3-D space, and for longish distances. The biggest threat to any submarine is the possibility of detection because of the noise made by the equipment and systems inside the vessel. So the ability to 'listen well' and make as little of 'self-noise' as possible are the key differentiators in submarine design and building. This self-noise can be heard by enemy submarines and ships at stand-off ranges using sonars to pick up such transmitted noise (including self and propulsion sounds) and use the frequency content to interpret the type of vessel they are coming from, whether enemy or a sister vessel from their own fleet. Once identified and classified as hostile, the submarine sends out powerful sonar (sound) 'pings', which travel far and get reflected from hulls of ships and submarines in the vicinity. These reflected waves are used to 'confirm' the presence of a submarine and its location, and target it immediately. An acoustic transparent shield, known as the sonar dome, protects the sonar from waves, currents and marine biology while allowing high noise transparency. The design and engineering of these systems is done in Powai, and high-precision manufacture is done at the Ranoli facility. This facility in Vadodara specializes in high-precision, thin-wall titanium and zirconium manufacturing for sectors across industries. This technology is also used to manufacture a submarine's sonar dome.

'All the exotic materials and alloys fabrication is done in Ranoli,' says Trivedi. It is Ranoli to where we set off, driving one late evening from Hazira to Vadodara. It is here that the BrahMos missile airframes and launch canister shells are produced in advanced composites—a contribution by L&T to substantially indigenizing the BrahMos missile. A centre of education, Vadodara houses both L&T's Knowledge City and, on its outskirts, the Ranoli works.

5

Knowledge Is Power

IF HAZIRA IS L&T's muscle, Knowledge City in Vadodara is its brain. Hazira and Knowledge City have one feature in common: a green cover that transforms the complex into a serene campus where engineers and designers work in tranquillity. Like Hazira, Vadodara's Knowledge City was a milestone for L&T. Naik explains its genesis: 'From Hazira I shifted attention in 1993 to Vadodara. The reason we selected Vadodara was it was not far from Surat. Engineering and design should not be too far from manufacturing. Of course, today, with computers, you can transfer anything from anywhere. The objective of our Vadodara complex was to get into the projects business. We started with hydrocarbons in 1997 because we had signed an agreement with Chiyoda, the Japanese engineering company. We formed a joint venture. I formed many joint ventures, but never with 49 per cent, always 51 per cent. It is against my policy to do a JV with anything less than 51 per cent (for L&T). At that time we started a power EPC (engineering, procurement and construction). We built an entire power plant for which the core engineering came from a JV, L&T-Sargent & Lundy.'

At Vadodara, L&T initially bought seven acres of land from Gujarat Industrial Development Corporation (GIDC). It created a light engineering workshop, similar to the one in Powai, which was later closed. A JV with Niro was formed. 'Previously the work was being done in Powai,' says Naik. 'Niro did not want to continue manufacturing so they sold it to us. We bought it and that was that. Now we do very sophisticated internals for all reactors. We do special material composites for aero activities. Anything which needs to be very light, very durable, very solid, which can withstand pressure, is done at Vadodara.'

The land L&T bought in Vadodara was in a location where stood a village some distance away. 'One village was expanding this way and the other village expanding that way,' says Naik. 'This is now Knowledge City but I am talking of the old land. I wasted three-four years trying to pursue matters, but could not succeed. Through various notifications following the proper acquisition process, we finally got this land. Originally we were looking for 25 to 30 acres at the place we first earmarked, which we abandoned. Now, when the authorities asked us how much land we wanted, I asked them how much can you give? They said, 110 acres. I'll take it, I said, and that land is a boon today. Now we have three facilities in Vadodara.'

Ashok Monga heads infrastructure and services at Knowledge City. As in Hazira, Naik's green thumb is in evidence everywhere here too. Serene, calm and well laid out, the sprawling environs of Knowledge City have been meticulously planned. Around 4,000 engineers and other staff work in here. 'Mr Naik's vision to buy this piece of land was farsighted,' says Monga, an intense man with fastidious manners. 'He had seen many land parcels around Vadodara before he identified this land. In phases, he acquired 114 acres, when there was absolutely nothing here. The price of land at that time was Rs 10 per square foot.'

Once again, as in Hazira, Naik struck a good bargain. After L&T set up Knowledge City, the price of the land has gone up by over one hundred times. Knowledge City has proved to be an astute investment in terms of both engineering excellence and real estate. Naik insisted on contiguous residential quarters. Several hundred staff who work in Knowledge City live in neat blocks of flats on the campus. This arrangement is in synchrony with Naik's 'walk-to-work' philosophy.

As Monga takes us around the spotless campus in buggies, he describes how Naik created the Institute of Project Management (IPM). Associated with IPM is the Power Training Institute, which caters mainly to L&T Power. IPM services various other businesses, such as the construction group and the hydrocarbon group. 'Mr Naik's plan is that we dedicate a part of the area to a special economic zone where all the units doing predominantly export-oriented business can avail of the benefits,' says Monga. 'For example, if someone wants to do backend engineering of a ship or design an aircraft, we can do it here.'

Knowledge City has the L&T stamp on it: clean workplaces, uncluttered pathways, sports and recreational facilities, lush greenery, disciplined staff and comfortable flats on campus for executives. Women have their own sequestered living spaces. There is emphasis placed on their safety and on a gender-neutral, congenial work environment. Naik places great emphasis on skill building and training. In Vadodara's Knowledge City I saw young village boys from poor families being taught vocational skills to help them become productive members of society.

As one Vadodara-based executive explained: 'Training is essential to L&T's business. We offer several training programmes for employee development and skill building to meet various facets of the organization's growth and performance. With this in view, Mr Naik sowed the seeds of the Institute of Project Management (IPM) in early 2000. L&T IPM was conceived in 2008 as an academic body that seamlessly integrates itself with practising managers to create and disseminate project management learning for present and future project managers. Mr Naik has mandated that L&T IPM develop a premier world-class education centre for creating global project management professionals, thereby making Larsen & Toubro a centre of excellence in project management. This will be achieved by providing state-of-the-art infrastructure and a learner-friendly atmosphere with innovative pedagogy to create a pool of world-class and socially responsible project professionals.'

—w—

K. RAVINDRANATH, SENIOR vice-president and a director on the board of L&T Hydrocarbon Engineering, has been with L&T for forty years. I meet him in one of Knowledge City's well-scrubbed buildings. A genial man with expressive eyes, he speaks in a soft but precise monotone. 'We do turnkey projects in oil and gas right from upstream to downstream. We do a lot of work in the Middle East, and we also have sizeable operations in India. Upstream is engaged in offshore and onshore oil & gas production and processing, downstream is petroleum refinering, petrochemicals and fertilizers. We handle turnkey gas projects in which values could range between Rs 500 crore and Rs 6,000 crore for a single contract. We try to have profit margins in the double digits, but that's not always possible—our margins vary from project to project.'

L&T is currently working on an $800 million project in Kuwait, a $1 billion project with Saudi Aramco and a $400 million project in Oman. The business expects to achieve a 50-50 per cent domestic-international balance. L&T has its own offshore yards. Apart from the yards in Hazira and Kattupalli (near Chennai), the company has a yard in Oman which caters to the Middle East and Africa.

Ravindranath says pointedly: 'If you do your own engineering, you have control. In turnkey projects that's very important. In fabrication too we have our own platforms, we have our own yards where we can fabricate equipment. We have control as we have our own workshops. In the new J3 Jamnagar refinery which Reliance Industries is setting up, the majority of the construction work has been done by our hydrocarbon construction group. At this point of time we have 38,000 workmen operating there. Bechtel EPC is the prime contractor. It's important to have a trained workforce in all disciplines and to take care of their safety. We have our own safety school.'

The hydrocarbon offices in Vadodara have 1,000 engineers and project management staff. The Mumbai centre is dedicated to offshore and Vadodara to onshore. The engineering centre for offshore, driven from Bengaluru, is a joint venture between L&T and Chiyoda Corporation, Japan.

As an L&T veteran of four decades, Ravindranath's views on Naik are forthright. 'When I saw Mr Naik for the first time he was a young mechanical engineer heading the workshop at deputy manager level in Powai. The way he gets into new areas, the speed with which he makes decisions and the manner in which he understands details is amazing. I have seen many leaders in my long career, but he stands out in terms of personality, entrepreneurial ability and grasping capacity. He is farsighted and picks up from the environment. He picks up from others and then he introspects and adapts ideas.'

Ravindranath continues thoughtfully: 'He is a restless man. He needs to do something different, being an all-rounder from the beginning; in school and college he was a student leader, so the leadership quality has always been with him. But when he joined an organization he was stepping into new things; plus, he was not satisfied with the way things were. There was a bit of mediocrity in the organization. He wanted to break that. Today too it's still very difficult to satisfy him, but he gets us excited just by pushing us. He pushes you hard. Some people may not like it at that point. But he teaches you to question yourself, and you have to prove yourself to him. I worked very closely with him for three months when he became chairman. I have never seen a person forget time and everything else and put in such tremendous effort with so much energy and self-motivation. He rates his own meetings and rates his own staff. He will say that in this meeting I give myself 7 out of 10, or 6 out of 10. Or that today's meeting was useless. He talks like that. Self-analysis and introspection happen with him on a continuous basis.'

L&T's RANOLI facility near Vadodara too has the Naik signature all over: green landscaping, spotlessly clean interiors and a sense of quiet efficiency as engineers, designers and workers go about their business. Mukesh Makwana heads VHEW (Vadodara Heavy Engineering Works). 'Ours is a small unit compared with Hazira,' he says. 'We have around 450 staff. We started in 1993. At that time it was a joint venture with Niro, the Danish company. Mr Naik's dream was to expand L&T's horizon in this region. In 1996, Mr Naik decided to separate from the partners. This then became L&T's own unit. Composites occupy one bay and metallics the other three bays.'

The Ranoli facility is spread over eight acres. The workshop takes up around two acres. Over the years the Ranoli facility has helped produce missile and UAV airframes and satellite deck plates. The supersonic BrahMos missile airframe and launch canister are its signature products. The Ranoli unit makes the components and other parts which go directly into missiles as well as space launch vehicles.

As we tour the facility, Makwana and Vijaykumar's team shows us two missile airframe sections – the F1 and F2. 'We make the airframe, in advanced composites,' Makwana says. 'Many of the metallic parts are made at our Coimbatore facility, adding up to L&T's total contribution of about 30 per cent of the BrahMos missile by part count. We produce launch systems and fire control systems at the Talegaon complex. For satellite deck plates, we produce honeycomb structures with lightweight aluminum honeycomb panels. We are also participating in the GSLV programme, where the honeycomb panels are used as instrumentational panels at different levels. Around 10,000 small and big parts have been delivered over the last ten years for helicopters. With these products we contribute to the country's advanced helicopter programme. We have now joined the LCA (Light Combat Aircraft) programme. The wings are being assembled and integrated at L&T's Coimbatore unit for the Tejas fighter. That's not all; we partner Israeli Aircraft Industries for production of UAV airframe subsystems and export these advanced composite products—that's a first in India.'

As at Hazira, the camaraderie in L&T's Ranoli facility is infectious. The engineers, designers and technicians all seem aware that they are a part of something exceptional, at the cutting edge of technology. 'The sonar dome involves working with thin titanium,' says Makwana. 'We then send it to a classified customer location where L&T does further work. We have also made and exported dry canisters to the US. They are used by existing nuclear power plants to safely store nuclear waste and keep it out of harm's way. We were the first Indian company to meet the requisite standards and overcame international competition to build and export these canisters to the US.'

WHILE HAZIRA grew and prospered, L&T did not lose sight of matters closer to home. Says Naik. 'We needed to be able to do things that others were not doing. I dropped carbon steel, dropped stainless steel, I brought in alloy steel, I brought in very advanced fabrication material. Then I went on increasing the thickness, from 6 mm to 20 mm. Then we brought it to 50 mm. Now we do anything more than 100 mm, and with different materials and different applications, different industries. The number of players in India was minuscule. In fact, the number of players around the world was very small. Obviously, your competition becomes a little less once you climb the tree. You then get a better price. This is how we turned heavy engineering around.'

Naik's passion for L&T emerges in every conversation. 'I have spent over fifty-three years at L&T working nearly eighteen hours a day,' he says. 'That's like 106 years of my life. L&T is my home, my passion, my temple.' Ethical values have been non-negotiable throughout Naik's career. L&T too has long pursued ethical manufacturing. It was a pioneer in clean fuel projects for refineries.

Fears over global warming and climate change led every country to sign time limits for clean fuel. L&T went directly to Euro 3, norms, bypassing Euro 1 and Euro 2 as early as in 1997. The company got qualified in 1996 and in 1997 it won seven out of twelve projects – over half of all the clean fuel projects on offer.

'In 1997 we had started the clean fuel projects and completed all of them in 2001, in four years flat, earning a good name,' says Naik. 'That is how the hydrocarbon division started. It began with our engineering JV company, L&T Chiyoda. Using that as a strength, we got qualified for clean fuel. In 1992, when the Licence Raj was lifted, we got into offshore work. Knowing that some day we will get into offshore, although our licence was rejected three times in the 1980s and 1990s for offshore, I said we must put in Rs 5 crore to develop an offshore yard with qualification from ONGC. We already had a nuclear licence, so the offshore licence was a formality from the government. Then we continuously pitched with ONGC. Our ECC was already doing erection and construction. So I said we will take one piece from here, fabrication from there and engineering from our joint venture companies. Then we would need a procurement office. We put all of this together and decided to do it.'

The concept of moving from fabrication to turnkey execution of an entire plant was another turning point for L&T. Naik recalls: 'We were basically manufacturing equipment. In 1979 I started thinking of making a boiler. I had started my career with package boilers. I knew that it is nothing but boiling water creating steam, pumping that steam at very high pressure on a turbine to rotate the turbine to finally generate electricity. So I thought, why only BHEL? Seeing BHEL reaping the benefits from all the nominated projects, I said, let us also work on this. But the idea was rejected three or four times. Then I too forgot about it. I should not have. The story would have been different if I had started ten years earlier. I used to see power plants and think to myself, a lot of that power equipment we can make.' As L&T moved up the value chain from making equipment to setting up turnkey projects, Naik's objective of transforming the company would soon be met.

—ııı—

A HABIT Naik has long cultivated, as Ravindranath pointed out, is introspection on the day's work. Every evening he notes down what could have been done better. 'And the next day I think about how I should improve,' says Naik. Yet the spirit of 'just doing it' infuses much of Naik's actions. He carefully thinks through everything, but he still prefers action to words. 'I started my career in L&T in the workshop and in planning,' he says. 'I used to spend a lot of time at the workshop. Even in Nestor Boilers I started in the workshop. I would go to a worker, talk to him, ask him, what's your father doing, how's your mother, brother, wife, etc., where are you staying. So I got to know everyone personally. I still remember a worker called Johnson in Nestor Boilers. He was a fitter and a union leader, but he loved me. I was a tough guy but very approachable. Today we are sitting here and someone knocks on the door, he will be able to come in. It's an open house.'

Reminiscing on L&T's growth, Naik says he had a rough time when he came to the workshop, initially. 'But three years down the road workers started appreciating me because they all felt that justice was being done,' says Naik. 'They all felt that L&T would have been in trouble had L&T not been fair to them. Balasaheb Thackeray in those days was like a tiger, and certainly Holck-Larsen took note of that fact. In 1975 there was a conflict between the Communist and Shiv Sena unions. A foreman was killed. The GM there could not do much. Later another GM was appointed at Powai. He literally ran to my office and hid there—just as Chandran had done ten years ago in the 1960s—because the workers were marching towards his office. They had already crossed the gate. I said it does not look good, you hiding here, you should sit in your office and talk to these workers. What are they going to do? The GM used to call me Raja; he said he was not going to move from my office. He then said, 'You know what your value is to the company? You should sit on one side of the weighing scale and on the other it should be all gold. You are to be weighed in gold. That is your value.'

Naik went to the gate where the workers had gathered. 'The only man acceptable at the gate was me, nobody else from management,' he recalls. 'I went there and quietened them down and told them not to create trouble. It's not going to lead anywhere, I told them. They kept quiet and went home. The situation was defused for the moment. In the past forty years since then, except for a three-and-a-half month closure in 1977-78, there hasn't been a union strike in Powai.'

Finally, the Shiv Sena union was embedded fully in L&T and the Communists were out. Naik was looking after the workshop at the time, but the union agitation had taken place in the switchgear department, not in the workshop. 'Once, trouble happened in my workshop, and I suspended three people,' says Naik. 'A scuffle took place in the switchgear department. It was between two rival union leaders. The foreman was pushed during the fight and he fell down. I got a message in my room. I went running there. Many people avoid going to a trouble spot, but I went there, told them to calm down, went to the labour office myself and said, suspend these people for creating trouble and commotion in the company. Everyone involved in the scuffle should go. This happened in the morning at 9.30. I went back at two in the afternoon and asked for a letter to be issued to the trouble-makers that day itself; they cannot come the next day to the office or to the workshop.

'Management called me and asked, will there be any trouble? I said if there is trouble we will have to face it. I said 99 per cent there will be no trouble because I have a good hold on them and they will follow me rather than follow their union. At three in the afternoon, I was told by the management, you can have the letter. Around 3.30 p.m. I got the letter and had it issued to the trouble-makers while they were leaving the premises at 3.55 p.m. The shift closure was at 3.50 p.m. They were given the letter as they left the building.

They were out: they could not come back the next day. They could come to the gate, but not step inside.'

That was the last incident in the history of inter-union rivalry in L&T. Naik says: 'In their subconscious mind, they had no fear of management. Since the Shiv Sena came, I must have dealt with seven different labour committees in the past forty years, maybe even eight, and all of them had respect for me. Finally all of them said, whatever Naik *saab* says we will agree. In this very room they came to meet me. I have my own style of telling them things, which I can't repeat in front of an audience! In a maximum of twenty minutes everything was solved. The new union agreement got signed within ten days and it was linked to productivity improvement.'

IT IS this unique quality of blending toughness with empathy that lies at the heart of Naik's success. But even as his career blossomed at L&T, India's macro-economic factors began to falter. Soon though, a new era of reforms would transform the Indian economy. In the first week of July 1991, the rupee was devalued twice. A fresh trade policy was announced. On 24 July, the government declared a new industrial policy that would in three years lead to an end to industrial licensing. On 29 February 1992, a leap year, Finance Minister Manmohan Singh presented a historic budget that changed the course and trajectory of the Indian economy.

Private industry was permitted to enter sectors that had been the preserve of public sector companies. Automatic permission was granted for foreign direct investment (FDI) of up to 51 per cent equity in certain priority industries. The peak rate of import duty was slashed from more than 300 per cent to 150 per cent. The Monopolies & Restrictive Trade Practices (MRTP) Act was amended, enabling large companies to embark on capacity expansion or diversification without seeking prior approval. The government accepted the major recommendations made by the Tax Reforms Committee.

These reforms paved the way for an era of economic growth and prosperity. L&T moved quickly to seize the opportunity. The services sector emerged as the pivot of the new liberalized economy. Services had been growing at a fast clip since the 1980s, but it was liberalization in the 1990s that unleashed the full potential of India's economy.

As the stock market boomed, however, L&T would become the target of unwelcome corporate attention. It would result in a trial by fire for Naik.

6

Winning Stakeholder Trust

BUOYED BY THE success of his Shaw Wallace acquisition, Dubai-based Manu Chhabria, the peripatetic takeover tycoon, had begun shadowing L&T in 1987. He bought L&T shares from the open market. Soon he had acquired a stake of nearly 1.5 per cent in the company. The Ambanis, meanwhile, were also eyeing India's largest engineering and technology firm, then significantly undervalued, with a market capitalization of around Rs 1,000 crore. Alarmed by the Chhabria onslaught, L&T chairman Narottam Desai sought out Dhirubhai Ambani as a white knight. He urged Dhirubhai to invest in the company as a counter against Chhabria. The Ambanis promptly acquired a 12.5 per cent stake in L&T. Mukesh Ambani and younger brother Anil Ambani joined the L&T board. In April 1989, Dhirubhai took over as L&T's chairman.

But the redoubtable Dhirubhai had not reckoned with the political atmosphere of the time. Government-owned financial institutions held a pivotal stake in L&T. Much therefore depended on how they reacted to the Ambanis' entry into a company closely involved with the government's nuclear, space and defence programmes. The Reliance group was at the time L&T's single largest private sector customer. L&T had built Reliance's Patalganga plant and would soon build two major manufacturing facilities for the group – a petrochemicals complex at Hazira and a petroleum refinery at Jamnagar.

Meanwhile, Indian politics was passing through a period of instability. Prime Minister Rajiv Gandhi lost the Lok Sabha election in November 1989. V.P. Singh assumed office as prime minister. Former State Bank of India chairman D.N. Ghosh replaced Dhirubhai as L&T chairman in April 1990. V.P. Singh's minority government soon collapsed and was replaced in November 1990 by another minority government led by Chandra Shekhar but supported by the Congress from outside. Ghosh resigned as L&T chairman in February 1991. Following Rajiv Gandhi's assassination in May 1991, a Congress government took office with P.V. Narasimha Rao as prime minister. It seemed initially well disposed towards Reliance. The Ambanis now tried to make a comeback. According to one report, 'They had enough shares and proxies to vote Dhirubhai back as chairman and appoint Mukesh as managing director. But following pressure from the Opposition, Narasimha Rao decided to stay away from the corporate battle.'[1]

By then the Ambanis too had come to terms with the inevitable: the Congress government would not support them. They decided to stay on in L&T as silent investors through the 1990s.

DHIRUBHAI AMBANI once had big plans for L&T. After Hazira went on stream he realized the company would have gained significant experience in building crackers. But Dhirubhai is also believed to have worked out a deal for full transfer of the cracker technology to L&T – technology which was the preserve of a handful of multinationals at that time. This would have enabled L&T to independently bid for petrochemical projects anywhere in the world.

It was Naik, then general manager, who took Dhirubhai and Mukesh around the L&T shopfloor at Powai. In an interview with

[1] *Business Standard*, 17 September 2014.

Sucheta Dalal, editor of *Moneylife*, Naik said: 'I never understood what was going on in the inner group of five-six people. I was one step away from it all till I entered the board in 1989. In 1988, I took Dhirubhai and Mukesh on a shopfloor tour of our Powai works. They never interfered. They understood that I am my own man and I always had an arm's length relationship with them; but at the same time they respected me as a professional. They used to take my advice on petrochemical plants, particularly reactors, even before they came in as shareholders of L&T. In 1986, Mukesh had requested me to look into the leakage in the Patalganga plant which L&T had built.'

Throughout the tug of war between RIL and L&T, Naik played the role of a mediator. He had the Ambanis' trust. And L&T's top brass reposed full faith in the man who was rising rapidly up the company's hierarchy and whose loyalty to L&T over the past twenty-five years had been beyond reproach.

In 2001, Grasim was India's third largest cement producer, with an annual capacity of 13 million tonnes. L&T was at the time the largest cement producer, with a capacity of 18 million tonnes a year. By then L&T's market value had climbed to Rs 8,350 crore, having grown considerably under the stewardship of Naik, who had been CEO for over two years.

In November 2001, in a surprise move, Reliance sold its shareholding in L&T to the Aditya Birla Group. Naik was in Chicago on business. He retells the story, adding context to it. 'I received a call at 2.20 a.m. from my colleague, the late Mohan Karnani. His first words, were: "*Maalik badal gaya hai.*" That was the first time I came to know that I had a *maalik*! I asked him what had happened. He said the Ambanis had sold all their shares in L&T to Kumar Mangalam Birla, around 10.5 per cent. Anil Ambani called me a few minutes later. Anil said that since L&T had never wanted them, they were going—"We have sold our shares to Kumar Mangalam Birla." I did not reply directly to him, but made general talk. Then at 7 a.m., Kumar Mangalam called. He said, Naikji, you did not come to us, so we are coming to you. His father, Aditya babu, had tried from 1976 till 1993 to persuade me to join the Birlas. He once told Dhirubhai, light-heartedly, I am going to take Mr Naik away from you. He said this in front of me at a function soon after the Ambanis had bought a stake in L&T. So later I told Aditya babu that we are an independent company. During Anil Ambani's wedding, standing just in front of me was Aditya babu. He was talking to Dhirubhai. He saw me and he immediately told Dhirubhai again, this man I am going to take him away. As if I am available to whoever wants me!'

IN WINDY Chicago, Naik wrapped up business and left for Mumbai immediately. He took a flight from Chicago's O'Hare airport and was back in India the next day. Holck-Larsen had already phoned Kumar Mangalam Birla, with whom Naik had developed a rapport. 'Aditya babu had given Kumar Mangalam only a few names with whom, as he said, "we should never lose a relationship",' recalls Naik. 'When Kumar Mangalam got married, only family members were invited. From L&T I was the only one invited. It was a close relationship and has remained so.'

In those turbulent months sixteen years ago, however, the tension was palpable between the two. Says Naik: 'I asked Kumar Mangalam, why have you bought this shareholding in L&T? He said L&T is a grossly undervalued company, there is a lot of money to be made. Then he asked if he could meet Holck-Larsen. So we all met. Three months later Kumar Mangalam started buying shares in the open market. L&T's stock price went up and up. From Rs 178 it started rising. People said he is buying in the market. I realized then that he is buying because he wants to take over L&T. So I went to Kumar Mangalam and asked him, why are you buying? He said, I had told you, there is money to be made. S. Gurumurthy came to my rescue; R.V. Pandit also came to my rescue. I was a man from the village. I did not know a single secretary in the government or even the chairman of LIC. I did not know any minister or politician,

I knew nobody. I was sitting here, doing my job as a professional, trying to change the company, make it entrepreneurial, transforming the company.'

Gurumurthy took Naik to meet Prime Minister Atal Bihari Vajpayee. He then took him to see Deputy Prime Minister L.K. Advani and Defence Minister George Fernandes. Says Naik: 'Fernandes was like me, a working-class man. He understood what L&T is. He said L&T cannot be sold – and remember, he was NDA Chairman at that time. He told Vajpayee: we cannot sell L&T. Now don't forget that the BJP had a cordial relationship with the Birlas. I had nobody. I am a man from the village. I wanted to sell our cement division anyway. It was not something we wanted to grow. So I brought an offer from England to buy our cement business. Kumar Mangalam got worked up as he had come in only to buy cement. And here I had created a competitor. In meeting after meeting there was a stand-off.'

As tensions rose the government became concerned. 'R.V. Pandit [the well-connected veteran publisher] called me from Delhi,' recalls Naik. 'He said he was visiting the finance ministry. Everybody is upset with you, all meetings are at a standstill, he said. No business is being transacted.'

By now the Birlas had brought up their stake to 16 per cent in L&T. Finance Minister Jaswant Singh told Kumar Mangalam not to buy any more. The share price was now Rs 220. Birla stopped buying at 16 per cent. Government institutions stopped at 37 per cent. Slowly, the government shareholding came down to 30 per cent. Those were fraught days for Naik and L&T. He had taken over as CEO barely three years ago and now found himself embroiled in a corporate battle with one of India's most respected and gilded business houses. Naik flew to Delhi. He told a senior government secretary he was now willing to sell L&T's cement division to Birla without competition. There was a caveat though: he asked the government official to put it down in writing that L&T

should sell the cement division to the Aditya Birla Group without competitive bidding.

'The government secretary suddenly fell quiet,' recalls Naik. 'He asked me if I wanted tea or coffee. Then we talked a bit and the meeting was over. The stand-off continued for two more months. One day the banking secretary, a lady, called and asked me if an L&T board meeting could happen that day. All meetings had been at a standstill. She said she would give me a one-line note okaying L&T selling cement. I said yes, provided there is competitive bidding. So they found a way to do it. They got the valuation done by the government credit rating agency ICRA. They said: whatever ICRA says should be acceptable. ICRA did the valuation at Rs 310 against the market price of Rs 220. They told me to now work it out with Birla. What should be the price component of engineering and of cement? We had many bilateral meetings. Gurumurthy was present, but most of the discussions were between Kumar Mangalam and me. We negotiated the value-split; how much of the Rs 310 I should take, how much he should take. The original price at which the employees were given stock options in 1999 was Rs 178. We did not give any concessions to them whatsoever. That was the market price and we gave the stock options at that price. Around 5 per cent of the L&T stock was given. Then we gave another stock option of 5 per cent in 2003. And then once more, another 5 per cent in 2006. Always at the market price. But our board directors did not get stock options after 2003. Only our employees were given them. About 200-250 employees got stocks in 1999, around 700-800 in 2003, and 2,500 employees in 2006.'

NAIK STOOD firm throughout the negotiations. 'I told Gurumurthy that we cannot do any deal till the remaining shareholding comes back to us. The L&T Employees Welfare Foundation was then formed, and the structuring was done. Gurumurthy negotiated with the government that L&T should be allowed to give a loan to the L&T Employees Welfare Foundation to buy shares in L&T. I went to a bank, deposited the shares, mortgaged them, and worked out the entire scheme.'

It's important to understand the financial architecture of the scheme. Under the Integrated Scheme of Arrangement, approved by the stock exchanges, SEBI, the Registrar of Companies, shareholders, creditors and the Bombay High Court, L&T's cement business was demerged. The L&T Employees Welfare Foundation (Trust) acquired the 14.95 per cent stake in L&T held by Grasim Industries Ltd and its subsidiary, Samruddhi Swastik Trading & Investments Ltd in 2004 for around Rs 446 crore. L&T, its shareholders, creditors, Grasim, its subsidiary, and the Trust were parties to this Scheme of Arrangement.

Crucially, SEBI had granted exemption to the Trust from the requirement of making an open offer under the provisions of the erstwhile SEBI Takeover Code to facilitate its acquisition of L&T shares from Grasim. SEBI noted that these shares would be held in perpetuity by the Trust to ensure that L&T retains its ownership and management character. The purchase of L&T shares was financed by way of a loan of Rs 275 crore from L&T to the Trust, bank borrowings by L&T Welfare Company Limited (LTWCL) totalling Rs 150 crore (Rs 105 crore from Bank of America and Rs 45 crore from HSBC), and voluntary contributions to the Trust from employees of the L&T group (Rs 21 crore).

The Trust had agreed to give a tax-free return of 5 per cent on the contributions made by employees. The manner of providing this return was left to the wisdom of the trustees. Since the dividend was tax-free in the hands of the recipient, the trustees felt that issuing preference shares to employees against their contribution would be beneficial to them. The Trust subscribed to the preference shares of LTWCL and held them through L&T Employees Welfare Foundation Private Limited (LTEWFPL) on behalf of the employees. LTWCL issued preference shares carrying a rate of 5 per cent cumulative dividend to the Trust. As per the terms of the issue, the preference shares were to be redeemed after a period of ten years from the date of allotment. However, the issuer (LTWCL) had an option to redeem the shares any time after three years from the date of allotment, while the shareholder (Trust) could seek repayment any time after seven years from the date of allotment.

Based on the instructions of the Trust, LTEWFPL allocated the beneficial interest in the preference shares to employees based on the contributions made by them. The dividend received was utilized initially to repay the loans taken from the banks and L&T, as well as to pay dividend on the preference shares. LTWCL declared a dividend of 5 per cent on the preference shares till 2006, and 6 per cent from 2007, until the time these preference shares were redeemed in 2009-10. The beneficial interest in these preference shares was revoked from the employees in three tranches on 28 February 2009, 31 December 2009 and 30 November 2010. The employees were repaid the principal amount, along with proportionate dividend at 6 per cent per year.

AS NAIK says today, with a smile: 'That's how the L&T Employees Welfare Foundation shareholding in L&T became 14.9 per cent. So now there was around 15 per cent with individual employees as stock options and nearly 15 per cent with the employees' foundation—30 per cent in all.' The L&T's Employee Welfare Foundation had ringfenced L&T from future takeovers. Analysts agree that Naik's innovative and complex financial engineering to create the L&T Employees Welfare Foundation will go down in Indian corporate history as an unprecedented achievement.

'You will be surprised to know that today our employees welfare foundation has several hundred crore rupees,' says Naik. 'All out of nothing ... zero. Plus all employees got stock options, plus we became the owner, the largest shareholder in L&T, plus we reduced the debt and became an AAA-rated company and I brought down the equity. Therefore, after adding a lot of value, we could give four bonuses—a 1:1 bonus in 2006, a 1:1 bonus in 2008, a 1:2 bonus in 2013 and a 1:2 bonus in 2017. That is how so many employees of L&T have become millionaires and *crorepatis*.'

Once all the paperwork was done, L&T and the Aditya Birla Group issued a public statement in July 2004 that the process of implementing the scheme of demerger of the cement division of L&T as approved by the Bombay High Court was complete. Grasim had acquired a majority stake in UltraTech CemCo Limited, the demerged cement business of L&T, effective 14 May 2004. Accordingly, the cement business undertaking was transferred to and vested in UltraTech CemCo Limited. Grasim had made a successful open offer bid for 30 per cent of the equity of UltraTech with a view to taking management control. Concurrently, Grasim acquired an 8.5 per cent equity stake in UltraTech from L&T. Grasim and its associates sold 14.95 per cent of their holding in the demerged L&T to the L&T Employees Welfare Foundation.

Naik smiles, his face creased in mirth: 'I tell you, the ladies are more grateful then the men. One was forthright in telling me: "I am from Kerala, we used to take forty hours to reach Kerala, now when we go on holiday we are able to reach in two hours by air, thanks to Mr Naik giving us stock options." I was once in Austria, and visiting an exhibition. When we were about to get back into the car three people came towards us. An ex-employee of L&T greeted me and said he had sold 300 shares of L&T and toured the whole of Europe with the money. Both he and his wife thanked me.'

Naik recalls: 'After signing the cement deal, Kumar Mangalam extended his hand to me and said "history should never, never forget you. You know what you have achieved: employee ownership of the company." Nobody had believed it possible. In post-Independent India it has never been done, and shall never be done. So If anybody tries to attack L&T again—and so far people have not tried as I am still here, people know that I am a fighter—then

I am the guard at the gate by way of managing trustee of the L&T Employees Welfare Foundation.'

SWAMINATHAN GURUMURTHY, who played a key role in the negotiations between Naik and Kumar Mangalam Birla, wears many hats. He is a chartered accountant with a flourishing practice. As president of the Swadeshi Jagaran Manch (SJM) he is close to Prime Minister Narendra Modi and senior BJP leaders. Following Cho Ramaswamy's death in December 2016, Gurumurthy took over as editor of Cho's *Thuglak* magazine. He is also a columnist for *New Indian Express*. His office in Chennai is quietly functional. The tight security at the entrance is testament to the key role Gurumurthy plays, usually under the radar, in economic and strategic government policy.

His office is spacious but spartan. Gurumurthy reveals a laser-sharp mind that misses nothing. During the tense face-off between the Birla group and L&T, Gurumurthy was a mediator between Kumar Mangalam Birla and Naik. 'The initial move came from Mr Birla,' says Gurumurthy. 'Earlier, Mr Birla, Nimesh Kampani (of JM Finance) and I met. There were several meetings. Afterwards, Mr Birla called me and said he was in a difficult situation and could not continue like this for long, so can you talk to L&T. I approached Mr Naik. I asked him what was on his mind. He asked my advice. I said L&T has got into the cement business under certain circumstances but the business is actually a burden. I could see L&T going places without cement. He arranged a meeting of all his executives and working directors. I had a discussion with them before I proceeded to meet Mr Birla. There were two critical issues. One, L&T is a working capital-driven organization, it's not a fixed capital organization. So L&T has to have rolling assets, it does not need fixed assets like cement. Two, by divesting cement, L&T's balance sheet would improve hugely. This too was on Mr Naik's mind. These were the two critical points which convinced the L&T executives to sell. L&T was borrowing money and was short of working capital. Unless you have liquid money you can't have projects with profitable margins.'

Gurumurthy says Naik has a multi-dimensional mind: 'He is an engineer, a chartered accountant, a lawyer, he is everything. The man's capacity is immense. He can not only understand what I am thinking but he can add to it.' The most important part of the negotiations between L&T and the Birlas was secrecy. Both are listed groups. 'Everything was kept within a small circle of senior executives to avoid leakages,' says Gurumurthy. It was decided to allocate a small portion of the capital to L&T and a large part of the capital to the cement company, and not irrationally but on the basis of the fixed capital requirements of the two businesses. The fixed capital requirement for cement is very high and rolling capital requirement is higher too, so it was decided that we should appropriately divide the capital between the two.'

The L&T Employees Welfare Foundation was conceived entirely by Mr Naik, says Gurumurthy. 'In the other matters I may have contributed, but basically it was Mr Naik's idea that the Birlas' share of around 15 per cent in L&T should come to the L&T Employees Welfare Foundation. I told Prime Minister Atal Bihari Vajpayee that this is in the national interest, so it has to be done and the financial institutions must support it. The prime minister was quite graceful, and he went through the whole issue threadbare. He had the details examined, and everyone felt this is the best way. The point that really impressed them was the firewalling of L&T so that no evil eye could be cast on it in the future. This convinced Vajpayee's NDA government that this is in the national interest, as L&T is not only a commercial organization but also heavily involved in defence manufacturing.'

Gurumurthy continues animatedly: 'In the last meeting, we sat down together and in two hours sealed it. Today L&T employees are the biggest gainers, along with L&T and the Aditya Birla Group.

The advantage L&T got was due to the honest way in which the deal was worked out. L&T gained in terms of ringfencing itself and major improvement in its financial parameters: earnings per share (EPS), price-to-earnings (P/E) and debt-equity ratio. If L&T had not been managed by very honest professionals, all these advantages would not have come to L&T, somewhere they would have been lost. But theirs was a totally transparent, committed and loyal team, led by Mr Naik. L&T is like a clan. The loyal attachment to the company cannot be breached.'

Newspaper headlines following the announcement of the deal said it was a win-win for L&T, the Aditya Birla Group and, of course, L&T employees. 'I'll put Mr Naik's role at number one,' says Gurumurthy quietly. 'He understood it so well and he had the capacity to steer his team. I had a discussion with the team, including the CEO of the cement division that was being demerged, and explained the logic of the whole plan to them. The top management of L&T was completely on board. Mr Naik was highly respected for his integrity and commitment to L&T and its people.'

The hidden value unlocked for L&T through the deal was its huge investment in cement. If those funds were invested in L&T's engineering and other non-cement businesses, they would deliver several times the return of the cement division because funds could be rolled over faster. L&T requires a rolling stock of money. With cement the money is frozen. The Birlas would also have had the same problem if this was the first cement capacity they were buying. But they were just adding to their already large cement base. By acquiring the cement plants of Jaiprakash Associates Ltd for Rs 16,199 crore in June 2017, UltraTech now has a cement capacity of 93 million tonnes.

But for L&T, as Gurumurthy points out, 'The deadweight goes away. The separation was advantageous to both companies. L&T's cement capacity could not have been enhanced without further large investment. Plus it is not their prime business. Remember why L&T got into the cement business in the first place in 1977.

There was a huge cash premium on cement prices. Large amounts of black money were being generated. George Fernandes, a minister in Morarji Desai's government, called the L&T management and told them to start cement production because he knew L&T could be trusted not to sell cement in the black. This is why L&T got into the cement business! It was not L&T's natural business. They may have consumed cement but it does not mean they have to manufacture it to consume it.'

Gurumurthy turns thoughtful when he says there are two men today he admires most: Prime Minister Narendra Modi and L&T chairman Anil Naik. Why does he say that? What common attributes does see in them? 'With each of them my relationship is different, of course,' Gurumurthy says. 'Ideologically, as a friend, and though there are areas where we clash, I have great respect for Prime Minister Modi. The Birla-L&T issue was my first major exposure to Mr Naik. He is fiercely honest. My test of anybody in the world is honesty. Besides, Mr Naik's capacity to understand issues is amazing. He is always one step ahead of his financial people. One step ahead of the tax professionals. He has an amazing mind and is a multi-dimensional personality. Honestly, it is impossible to find people like him.'

7

The Entrepreneurial Visionary

WITH THE AMBANI saga of the fight for control of L&T yet to fully play out, the company prepared for a change of guard in 1994. CEO and managing director U.V. Rao was retiring. A search committee was appointed by the company's board to find a successor. All the candidates were internal; no outside candidates were called. Significantly, in 1999, when CEO S.D. Kulkarni retired after a five-year term, external candidates were considered.

Several newspapers speculated in 1994 on who among L&T's insiders had the best chance to succeed CEO Rao. Then fifty-one, Naik was the consensus candidate to head L&T. He had long been regarded as the favourite to take over from Rao. Naik himself expected the job in 1994, but shrugs today, calling it one of those twists of fate that he didn't get it.

In a last-minute decision in 1994, the board leaned in favour of seniority. Naik had joined the board fairly recently. He was clearly disappointed at not having got to head L&T in 1994. Had he done so, many of the projects he initiated when he did finally become CEO in 1999 could have propelled L&T earlier into a steep trajectory of growth.

On CEO Kulkarni's retirement in 1999, a search committee was again formed. 'It was a board-appointed committee, but this time the board decided to also call outside candidates,' says Naik. 'A professional firm was appointed. They had three names from outside and two or three from within L&T. Founder Holck-Larsen's voice became all-important. He spoke up for me. I was appointed CEO a few weeks before the completion of the incumbent CEO Kulkarni's term. Even based on seniority, this time the choice was clear—I was now fifty-six and had spent thirty-four years in L&T.'

Though he had been informed of the decision, Naik was formally appointed CEO and managing director on 28 April 1999, six weeks before he turned fifty-seven. Naik says: 'While I missed becoming CEO in 1994, I was constantly engaged with the company's plans. I was in the CMC (Corporate Management Committee) and voiced my views strongly. On becoming CEO, I set a 100-day plan.'

Naik is animated as he recalls those early action-packed days: 'In the first 100 days merit, merit and merit should prevail—that was my objective. How do we drive merit? From being seniority driven to becoming merit driven, this was my number one priority. Number two was that we must make a five-year strategic plan, which we had never done before. So the first five-year strategic plan was conceptualized. The preparations for that were launched. We had to come up with a vision statement to make L&T a more international company and not a frog in the well. That was our number three priority. Number four was weeding out non-performers. If there are people who are non-performers, we should, with as much humaneness as possible, let them go. The same applied to unionized workers. For the first time ever, a voluntary retirement scheme (VRS) was launched to promote merit and reduce inefficiency. Later we launched the Blue Chip and Lakshya 1 and Lakshya 2 strategic plans.'

AFTER THE VRS was successfully implemented, the focus shifted to transforming L&T into an Indian multinational. The vision statement stated explicitly that L&T would be a professionally managed Indian multinational company. 'The word multinational came to the forefront for the first time in the history of L&T,' Naik points out. 'We were committed to total customer satisfaction and enhancing shareholder value. The term shareholder value too was adopted in the vision statement for the first time in the history of L&T. Since we were anyway professionally managed, we were very happy to be called a professionally managed company. Little did we realize then that while it is fine to be professionally managed, we should also be entrepreneurial to increase value for all stakeholders, not just do very good work and make losses.'

On assuming office as managing director and CEO, Naik made it clear that an L&T-ite should be innovative and entrepreneurial. The concept of empowering employees, creating value and achieving global benchmarks was introduced and articulated, along with an emphasis on encouraging an entrepreneurial mindset among employees. Naik had been mulling over these ideas well before he became CEO. 'When I got the chance,' he says, 'I pledged that in the first 100 days I will launch these initiatives one by one. L&T shall foster a culture of caring, trust and continued learning while meeting expectations of employees, stakeholders and society. This comprehensive vision statement inspired the company to structure its future strategy.'

Four months after he was appointed managing director and CEO, Naik wrote a letter on 26 August 1999 to L&T's shareholders, outlining his vision for the company's future. It is important to read the letter in full for the clarity it displays of Naik's thinking, at a time when India's economy was at an inflection point after a year of Atal Bihari Vajpayee's government:

Dear shareholder,

I am happy to write to you on behalf of the L&T Management and express gratitude for the support and encouragement that has enabled the Company emerge amongst the front runners, while contributing significantly to nation-building.

Your company enjoys leadership position in several businesses:

Heavy engineering – encompassing manufacture of high technology equipment for process, power, and aerospace industries.

Project execution – covering all aspects of engineering, procurement and construction for core sector industries.

Turnkey construction – proven record of using innovative technology to handle complex projects for industries and infrastructure development.

Cement – largest manufacturer and exporter of cement and clinker, with aggregate capacity of 12 million tonnes.

Electrical – offering the widest range of low-tension switchgear, through the most widely dispersed network of stockists.

In addition, in the Information Technology business, plans are under way to accelerate the growth of L&T's wholly-owned subsidiary, L&T Information Technology Limited. Our tractor project, a joint venture with Deere &Co., USA, is on schedule, and roll-out of tractors is expected in early January 2000.

In the past few years, we have taken some initiatives in restructuring our operations to enhance competitiveness and profitability. We spun off manufacturing of excavators into a joint venture with Komatsu, divested our shipping business and discontinued manufacture of computer peripherals and footwear.

In recent weeks, we have brought together operations of all diversified industrial products and machinery to achieve greater synergy. Our heavy engineering facilities at Mumbai, Hazira and Kansbahal have been integrated. The EPC and construction business will be aligned so as to enhance our capabilities in executing large size projects. In order to leverage our financial resources, we plan to set up two independent subsidiaries for power and infrastructure projects.

Your company has worked towards harnessing Information Technology to enhance its capabilities. For instance, a large number of business units have implemented Enterprise Resource Planning (ERP) systems. We are in the process of implementing a new IT-driven Management Information System that will effectively interface performance with value creation.

In today's context, it is imperative that there is greater transparency in business practices. You may have observed that the current Annual Report (1998-99) provides you with more information about your Company. A meeting of the Board of Directors was specially convened to discuss the issue of good corporate governance. The Board decided on measures to introduce greater transparency in line with CII's recommendations on a desirable Code of Conduct. While a majority of these recommendations are being practised by your Company others will be implemented in the future.

While these initiatives will create value, more needs to be done. We will have to periodically review our business portfolio and strategies for continuous enhancement of shareholder value. This is my mantra for the future. We expect this will result in L&T becoming a premium conglomerate.

To further assist us in our plans, we have appointed two international consultancy organizations. The Boston Consulting Group (BCG) will review our business portfolio and revalidate our strategic plans. Nine of our own tasks forces, comprising over 70 senior executives, are working in tandem with BCG. The other consulting firm, William M. Mercer, will focus on people-related processes and enable the human resource of our organization to realize its fullest potential. The final aim is to create a robust organization which will become a benchmark in terms of value creation, corporate governance and business practices.

I look forward to your continued support in the new millennium.

Yours faithfully,
A.M. Naik
Managing Director&
Chief Executive Officer

As his letter suggests, Naik pays fierce attention to detail—not only to the heavy engineering and manufacturing businesses he has nurtured but even to the content and design of the company's annual reports and their condensed version—the annual reviews. Nothing escapes his hawk-eye.

Meticulous planning is a hallmark of Naik's management style. Executives say he plans every hour of the day, often every minute, going into the minutiae of projects, timetables and travel schedules without losing sight of the bigger picture. Macro- and micro-management rarely go together. In Naik they cohabit comfortably. Since Naik took over as managing director and CEO in 1999, L&T has developed and implemented rigorously a five-year strategic planning process. The Naik folklore in L&T is that even before he was formally anointed CEO, he had the 100-day work plan ready. As CEO he hit the ground running.

Naik summarized his 100-day plan of 1999 succinctly: '1) I wanted merit to come back; I wanted a change from seniority to meritocracy. We took initial action and did whatever was required to be done; 2) Create value for all stakeholders which was never a focus earlier; 3) L&T should become more outward looking, more international; 4) In becoming a meritocracy, if we have to remove inefficient people in a humane manner we should, so we declared a VRS. We did not remove staff but said if anyone wants to go, they can go. Around 600 people went; 5) The first five-year strategic plan was launched. We said the vision statement will be prepared by 1 November 1999, and we will hire a consultant. Boston Consultancy Group (BCG) was selected. All of this was done in the first 100 days.'

PATHIK KOTHARI looks after corporate strategy and change management at L&T. He expounds on L&T's five-year strategic plans: 'When Mr Naik took over in 1999, as a part of Project Blue Chip we decided to revisit L&T's vision. Some basic goals and objectives in the company's vision had been codified in 1995, but the first full-fledged vision statement was formulated in 1999. While this statement embodied the thinking and direction of Mr Naik, its final expression was the result of the collective effort of 7,500 senior L&T staff drawn from across the country. Soon after he took over as CEO, Mr Naik travelled to virtually every major workplace of the company to enunciate his goals and enthuse executives across L&T to achieve them. Four distinct points emerged in the new vision. One, that we want to make L&T an Indian multinational. We were virtually a domestic company with around 3 per cent global business at that time. Last year our international business was 34 per cent of total revenue. The second distinct aspect of the new vision statement was that while L&T was considered a highly respectable company, it was not the shareholder's favourite. So we brought in a second criterion—enhancement of shareholder value. The third aspect is when you enhance shareholder value you constantly create value. So we added that criterion: constant creation of value. Finally, we introduced the concept of global benchmarks: anything that we do has to be globally benchmarked. Mr Naik gave direction to this vision: first comes people, then comes strategy, then comes process. The results you see today are an outcome of all this.'

Kothari is an L&T veteran. He calls Naik an inspirational speaker who mesmerizes audiences, 'At the end of the day people feel extremely charged,' says Kothari. Talent was always at the top of Naik's agenda. In 1999 nobody was talking about talent, he says. Mr Naik, however, focused on HR and on developing and attracting talent. 'Top people were not staying on in L&T,' reveals Kothari. 'The whole definition of HR in those days was based on seniority, not merit. Mr Naik changed that. We engaged the services of William Mercer, global HR consultants. They called it their 3P model, where they study people, potential and performance.'

Lakshya is an acronym. Kothari engagingly explains its genesis: 'L stands for lean. L&T was considered a bureaucratic organization. Things were moving slowly here. If you reduce the fat in an organization it becomes lean. A stands for agile. During the strategic journey you need to remain agile—agile for the threats that may come your way and opportunities too that may come your way. You can't have an emotional attachment to a business. K is for knowledge. How do you distinguish L&T from others? There are so many civil contractors, so why is L&T different? So we said whatever we do, we will do it with knowledge in a way that we monetize knowledge. S is for speed and scale. L&T was considered a steady but slow organization. We had to work on that. H is for humane. Whatever we do, we will do it in a humane way. Even if we have to come out with a VRS, we will give employees time to stabilize. Y stands for yielding value. Anything we do should result in a good yield. Finally, A stands for being action-oriented. If after doing all this, you don't take action, then there is nothing! That is what defines Lakshya.'

As L&T's global business grew from 3 per cent of total sales in the late-1990s to 34 per cent today, the need for global talent too was acutely felt. The composition of L&T's businesses was meanwhile changing. It was developing more project-oriented business lines. Projects, though, carry an intrinsic risk. 'Hence, in 2005,' says Kothari, 'we evolved a risk management structure and processes. Without risk there is no reward. You have to manage risk in projects—but what are the governance mechanisms? How do you carry out an evaluation of a project? All this was considered. We also appointed a chief risk officer (CRO).'

Defence was incubated when L&T was still mainly a construction company. 'But in L&T our thinking always is: what else can we do?' says Kothari. 'So we created Infrastructure Development Projects Ltd (IDPL) to handle large infrastructure projects. We also realized that there were things we could have done better. In every successive strategic plan we look at PDCA (Plan, Do, Check and Act) so that the next plan is better than the earlier one. We realized that we need to place more focus on implementation. We came up with a series of set processes in the organization, which we call Rigorous Programme Management. The operating company idea was to create an internal board structure across synergistic divisions. From Operating Companies (OCs) evolved Independent Companies (ICs), which were an important enabler of L&T's growth. Because then there is internal competition: you are one IC, he is another IC—both can be benchmarked with global peers. It was a kind of internal listing.'

Lakshya 1 (2005–10) was a good period for L&T operationally. At the end of it, turnover climbed to Rs 47,000 crore. Lakshya 2 (2010–16), was even better: turnover more than doubled, to over Rs 1,00,000 crore. Systematic planning and organized processes turbocharged L&T's top line, though external factors and large up-front investments in defence, nuclear and shipbuilding slowed profit growth.

Of the group's main subsidiaries, L&T Infotech, now known as LTI, and L&T Technology Services were listed in 2016, within two months of each other. L&T Finance had been listed earlier, in 2011. The group, however, recognizes that it cannot list every company in its fold. 'If we vertically split every business, then L&T itself will vanish,' says Kothari. 'So even at the strategic planning stage we realized that we need to list 30-40 per cent of our business, but that 60 per cent should be the core under the parent company. Otherwise, rather than creating value, we will destroy value.'

Ruminating on his long association with Naik, Kothari says: 'I have had the good fortune of working closely with Mr Naik ever since he took over as CEO in 1999. He is adept at macro-strategy formulation and micro-level implementation—a rare combination. According to him, the real skill lies in implementation. Added to all this is Naik's ability to think far ahead of his time and foresee with accuracy what will happen if a particular strategy is implemented. Naik is also a firm believer in thorough planning.' Adds Kothari: 'In his own vivid imagery, "if you want to kill a goat, prepare as if you are going to kill a tiger".'

Naik's attention levels are extraordinary, as L&T's managers have often discovered to their discomfiture when he detects the minutest inconsistency even in hour-long presentations. Says Kothari, with a smile: 'L&T managers are used to Mr Naik's signature style of keeping abreast of developments. Typically, when Mr Naik calls you on your mobile, you need to be immediately on full alert. "Where are you?" will be his first question. Other searching questions will follow in rapid fire, giving him a full picture of the status of the project you are handling.'

Avant garde management gurus suggest using operational research models with multiple variables. 'Mr Naik does this processing in his mind,' says Kothari. 'He can appraise situations, crunch numbers and rapidly come up with the likely result. He has the remarkable ability to "switch-on" and "switch-off". He could be deliberating on crucial industrial relations issues, and minutes later in the next meeting, he can immerse himself in strategy, with no overhang of the previous issue.'

L&T deals regularly with almost every major global strategy firm, but Kothari avers that none of the heads of these marquee firms seems to be able to match Naiks's speed or cope with his incisive logic. Naik's working style is to delegate completely but monitor closely. 'The remote control stays in his hand,' says Kothari. 'He inspires and challenges you, and when you are nearing the goal, he has no compunction in shifting the goal posts! It makes you go that extra mile.'

IN FEBRUARY 2000, Naik's team made a presentation to the board of directors on what L&T should look like in the next five years. L&T should, first and foremost, think like a multinational company with global benchmarking. It took Naik two or three years to change mindsets at L&T. Seniority had been entrenched for decades. Merit was the new mantra. The culture took time to seep in and percolate through the ranks. Several senior managers resisted change because, as Naik says, they themselves often lacked merit. Why would they want to upend a long-established system of seniority and move out of their comfort zone?

Earlier, as one L&T executive says, 'If you did well, you would be promoted in three years and if you did not do well, then you would be promoted in four years. So there was no incentive for high performers. Naik changed that thinking: "I said if there is an outstanding man, he will be promoted in two years. If somebody is not performing, he may not be promoted for five or six years or even have to leave. And if he is super-outstanding, he may be promoted even in one year." Earlier, executives of merit were also leaving. They said, what is the difference, we are getting promoted in three years and the others in four years!'

As the managerial centre of gravity shifted, Naik spent three days a week at the Powai office and three days at the company's south Mumbai office, L&T House, in Ballard Estate. Gradually, management operations were centralized in the glass-and-steel Landmark building in Andheri, north Mumbai, where Naik now spends much of his time. Landmark lies between suburban Powai and south Mumbai's Ballard Estate. 'My idea is that employees should be close to where the chairman is,' says Naik, 'because the chairman is the chief brand manager. When he gets new ideas he should be able to call an executive immediately and say let's do this.'

As ever, for Naik action spoke louder than words. 'We got on with our work,' he says briskly. 'It was time for our second five-year plan. The first five-year Blue Chip plan was getting over in 2005. We were working feverishly on the Lakshya 1 plan for 2005–10. From project Blue Chip, we retained the Strategic Business Unit (SBU) concept. Now we introduced the Independent Company (IC) concept with internal directors—no outside directors. When we launched project Lakshya 2 in 2010, we had everything working smoothly, as if the ICs were listed entities.'

With each five-year plan the corporate structure of L&T went through significant changes. In 2016, Lakshya 3, which runs through to 2021, incorporated as many statutory provisions as possible ensure the compliance listed entities must have. 'If the number of outside directors was less than what was required,' says Naik, 'then we immediately put up a red flag and rectified it. So that when we list a company, it is ready.'

Naik's spirit was unquenchable, his energy boundless. In 2006, when he was sixty-four, he went to Kullu Manali to see two hydropower plants. L&T's investment in one was Rs 115 crore and in the other, Rs 210 crore. 'When I went up the hill where the hydropower projects were,' Naik recalls, 'there were no railings. And for six months of the year the road is muddy. Though there are four-wheel drives, if by chance the vehicle slips, all the people die. So I made it a rule that we will not make any hydropower investment of less than Rs 750 crore. Then we can provide security to our people by spending on safety infrastructure. And today ECC itself will not bid for anything less than Rs 1,000 crore.'

INFORMATION TECHNOLOGY was a powerful driver of India's growth. Software exports rose exponentially. The availability of skilled labour at low wages encouraged foreign companies to establish back office operations in India. Investments flowed in from developed countries. The software industry prospered. Within a few years, India was acknowledged as the dominant hub for knowledge-based services. Indian infotech companies led the software export boom.

Recognizing the need to diversify in order to protect L&T's bottom line, Naik had turned his attention in the mid-1990s to infotech. 'L&T Infotech actually emerged from a strategy to stop IT engineers leaving L&T for technology companies,' concedes Naik: 'Attrition rates were very high. Our people were going to the booming IT services industry.'

How did L&T's own IT services business initiative evolve? A soft-spoken man with a distinctive mien, Sunil Pande is an executive vice-president and advisor in L&T's corporate strategy group. 'I have been with L&T for forty-five years,' he says. 'I have known Mr Naik since I joined the company in 1971, but I worked closely with him from 1998 when I was shifted to the power group. Mr Naik was responsible for the power business along with other portfolios. He was in charge of Group II, to which power belonged. Mr Naik decided to focus on areas which he thought could give good valuation to the company and enhance shareholder value. Infotech was one such area.'

L&T Infotech struggled in its initial years. Says Pande. 'After 2000, Mr Naik took personal responsibility for improving its business. I was picked in August 2000 and made country manager for L&T Infotech in the United States. I was in the US for around ten years, from 2000 to 2010. Mr Naik used to visit the US every quarter for about two or three weeks. He would meet every customer personally. He developed L&T Infotech's business from almost ground zero. He knew how Infosys had grown, how Wipro had grown, how TCS had grown. We had business in Europe too. But 70 per cent of IT business comes from America, so we worked almost 24x7 in those days.'

Pande adds unhesitatingly: 'I have not seen a person with so much passion and dedication, doing such hard work and with such close involvement in the business. Mr Naik is a man in a hurry. He wanted quick results. He knew that L&T's engineers and the quality of work we had done in hard-core engineering was much more valuable than what IT companies were doing at that time. Software firms were doing more body shopping, especially during Y2K. But he knew they had generated so much value for shareholders. So Mr Naik took it upon himself to make up for lost time. Of course he was a very hard taskmaster. Expectations were very, very high. He expected results overnight. In fact he would talk to me every day, morning and evening, take stock of things, review each case. He would insist on seven or eight meetings every day when he came to the US, and those meetings had to be at not less than chief information officer-level. We had to manage that. Besides, we also had to optimize time. So if we had fixed four meetings and in between, if one hour was available, then he would want to fill that up too. He would shuffle the meetings around. For example, we had to once juggle a meeting with the CEO of JP Morgan just so that we could complete more meetings. His expectations were extraordinary. It was very difficult to cope with those expectations. But we did.'

There were hiccups along the way too. In 2009, L&T bid for infotech services major Satyam Computers, which had collapsed after its fraudulent book-keeping had been exposed. Naik's idea was to strengthen L&T's Infotech's business with Satyam's ready-made blue-chip clientele. L&T Infotech had grown rapidly since the mid-2000s but now needed a dose of steroids to enable it to move into the top league of India's software firms like Infosys, Tata Consultancy Services and Wipro. Satyam seemed a good takeover target. In the end though, Satyam was sold to the Mahindras and L&T exited its investment with a profit.

GLOBALIZATION IN the 2000s opened up a cornucopia of opportunities for India. The government's tenth Five-Year Plan (2002–07) had set a GDP growth target of 8 per cent. India, in fact, grew at an annual average rate of 8.5 per cent during that period. And at the beginning of the eleventh plan in 2008, the country was amongst the world's fastest growing economies. Investments surged, the industrial sector expanded, and the savings rate rose.

L&T prospered in this salubrious economic environment. Naik, appointed chairman in 2003, was in his element. Globally, however, turbulence lay just around the corner. The financial meltdown originated in the US subprime mortgage market in 2007. It spread rapidly to the US financial sector. The crisis enveloped the international banking system and financial markets in other countries. By the end of 2008, most countries had slipped into recession.

Like India though, L&T was able to weather the storm without incurring significant damage. Quick to react to the changed environment, Naik pressed his senior executives to expand L&T's geographies to the oil-rich Gulf. The fall in oil prices after 2013-14 would, however, cause a downturn in orders from the Gulf region too. Once again displaying great agility, Naik focused on priority projects in the Middle East, like airports, roadways and metros, which are largely immune to sovereign budget cuts. L&T's eclectic business portfolio played a major role in its ability to sustain growth during these difficult times.

The government, meanwhile, undertook several measures to deal with the economic slowdown. It fast-tracked large infrastructure projects and stepped up core sector financing. This worked to L&T's advantage. Its Indian project footprint—from metros and highways to airports and power plants—expanded. In 2011, L&T restructured its business into nine verticals to enhance operational efficiency: power equipment, hydrocarbon, heavy engineering, infrastructure, building and factories, metals and minerals, electrical and automation products, electrical construction, and machinery and industrial products. Each unit would function as an independent company with an internal board to make investment decisions. Business heads and board members were appointed for each vertical. During the year, L&T Finance Holdings was listed on the stock exchange. It would be the precursor to other businesses being listed, beginning with infotech and technology services, as L&T's strategy of spinning off profitable businesses gathered pace.

WHERE DOES L&T stand in the global pecking order of infrastructure giants? Naik is unequivocal in his reply: 'We are actually bigger than Bechtel because they work in a high-cost economy. Using the purchasing power parity (PPP) methodology, L&T's $17 billion annual turnover is on par with Bechtel's $38 billion annual turnover, taking into account PPP-based costs and revenue.'

Nationalism and the desire to strengthen India's economy have been the driving forces in Naik's life. 'Deep down in my mind and heart, I have from the day I joined L&T I tried to do things that others don't do,' he says. 'To do things that will make India a very strong country – whether in infrastructure, defence, energy, power, nuclear or aerospace. There is not a single company in the world which can today say categorically that it does all of these and more.'

He swivels in his chair and points to the far wall. 'See, in this boardroom there is a flag there on the table. If you go to my office room, there is a flag there too and on my jacket lapel also a tricolour flag. In my home too there is an Indian flag. It keeps reminding me of the nation. I put it on my jacket and go all over the world. It keeps reminding me – don't forget your country. So my mission has been somewhat accomplished, though there is a lot still to be done; there is never an end in our country which has so many poor, deprived people.'

Recognizing his contribution to India's infrastructure and strong sense of service to the nation, the government awarded Naik the Padma Bhushan in 2009. He recalls the moment with pride: 'I have been deeply involved in several activities, and the government thought it fit to recognize somebody who is doing a good job in the corporate world, is a professional manager, not an owner, and who is not making money for himself but for all stakeholders. At the same time he is involved in society, always looking to make India a strong country, whether, as I said, through defence, nuclear, aerospace, infrastructure, energy, whatever. All of these activities are oriented towards making India strong.'

Naik has clear-headed views on the Indian economy. 'During Indira Gandhi's tenure,' he says, 'India was a government-driven economy with hardly any freedom to do what you wanted to do in the private sector. The Licence Raj made it virtually impossible. Anything that could be made by government companies was closed to the private sector. But for those restrictions, L&T would have moved ahead much faster. We applied for a mining machinery licence in 1975 and got it only in 1979! We applied for a boiler licence in 1979 and did not get it till 1981. When we applied for a licence for offshore platforms, we didn't even get it! India had to import so much because government companies simply could not deliver. So a lot of things did not go well during the Licence Raj. We were a victim of that, just as many other companies were. Once liberalization set in under the Narasimha Rao-Manmohan Singh dispensation, things improved gradually. By 1995-96, the Licence Raj was more or less over.'

As India's economy opened up, all boats rose with the tide. So did L&T's. But impediments remained. Bureaucratic decision-making was slow, regulations onerous. In an article for *Business Today* on 16 November 2008, Naik wrote:

> It will help to start by understanding that the manufacturing sector covers a very broad spectrum, with products that range from bicycles to automobiles to steel plants and nuclear reactors. To offer a broad forecast on all these sectors will actually necessitate an understanding of the larger economic outlook for global growth. It is necessary to recognise that in a globalized economic environment, the business outlook for any particular product will depend on the global 'demand-supply' balance for that product. Global manufacturing facilities seek market opportunities across the world. For most products, there is production overcapacity at a global level, which was built up over the last decade or so in response to a boom in global growth and increased levels of per capita consumption.
>
> The growth of the manufacturing sector will be largely influenced by the growth of the global economy, which, in turn, depends on the easy availability of credit at viable costs. Paradoxically, the creation of capital depends on a high savings rate; the infusion of capital into the economy without matching increases in the production of goods and services will be inflationary. However, easier access to and injection of capital may be necessary in the short term to prevent economies across the world from stalling. In the longer term, it will require discipline across societies to change their habits and shift spending from wasteful consumption to investment. Similarly,

> there will be increasing business opportunities for products that meet the changing requirements of customers. This basic business truth has always been applicable; in turbulent times, the urgency and recognition of this is far more acute. We expect the Indian economy to continue to grow faster than more mature markets, even though there may be a temporary downturn arising out of the global slowdown, and the higher cost and tighter availability of capital.

—ω—

BY 2009-10 it looked as though India had emerged unscathed from the global economic downturn. The Indian economy was still robust, with GDP growth at 8 per cent. Subsequent years, however, showed that contrary to conventional wisdom, India had become increasingly integrated into the global economy. For example, between 2011 and 2014, as the world economy slowed, Indian economic growth too sagged. It showed little sign of immediate revival, with growth flattening out.

In October 2010, following the global financial meltdown in the wake of the sub-prime mortgage crisis that led to the collapse of storied American investment banks like Lehman Brothers, Naik recognized the need to sculpt a new growth strategy for L&T. On 23 October 2010, he issued a detailed memo to L&T's top management outlining the tasks ahead. It is important to study the memo in its entirety to get a sense of Naik's thinking at a critical juncture in L&T's evolution in a challenging international economic environment several years ago:

> We had initiated the process of developing our strategic plan for the period 2010-15 (Lakshya 2015) in September 2009. The process defined the strategy and strategic initiatives for each Business Unit (BU) and carried out a detailed assessment of our Portfolio, Organization Structure and Capital Structure. The assessment reveals significant opportunities across all our business segments and the need to refine our organizational model – one which would facilitate growth through greater levels of empowerment and

delegation while retaining accountability. This is even more critical as our plans call for growing aggressively on a large revenue base. Considering this, Management has decided to restructure L&T into nine Independent Companies (ICs).

These ICs will comprise synergistic Strategic Business Groups (SBGs) and Business Units. All related Subsidiary & Associate Units (S&A Units) would form part of the respective IC. Each IC will have its own board consisting of representatives from the L&T Board, executives from the IC and external members who will bring a greater degree of accountability and governance in operations. The external members will typically be industry experts, academicians, etc identified in line with the needs of each IC.

Each IC would be encouraged to establish its organizational structure and processes as if it were a market-listed company. ICs will have greater freedom in defining the compensation structure and other HR policies. However, only certain processes/policies will continue to be driven from L&T Corporate.

Strategic Business Groups will be synergistic groups of like businesses that can over time evolve into ICs. The head of an SBG may be a member of an IC Board and will be accountable for the performance of the businesses in the SBG. Similarly, Business Units are likely to evolve and grow into SBGs.

The following businesses, which are housed in a respective Subsidiary Company, will continue to operate as before:

1. IDPL;
2. Power Development;
3. Hyderabad Metro;
4. Financial Services;
5. IT;

Formation of these Independent Companies and Corporate Centres will require substantial organizational restructuring and changes in processes and policies. This process will be completed by March 31, 2011 progressively, as each business gets ready. The budgets for FY 2011-12 will be drawn up as per the new organizational structure.

> Management believes that the formation of ICs would empower businesses to capture opportunities, enhance competitiveness, attract talent, create opportunities for leadership development, increase accountability and strengthen performance culture. We are venturing into this large-scale, high-impact organizational transformation in the near future. Considering the importance of this initiative, all concerned are requested to provide necessary guidance and support for the effort.

Naik's memo set the agenda for L&T in a world beset by uncertainties, economic and political. It would serve as an important template as the company moved into a new orbit of growth and business diversification.

JUST WHEN it seemed the worst was over, another financial crisis rocked the world. The global economy suffered a new bout of recession in 2011-12 following the sovereign debt meltdown in Europe centred on the euro and debt-ridden Greece. Domestic factors, meanwhile, stymied the country's progress. Measures taken by the UPA government to inject a fiscal stimulus to the economy during the 2008 global financial crisis had caused macro-economic imbalances. Investments fell in several sectors. Inflation surged. All these developments coalesced to plunge the economy into a downturn. Growth decelerated to 6.2 per cent in 2012-13. It would fall even further in 2013-14 before stabilizing under a new government.

While the country grappled to reverse the slowdown in 2012, L&T engaged in a slew of measures to increase efficiency, cut costs and rebalance its portfolio of assets. Investor sentiment had been dampened by high bank interest rates. Key projects were being postponed. The government had pledged additional spending on infrastructure, but those investments dipped because of rising inflation and multiple interest rate hikes that ballooned costs. Banks with stressed assets reported alarmingly high non-performing assets (NPAs) and reduced corporate lending.

L&T cut its order growth guidance. While its order book had increased significantly between 2004 and 2011, the company's global presence was largely restricted to the Middle East. Now it aggressively began to court orders in the Far East, Africa and South America. Offices were opened in these regions. L&T also started to analyse opportunities in member-nations of the Commonwealth of Independent States (CIS) and established an office in Istanbul, Turkey, which straddled the Eurasian geography. Revenues and profits gradually improved as Naik's third term as chairman unfolded between 2012 and 2017.

New challenges lay ahead. Shipbuilding beckoned.

8

Kattupalli: A Rising Tide

DRIVING FROM CHENNAI to Kattupalli takes just over an hour. Lush greenery greets you as you enter L&T's 1,225-acre campus. As with most projects, Naik wants L&T to be asset-light. Hence the decision to sell the port section in Kattupalli to the Adani group. Running a port is not part of L&T's priorities. Building ships at Kattupalli certainly is.

Kattupalli's multi-disciplinary facility comprises a shipbuilding yard, a modular fabrication yard for hydrocarbon projects, and associated units. The Kattupalli shipyard is an example of how Naik thinks ahead and builds for the future. The Kattupalli facility entailed high capital expenditure in anticipation of large orders from the ministry of defence (MoD). The shipyard is well suited to meet India's defence needs since it incorporates the latest technology in shipbuilding, including a unique shiplift that was designed and manufactured in-house. The shipyard is capable of manufacturing warships (frigates, destroyers and corvettes), submarines and other vessels. With the defence sector opening up to the private sector—albeit slowly—Kattupalli is brimful of promise. Naik has repeatedly said that once defence orders materialize, the Kattupalli facility could, like Hazira, become a key asset for L&T.

Rajendran Urikouth, vice-president of L&T's commercial shipbuilding, is a loquacious and self-assured man. He was associated with the shipbuilding business from the initial days of L&T's foray in 2005. 'We started with a business plan, then we started looking for a shipyard,' he explains. 'We saw almost a dozen locations all over India, from Kandla to Vizag and Paradeep on the east coast. We finally zeroed in on Kattupalli in 2006.'

The advantage of Kattupalli is its vast expanse of land. L&T's objective was to build a shipyard as big as those of Hyundai and Samsung in South Korea. The first priority was land, followed by infrastructure, and finally, proximity to a workforce with technical knowhow. Based on these criteria, Kattupalli struck Naik as the ideal choice.

'Getting 1,225 acres near a metro is almost impossible,' points out Urikouth. 'Besides, we have an operating port right next door, and Chennai has been catering to the marine fraternity since time immemorial. In 2005-06 the shipbuilding market was booming. To set up a shipyard takes time, a minimum of two to three years. In Hazira we have a facility with a riverfront. We set up a medium-sized shipyard there to start off with. The idea was that by the time Kattupalli is up and running, our people would have the required experience and exposure. We first converted 20 acres of land in Hazira next to the Tapti river and initially made vessels that were 80 to 90 metres in length. We started scouting for orders in 2006 itself. We received an order for a heavy lift vessel and for four vessels from a Dutch company, then another two with a big shiplift facility. The Dutch gave us another four orders. We thus started with more than ten orders in hand. Four were delivered on time and the others, because of delays and the market crashing, were foreclosed midway. But by the time we operationalized the Kattupalli shipyard, the first ship had been delivered in 2010 from Hazira. We started locating to Kattupalli around 2008. Land had been bought in 2007-08. Construction began in 2010. We got consent to operate in 2012. With prospects in the defence sector brightening, Mr Naik decided to focus on naval vessels.'

DEFENCE REQUIRES a sophisticated approach. It is more skill-oriented than commercial shipbuilding. Technical knowledge and precision are essential. Urikouth is a naval architect from Cochin University. He has a BTech. in naval architecture and an MBA. Urikouth worked in Mazagon Dock for thirteen years. He left because of the way, he says, the public sector works. He was with Western India Shipyard for three years, then with Dempo in Goa, where he was head of shipbuilding. He returned for a while to the public sector before joining L&T.

Urikouth recalls with a smile the events leading to his association with L&T: 'When Narendra Modi was chief minister of Gujarat, he had invited Mr Naik to see the Gujarat government's shipyard. Mr Naik ultimately decided not to buy the shipyard but hired me! I joined L&T in July 2005.'

Of the 1,225 acres in Kattupalli, L&T has handed over 350 to the Adani group for its port there. Currently managed by the Adanis, the port will be sold to them once all legal formalities are completed. K. Venkatesh, chief executive and managing director of L&T IDPL, puts the matter in perspective: 'The Board of L&T, in its strategy to become asset-light and streamline portfolio investments, decided to exit the ports portfolio in 2014. Consequently, after exiting Dhamra port in June 2014, a decision was taken to exit Kattupalli port too. The process of demerging Kattupalli port after obtaining the necessary permissions from state and central government authorities is in the final stages. A strategic investor has been identified and terms of sale agreed upon. The Tamil Nadu government has approved the sale of shares to the strategic investor after demerging and converting the port, currently a division of LTSB, into a separate company. The sale of L&T's interest in the port, when completed, will help reduce debt and improve return on equity for the group.' Naik reiterates that running ports and metros is not L&T's business. He is keen to exit businesses which are asset-heavy and require excessive management time.

In Hazira, huge plates are cut for nuclear reactors, Urikouth explains. For shipbuilding though, much thinner, finer plates are needed to be cut. To master the overall technology in shipbuilding, L&T underwent three years of productive collaboration with Mitsubishi Heavy Industries, from 2011 to 2014. More than thirty of the Japanese firm's executives lived in Chennai and worked at Kattupalli. All were Japanese nationals. 'We would sit with our design experts and production people to plan the shipbuilding process and methodology and the ship itself,' recalls Urikouth. 'We had also sent our team to Mitsubishi's shipyards in Japan. They were trained there for three months in design, production and quality. The knowledge they dispensed to our people was extremely valuable.'

Admiral J.S. Mann, who heads shipyard operations in Kattupalli, joined L&T in September 2015. Over lunch, in a room overlooking the Kattupalli facility, he spoke of the challenges his team faced: 'At that time we were working on one of the Indian Navy's largest ships, INS *Jyoti*. It was very challenging. That was also a transition period when L&T had decided to bid only for defence work. Our prime customers were the Indian Navy and the Coast Guard. When you build warships, the first things are the weapons system and the propulsion system. These are extremely sophisticated, and the specialization required for their design and production are quite different from what we do for commercial shipbuilding. Besides, the tolerances are very fine here. Our biggest challenge earlier used to be erecting the blocks, which we have now overcome. We are on schedule or ahead of schedule in all our work. It takes time for a shipyard to graduate to a stage where you start building ships on schedule, because the design as well as production has to proceed simultaneously. Since we work for the navy and coast guard, there's no leeway for error.'

Admiral Mann, a distinguished looking man with a baritone voice, joined L&T after retiring from the Indian Navy. 'Earlier, I was project director of a strategic naval project at Visakhapatnam,' he says. 'I was operating from the navy's headquarters in Delhi. Mr Naik's nationalist dream was always that L&T would be the first private company taken on board by the Indian Navy, and that too for its strategic programme.'

Admiral Mann reveals that the *Arihant* nuclear-powered submarine programme started in the 1980s. Once the initial prototype design stage was over, production began in the late 1990s. 'You can imagine the vision Mr Naik had,' he says. 'We would build the blocks in Hazira, take them by barge all the way to Visakhapatnam, and in Visakhapatnam load them onto the dock, then join them together and the submarine finally got its shape. I have seen first-hand when I was in the navy, L&T evolve to a stage where it can handle any type of sophisticated equipment, install it, integrate it in the system and commission it. And there can't be anything more sophisticated than a nuclear-powered submarine. The lessons learnt from INS *Arihant* have been applied to subsequent platforms.'

Says Urikouth: 'One of the core principles being addressed by Mr Naik every time he comes to Kattupalli are quality and on-time delivery. If you take five years for a submarine, then the navy is not going to come back to you. If you deliver on time, as we did the coast guard ships, which we built two years ahead of schedule, they'll come back.'

Naik's nationalism is embedded in his DNA. It has imbued many of his strategic decisions, including Hazira and Kattupalli, both of which strongly serve the national interest. He says: 'India has a very long coastline. We need to protect it with a strong navy and a strong coast guard. They need lots of ships. For a long time, in line with our commitment to build a strong nation, we had been planning a shipyard that can build defence ships and submarines. We located this spot at Kattupalli. It is one of the largest Indian shipyards, 1,225 acres of land, with huge potential for expansion. Two or three years down the line, you will see this shipyard full of warships and—hopefully—submarines. We have a 21,000-tonne shiplift—one of the largest in this part of the world. And six ships can be built simultaneously. Kattupalli will make a significant difference to India's future defence needs.'

The back story of how L&T dropped anchor in Kattupalli is particularly interesting. *Business Today*, in March 2008, wrote:[1]

> Finance Minister P. Chidambaram isn't quite known for his fondness for granting favours. But with A.M. Naik he was willing to make an exception. When he was looking for a location for a proposed shipyard and port, he went up to the FM. A week later, L&T had got a green signal from the Tamil Nadu government for the twin projects. Recalls Naik: 'He took me to the Tamil Nadu Chief Minister (M. Karunanidhi) and told him that he could have taken me to Andhra Pradesh, but the love for his own home state has brought L&T to him and they should be given all the cooperation. In a week we had the go-ahead. When it comes to L&T everyone speaks their heart out. They know we aren't working for our own self-interest, but are nation builders. That's the reason even the Prime Minister classifies L&T as the only national sector company.

The magazine's story added:

> Such a nationalistic vision and mission also works on Dalal Street. Today L&T is among the top 10 stocks trading on the domestic bourses, with a market capitalization of over Rs 1 lakh crore. And there's plenty more value that's waiting to be unlocked.

VICE-ADMIRAL B. KANNAN served the navy with distinction for forty years. 'I took charge at Kattupalli in November 2015,' he says, in the clipped tones of a senior naval officer. 'L&T makes torpedo tubes, rocket launchers, ship systems stabilizers, etc. These need structural engineering, mechanical engineering. They have to have accuracy and precision. It is a combination of these two for which L&T has unmatched capability.'

---

1 23 March 2008.

The Indian Navy has a specialized cadre of 450 officers and naval architects who deal with its design requirements. L&T's involvement in the navy's various programme goes back several decades. For the *Arihant* nuclear-powered submarine programme, once the prototype had been approved, the steel was first cut in 1998 by then President A.P.J. Abdul Kalam. L&T played an increasingly important role in the navy's nuclear-powered submarine programme. Many of the details on ongoing projects remain classified. However, all the construction and critical outfitting activity for India's nuclear-powered submarines are being done by L&T using home-grown technologies.

'After we build the hull, which is cylindrical,' says Admiral Kannan, 'we put the equipment, pipes and cables inside, and then they are all put together to form the submarine which operates at sea. This programme has given a huge push to indigenization with the participation of private sector industry. The *Arihant* nuclear-powered submarine was launched for sea trials in 2009. I was the director for the Indian Navy's submarine programme at that time. As Admiral Superintendent of Bombay Dockyard, I steered the programme. Getting the nuclear-powered submarine floated for the first time was a huge challenge. That was the time the navy worked closely with private industry and I developed a lot of admiration for the engineers and designers at L&T.'

Worldwide, submarine construction is today largely done in workshops. It is difficult for engineers to work on submarines because of space constrictions. Building in dry docks adds further complications. The submarines have to be kept in covered sheds so that high productivity is achieved and the equipment is not impacted by the weather. A nuclear-powered submarine has extremely sophisticated equipment and systems. While the hull was built by L&T, the equipment inside the submarine came from different sources—L&T, TCS, Godrej and Walchandnagar. L&T's job was to build the complete hull, install the different pieces of complex equipment and integrate them into systems. The entire outfitting was done by L&T. 'A special organization was formed, which was not under the navy's command, though the entire team actually comprised naval officers,' says Admiral Kannan. 'There were 350 officers in the programme. They interacted closely with L&T.'

TAMIL NADU'S coastline is well endowed with a deep waterfront, which is a boon for shipbuilding. When a ship is finally launched into water, the depth of the water is critical. 'Sustainable depth' is important; artificially created depth can be sustained only for a limited period of time. When L&T selected Kattupalli north of Chennai, the objective was to build a modern, green shipyard. The company had studied the models of other shipyards, global and Indian. It had taken advice from Japanese shipbuilding companies on how the shipyard should be laid out, and on the complex engineering required to build warships and commercial ships.

'You have to have a captive design organization if you want to execute projects in shipbuilding in as short a time as possible,' says Admiral Kannan. 'This was a major lesson for all of us in India, be it in industry or in the navy. We learnt by looking at how shipbuilding was done in the country from 1965 to 2005. We realized that there was not a single programme which did not suffer time delays. Every programme the navy embarked upon had a time delay. And of course there always was a technical reason. But the lesson we learnt was that between design and construction there is a huge amount of information which has to flow both ways to make sure the design meets the production requirement and vice versa.'

Admiral Kannan has implemented in Kattupalli the lessons he absorbed during his long tenure in the Indian Navy: 'Some of the designs are iterative in ships, so it's not possible for you to say, "I have finished the design, take it." It comes back for revalidation and changes. You have a very strong sense of knowledge and information. Even within the same organization, under the same roof, design and production cannot be 100 per cent concurrent.

The design has to lead by a few months or by half a year or, in some cases, one year. If you can minimize this period and enjoy maximum concurrency, then your shipbuilding programme will become more efficient, more productive. You will complete projects on time. It's never happened in India! For nearly forty years, from the mid-1960s to 2005, there were always delays. It has not changed even today, because you still have a design unit which is a separate organization, government, public or private, and so the design of the ship goes back and forth, the selection of equipment gets held up. Essential changes in equipment do not happen.'

This lesson of shipbuilding was quickly assimilated by L&T. A decision was taken in 2009-10 to have a strong in-house design team. It started in Powai and slowly expanded its activities to Hazira. Thereafter, a large part of the team shifted to Kattupalli. Today L&T has a design team at the shipyard comprising 150 engineers and naval architects. The company started operations with commercial shipbuilding. Significant capital was invested to build the shipyard. But with commercial orders not flowing in due to the global downturn, it was decided to utilize the infrastructure to cater to defence—from building warships for the navy to small fast boats for the coast guard.

Fortunately, underscoring Naik's foresight, the Kattupalli shipyard had fundamentally been built as a defence shipyard. It has a shiplift facility with a capacity to lift all the ships in the Indian Navy and coast guard except, obviously, an aircraft carrier. The second largest ship in the Indian Navy is INS *Jyoti*, a tanker which is serviced in Kattupalli. 'Dry docks are at a premium in the country,' points out Admiral Kannan. 'You ask for one, but you don't get it easily. The advantage of having a shiplift is to lift the ship and put it on land and then go out for the next ship and put it again on land. Meanwhile, the third ship can be put in the water. There's a huge amount of flexibility, but it's a very capital-intensive infrastructure, which is why it's important to speed up the production process.'

L&T has the right design infrastructure for defence shipbuilding—capacity-wise, capability-wise and technology-wise, says Admiral Kannan. 'The turnaround time is good. Defence orders did not come in initially. Around February-March 2015, however, L&T received an order from the coast guard to build seven offshore vessels. These are under construction. The ships are capable of carrying a helicopter too, which will greatly empower the coast guard in its critical duty of protecting India against a terror attack from the sea.'

L&T is, meanwhile, building the last of the 48 high-speed interceptor craft. They are ready two years ahead of time, waiting for the coast guard to take delivery of them. These were the first defence ships to be *ab initio* designed by any Indian company. Work began in-house at L&T's own warship design centre, then at Powai, before expanding into a full-fledged unit at Chennai to support the Kattupalli yard. Manufacturing was concurrent at Hazira and Kattupalli. The Indian Navy wished to evolve into a 'builder's navy' and not a 'buyer's navy' and steered the warship building programme with foresight from the early 1960s. It decided to design warships indigenously and set up a design directorate. It created a cadre of naval architects in 1962. This later included submarine design, culminating in the setting up of an independent submarine design directorate in 1987. Today India designs all its ships and submarines.

The government nationalized private sector shipyards in the 1960s, including Mazagon Dock and Hindustan Shipyard (which was earlier Scindia Shipyard). The government nurtured them to build complex warships and submarines, and by the 1990s they could deliver destroyers, frigates, corvettes and auxiliary warships. Gradually, public sector shipyards acquired organizational fat, leading to massive delays and mounting costs. New technologies required less manpower, nimble feet. 'They could not adjust,' says Admiral Kannan. 'That made them inefficient, apart from the fact they always relied on someone else to provide the ship design. Even today, at varying levels, except for Cochin Shipyard that saw global competition for commercial ships—it not being under MoD with order protection and therefore better than the others—the same situation prevails.'

J.D. Patil, a wholetime director heading the defence business and aerospace business at L&T, says: 'The government of India opened up the defence sector in 2001 for private sector participation and licensed L&T in 2002. We were among the first to get licences to design and build almost the entire range of defence systems across our locations at Powai, Hazira, Chennai and Kansbahal. The licences have been extended to our new dedicated complexes at Ranoli, Talegaon, Bengaluru, Coimbatore and Kattupalli, as also for a widened range of products and solutions.'

In 2015, the Kattupalli shipyard won two contracts, one for building seven offshore patrol vessels for the Coast Guard and a floating dock for the Indian Navy. Together these were valued at around Rs 2,000 crore. The yard also undertook a series of warship refits for the Indian Navy, the largest being the LST-L class and the navy's largest fleet tanker (next in size only to an aircraft carrier) as well as coast guard ships. These refits were delivered on schedule. The yard was also selected by OEMs and approved by the navy for upgrade and refit of Russian-origin Kilo class submarines, against strong competition from government-owned Cochin Shipyard and the private sector Pipavav Shipyard. Of the nine kilo-class submarines still in naval service, two are reaching life expiry, needing major refit, modernization and life certification at the Kattupalli yard. The extensive refit will not only extend the life of the submarines by a decade, but also upgrade their combat potential.

Another key project at Kattupalli is the design and delivery of twelve fast attack ships for the Vietnamese coast guard. 'We won the order from the Vietnam government, reveals Admiral Kannan. 'This contract has a line of credit from the Indian government. India sees a valuable friend in Vietnam amid regional uncertainties. The

Vietnamese visited five Indian shipyards and selected L&T after competitive bidding.'

Patil looks forward eagerly to the future. He says: 'Having launched the Naval FDN (Floating Dock—Naval) on 20 June 2017, ahead of schedule, and the first OPV (Offshore Patrol Vessel) in August, Team Kattupalli is raring to go. We are waiting for a go-ahead from the Vietnam government to start construction, and we anticipate new orders from the Indian Navy in the coming months.'

Kattupalli is recognized by the Indian government as a shipyard which can build everything, including even an aircraft carrier. But for that, concedes Admiral Kannan, 'We have to create additional infrastructure. The shipyard occupies more than 700 acres of land. We have used only a small part of it, the rest is kept for expansion. India's second aircraft carrier is being built at Cochin Shipyard, but it has taken many years. Ask Cochin Shipyard, and they will say delivery of the aircraft carrier will be in 2019. If you ask the Indian Navy, they will say 2021, so we have to take a mid-point and say 2020 for India's second aircraft carrier.'

What does Admiral Kannan make of Naik's management style in the context of Kattupalli? 'Being a military man, I am used to authoritative leaders,' he says. 'Some leaders I witnessed in the navy gave directions from positions of power. I used to wonder how they could do this when they were not endowed with much knowledge in that area or don't have much experience. I found a difference in Mr Naik. He is equally authoritative, very clinical in his approach, but it's all backed up with facts and a very strong consolidation of knowledge. He can tell what will happen two years from now. He has great vision. He has total commitment to L&T. You don't get leaders like him who live and breathe a company. This is a very complex field, technologically very complex. But even an activity like building warships—he could grasp it very quickly. He can give you details of submarines and battleships even though he is not a naval architect. I have spent forty years in the navy. I would find myself in shallow waters if I have to discuss construction methodology or design. But Mr Naik has a special gift to be able to grasp knowledge rapidly. If you don't keep pace with him, then be prepared to be pulled up. I have also interacted with our new managing director and CEO, S.N. Subrahmanyan, a number of times. A chemistry has developed between us over a period. We have solved problems locally together. He will make a fine leader.'

LOCATED IN the sylvan environment of the L&T Construction campus – a veritable oasis in metropolitan Chennai – L&T Infotech is an exceptional success story built on intensive marketing by the company in the US and Europe in the early 2000s. Chennai is one of the development centres for L&T's growing information technology business. Sudhir Shenoi, who heads ACE: Automation Centre of Excellence at L&T, says: 'Mr Naik has personally led the growth of L&T Infotech, transforming it from a company with an annual revenue of less than $50 million into a global player with a turnover close to $1 billion. Before 2002, L&T Infotech delivered services to its clients from various small rented offices. Mr Naik concluded his first visit to one of those rented offices by saying that L&T Infotech needed a new world-class development centre in Chennai to drive the growth of its international business. Mr Naik provided the required support to help L&T Infotech build its first exclusive development centre. This centre was located within the L&T Construction campus called Technology Centre-1. From then onwards, the company has shown exponential growth in Chennai. We have grown from a mere 250-plus-strong team to a staff of over 3,500 in about ten years.'

Displaying the courteous, calm efficiency that marks out L&T managers, Shenoi adds: 'This further resulted in expansion of two additional large development centres, which were called Technology Centre-2 and Technology Centre-3. Each of these is a marvel of design, engineering and construction, and have been showcased to potential global clients of L&T Infotech as world-class workplaces from where their extended teams would operate. Mr Naik's personal example of rising from a junior engineer to chairman of the L&T group has inspired our young engineers. This has resulted in a number of engineers choosing a long career with L&T Infotech, even during the period when the IT services industry had poor levels of retention.'

G.B. Pon Manivannan heads a key division of L&T Technology Services in Chennai. The firm had a modest start in 2009 focusing on mechanical engineering services, product engineering, process engineering and plant engineering. A centre in Mysore specialized in embedded systems and products. 'We felt that if we can integrate all this and make it a global company, offering our services to international customers, there was a big opportunity,' says the quiet but articulate Manivannan, sitting in the company's well-appointed conference room in Chennai. 'L&T Technology Services is a pure-play engineering services company. Almost all our customers are global. Around 55 to 60 per cent of our business comes from the US. Let's say we have aerospace customers. We then design the product, the aircraft parts, the assemblies, the components. In automotive we have a number of marquee clients—all are OEMs. We provide full product design, from conceptualization to the manufacturing "womb". Once the womb is generated, we also help them to manufacture the product. That is a part of manufacturing engineering services.'

With the United States and Australia restricting entry-level software engineers, IT services companies like TCS, Infosys, Wipro and Tech Mahindra, which rely on fairly low-skilled outsourced IT work, are at a disadvantage. L&T Technology Services' high-value engineering skills protect it from downturns flowing from political changes overseas. L&T Technology Services has designed the machinery and plant layout for Honda's new manufacturing facility in India. Nearly 20 per cent of the company's engineers, designers and technical support staff—around 2,900 –work at customer sites. For Nissan, L&T Technology Services is developing next-generation products, such as heat exchange cockpit modules. It focuses on verticals like transportation, industrial products, telecom, high-tech services, and process and plant engineering. These are supported by two horizontals across the mechanical and embedded parts.

New product development is another growth area. In Kenya, the firm was given the complete body of a bus and asked to come up with an India-specific design. Polaris is another client for which L&T Technology Services customizes products for Indian conditions. 'CAE (Computer Aided Engineering) and MES (Manufacturing Engineering Services) are our strengths,' says Manivannan.

L&T Technology Services has evolved rapidly into a cutting-edge engineering, research and development (ER&D) services firm. Meanwhile, L&T Infotech's product engineering services business and L&T's integrated engineering services were transferred to the company in 2014. L&T Technology Services provides solutions in product lifecycle management. The company has been positioned in the 'leadership zone' in eight industry verticals and two horizontal service offerings by research firm Zinnov.

As a pure-play ER&D firm, L&T Technology Services has an increasingly distinct edge over IT companies that offer plain-vanilla solutions in a US market which, under the Trump administration, is raising entry barriers. Its strong parentage is another asset. It gives the company access to the group's experience and expertise in multiple sectors as well as significant business opportunities. However, a large portion of the firm's revenue is dependent on a limited number of customers. Most of its customers are based in North America and Europe, rendering L&T Technology Services vulnerable to economic cross-currents in those regions and to turbulence in global financial markets. In addition, the company faces risks from exchange rate fluctuations and fierce global competition in the ER&D services market, but it takes these and other challenges in its stride.

L&T HAS embraced new-economy businesses with gusto. Many of its most successful subsidiaries are now in financial services, information technology, engineering solutions and realty. Together, these businesses contribute over 35 per cent to the L&T group's net profit. L&T Infotech is ranked India's sixth largest IT services company by NASSCOM (2015). The company is listed among the top twenty global IT services companies by the Everest Group. One of the L&T group's most profitable firms, it offers a wide range of services, including application development, maintenance and outsourcing, enterprise solutions, infrastructure management services, testing, digital solutions and platform-based solutions. Its client base comprises major players in banking and financial services, consumer packaged goods, insurance, media, entertainment, energy, process, retail, pharmaceuticals, consumer electronics, automotive and aerospace. North America contributes around 69 per cent of L&T Infotech's revenue. Europe accounts for 17.4 per cent and Asia Pacific just 2 per cent. India and the rest of the world contribute the balance.

The restrictions on H-1B visas have affected Indian software firms like Infosys, TCS and Wipro. These companies often offer entry-level coding services. The Trump administration says the firms pay Indian software engineers average salaries of $60,000 onsite, whereas similarly qualified US software engineers would receive an average salary of $150,000. In a reaction to the US move, Infosys announced it would hire 10,000 local American engineers for onsite work.

L&T Infotech's focus on high-tech engineering services, rather than low-value software services offered by most Indian IT companies, gives it a significant advantage in America's new protectionist environment. Complex outsourced engineering services, onsite or offsite, are far more difficult to replace than the basic software services offered by the traditional Indian IT firms. The US policy change has also forced companies like Infosys to upgrade their services.

In an interview in *Business Standard* on 16 April 2017, then Infosys CEO Vishal Sikka said:

> We had an astonishing experience with a client in Asia in the last quarter where we were able to eliminate a small team of lawyers by using our Mana software to analyse non-disclosure agreements and other contractual documents, only escalating exceptions to senior lawyers. In our lifetime, we will see Artificial Intelligence (AI) systems achieve skills so that any problem that can be mechanically articulated will be solved by them. For now, we have AI at a unique situation, where on the one hand it is eating the jobs of the past but on the other hand it is creating far greater opportunities for jobs of the future.

Naik was quick to spot the potential of engineering services in India. It has paid off handsomely. L&T Infotech's listing in July 2016 was well received. Apart from high-end technology services, L&T's entry into financial services has also paid rich dividends. L&T Finance Holdings was listed in August 2011. It now has a retail asset portfolio of over Rs 28,000 crore. L&T Finance Holdings Ltd offers a wide range of financial products and services through its direct and indirect wholly-owned subsidiaries, L&T Finance Ltd, L&T Infrastructure Finance Company Ltd, L&T Investment Management Ltd and L&T FinCorp Ltd.

For an engineering and technology multinational like L&T to venture into finance required a leap of faith. The company's IPO in 2011 was priced conservatively at Rs 52 a share. L&T Finance Holdings' then chairman, Y.M. Deosthalee, played a pivotal role in the company's growth before retiring following a stellar career. He was a longtime CFO of L&T and midwifed L&T Finance in its early years as it morphed into a multi-brand financial services company, nearly tripling its market capitalization in the six years since its listing.

CHENNAI IS the operational headquarters of a cluster of businesses grouped under L&T Construction, earlier known as ECC. Together they account for the single largest slice of the company's revenue pie. The 27-acre campus is the workplace for nearly 4,000 employees at Manapakkam. A large engineering and design centre features Shristi, a 3D studio with an immersive walkthrough of projects, a corporate museum—the Holck-Larsen Centre—and a convention hall. L&T Infotech and L&T Technology Services are located in an adjacent campus. Several manufacturing facilities have been relocated from Powai to the Chennai hub, which has gained in strategic significance.

Shamala Nadendla, a young woman with boundless energy, manages the Holck-Larsen Centre in the sprawling campus. 'The museum came into existence in 2004,' she says, as she takes us on a guided tour. Shamala recalls: 'In 2002, Mr Holck-Larsen was walking around our campus. Many of the buildings and blocks here are named after our directors. He mentioned that there was no building or block in his name. He was told that the L&T directors after whom the buildings and blocks were named had passed away. They were named posthumously. He smiled and said, "I can't wait any more." A year later, sadly, in July 2003, he passed away.'

The concept of the Holck-Larsen museum was mooted soon after. The L&T management decided to name it the Henning Holck-Larsen Centre. 'Unfortunately, during the floods in 2015 the entire campus was under ten feet of water, and every pedestal, every exhibit you see here got washed away, says Shamala, with a shake of her head. 'It was a huge disaster. All the awards had to be cleaned and then polished to get them back to their former pristine state. Then again, in December 2016, we had floods, and 100 trees were uprooted in the cyclone.'

Interestingly, Holck-Larsen's and Toubro's families do not own a stake in the company any more, nor do they hold any office. 'It was as if they had helped create this company and handed it to us to take care of and walked away,' says Shamala.

The Toubros have a farmhouse in Kodaikanal, which they visit every summer. On the way to Kodaikanal from Chennai, they spend a day in the museum, walking around. Toubro was a year older than Holck-Larsen, and passed away in 1982. 'They both believed in people,' says Shamala. 'Machinery comes and goes, buildings come and go, but people are the real assets, and that's the strength of L&T today. Mr Naik has been here for nearly fifty-three years and is a huge inspiration to all youngsters. He is very dynamic and hardworking, his memory is phenomenal. L&T runs in his blood. The passion he has for the company, nothing can match that.'

Shamala's eyes twinkle as she relates the story of Toubro's role in L&T's first-ever international project in the 1950s: 'The bridge in David Lean's classic film, *The Bridge on the River Kwai*, was built by L&T, only to be blown up, as per the script, in the climax of the film! The film's story, which is loosely based on a true World War II incident, is about a bunch of allied prisoners of war (PoWs) who are ordered by the Japanese to build two bridges—one of steel and the other of wood—over the River Kwai to move Japanese supplies and troops from Bangkok to Rangoon. Since the Thai jungles were unsuitable for shooting in, the film was shot in the jungles of Sri Lanka instead. L&T was contracted to build a bridge across the river Kelani in Sri Lanka.'

Shamala is replete with anecdotal nuggets from the film: 'L&T had to construct the main bridge for the movie set. But when the project was given to Mr Toubro in 1950 he was not told that the bridge is for a movie and that, as per the movie's climax scene, the bridge would be blown up. L&T went ahead, constructed a solid bridge and handed over the project. P.H. Mortensen, a carpenter by profession, led L&T's project, and the bridge he built for the film appeared like a "carpenter's masterpiece", with a steel structure and wooden cladding making it look similar to the real one in northern Thailand. An initial Rs 8 lakh contract that was signed finally worked out to double that amount, much to the ire of the producer, Sam Spiegel, who apparently shouted at Mr Toubro: "You won't get so much as a nickel out of me." Mr Toubro's calm retort was: "That's all right, but you will not be able to blow up the bridge as we have got an injunction against it." With Hollywood stars like Alec Guinness, William Holden, Grace Kelly and Jack Hawkins all kicking their heels doing nothing, Spiegel realized that he could ill-afford the mounting costs and thus agreed to a negotiated settlement. The shooting recommenced.

'When the film crew shot the climax scene, everybody kept their fingers crossed, waiting for action. But L&T's construction was so strong that when they tried to blow up the bridge it did not move an inch! The crew called Mr Toubro and asked him to loosen the structure as they needed to shoot the scene. What is seen in the movie is the second attempt to blow up the deliberately weakened bridge. The *Bridge on the River Kwai* released in 1957. It became an all-time hit, winning seven Oscars, and L&T had more than a fair share to contribute to its success!'

AMONG L&T's most successful new businesses is L&T Realty, the company's fast-growing and highly profitable real estate development arm that operates in Mumbai, Bengaluru, Chennai and Hyderabad. It also has sales and marketing offices in Singapore, Dubai and the US. L&T Realty has carved out a dominant position in the industry within a relatively short period of time. While the parent company's powerful brand has contributed to its success, the real estate division's focus on just a few cities, on signature projects, superior construction and timely completion, has helped it achieve a leadership position.

L&T Realty's market share in terms of sales in the micro-markets where it operates is now an impressive 50 per cent. Moreover, for each of its projects, L&T handles the engineering and construction, while L&T Finance looks after the financing needs of customers. Other associated activities such as sales, marketing and branding are also handled by in-house companies. The synergies help deliver excellent margins. L&T Realty's total portfolio across residential, commercial, mixed-use developments and transit-oriented developments (TODs) consists of over 62 million square feet.

Shrikant Joshi, CEO and managing director of L&T Realty, is a battle-hardened veteran. He worked with the real estate major Emaar and the IT services giant Wipro before joining L&T in 2011. An affable, self-assured man, Joshi says reflectively: 'Mr Naik worked in Powai, and he would look at the Hiranandani complex coming up in front of him. A seed was planted in his mind. As he saw Hiranandani prosper and expand, he said why can't we do this? That was one thought. Now, as a part of our ECC business, when we got contracts builders used to put up a board saying "construction by L&T" and charge Rs 300 per square foot as premium. We thought to ourselves: why shouldn't we build our own branded properties and take that premium?'

L&T's realty ambitions date back to 1996. Its first venture was Urban Infrastructure Ltd. L&T held 74 per cent equity in the company and HDFC, 24 per cent. L&T built L&T Infocity, a part of Hyderabad's High Tech City. Unfortunately, says Joshi, the realty business 'got tucked under a very big company, IDPL, which makes roads and other infrastructure. Realty was a subsidiary of IDPL and did not get the same focus. Nevertheless we still did small projects.'

Naik, though busy with Hazira and Kattupalli, never lost sight of the potential of realty. L&T invested in SeaWoods in 2007-08 in Navi Mumbai. 'The company may have overbid,' says Joshi. 'Then Mr Naik started looking out for somebody to head the business. That is when I met him in 2009 for the first time. He told me to come to SeaWoods and we would decide to do something big, not just one project. I was with Emaar, a real estate company in the Gulf. L&T was already doing work in the Gulf. I joined in June 2011. In the past six years we have grown to a very good size as a result of Mr Naik's foresight. Our profits are the highest among all L&T's subsidiaries, Rs 600-650 crore annually.'

Joshi says Naik is a quick decision-maker. 'For example, after

I joined in June 2011, I must have met him two or three times over twenty days, and then he tells me, we need to close Urban Infrastructure Ltd. Previously it had been valued at Rs 1,200 crore, so he picks up the phone and speaks to HDFC's Deepak Parekh, and says that either I buy you for Rs 300 crore (HDFC's 25 per cent stake) or you buy my 75 per cent stake for Rs 900 crore. Within twenty-eight days we had paid Rs 300 crore to buy HDFC's entire stake. We were then free to close the company. I had not seen this kind of decisiveness from anybody in my long career. In the meantime, we received an inflow through real estate divestments of Rs 4,000 crore. So as a group company, the capital which was locked up had now been freed up.'

One of L&T Realty's prestigious projects is in Powai. It is a 35-acre residential as well as commercial development that harks back to Naik's pet theme: 'walk-to-work'. The Powai complex has an IT park and medical centre to make it a completely self-contained work-and-live zone. With 62 million square feet under development, the return on investment will be, as it is for newer projects, 40-50 per cent. 'The plan is to stabilize overall returns to 20-23 per cent in the next three years,' says Joshi. 'However, older projects will bring down the current year's return to 17-18 per cent. The industry average is 20 per cent. Our total annual sales are around Rs 3,000 crore and, as I said, profits are now well over Rs 600 crore.'

HOW DOES Joshi, unlike others a relative newcomer to L&T, assess Naik's management style? 'I have spent only six years in L&T but I am the luckiest guy here because I get maximum time from him,' smiles Joshi. 'First, he is very passionate about his work, and his mind and my mind gel so we spend a lot of time discussing sales and profits. Even now, twice a week, he calls me. On key issues like design and master planning, he is involved. None of the business houses have been able to convert their industrial projects into real estate projects so easily as L&T has done.'

Joshi worked very closely with Azim Premji, chairman of Wipro, from 1983 to 1996. He says both Naik and Premji excel at micro-management. Both have called him at 2.00 a.m. to discuss work. Both never keep people waiting. Both are considerate. 'The difference lies in their persona,' says Joshi. 'Mr Naik knows how to relax and enjoy life as well as work hard. Mr Premji doesn't. Mr Naik watches movies, wildlife programmes on TV, he loves that. Whereas, for Mr Premji it is no TV, no movies, only news, no entertainment as such. Mr Naik is very social that way. Emotional empathy is also very high in the case of Mr Naik. I have seen that even if he fires people in a meeting, after the meeting is over he will make up in five minutes and the other person will go back home feeling good. Mr Premji would also fire people but he is absolutely polished and will give total respect to employees. Mr Premji will be angry, but later on he will say he was sorry that he had to blow up like that. Mr Naik is more emotional that way.'

Joshi recalls one particular incident: 'Once Mr Naik was very disturbed and had lost his temper at a meeting. When the meeting got over and everyone had gone off to work, I went to a meeting in SeaWoods. At 5.00 p.m. he called me and asked where I was. Typically, he will not make one call, but four or five! I was still a bit upset so I told him that I was in SeaWoods. Again, a second call came. He again asked me where I was. So I told him I was near IIT. Our then managing director K. Venkatramanan's mother had passed away that day and there was a prayer meeting. So he asked me if I was going to the prayer meeting in Juhu. I told him that I did not know his mother well so I would not be going. But from his tone I realized that something was playing on his mind. I asked him what it was and he said what he did earlier at the meeting was not right. He asked me to come home and we would have a drink together. This was just one year back. It was his way of showing regret for having lost his temper.'

Joshi has fond memories of Premji too. 'Incidentally, Mr Premji comes to meet Mr Naik quite often,' he says. 'Both are my mentors, so I once told Mr Naik, I want a photo of both of you together. Mr Naik said okay, come at 9.30 a.m. Mr Naik was to meet Mr Premji in the conference room but he told me to come to his office room. He called Mr Premji there and said, first let's do the photograph and then I will start the meeting. Mr Naik then told Mr Premji, this is Joshi from real estate. Mr Premji said he knows me, and recounted my entire career. I had left Wipro twenty-one years ago and yet he remembers every detail. So I thought to myself, how can I tell these two guys that I want to stand in the centre for the photograph? But Mr Naik himself asked me to stand in the middle. We took the photograph and then he started his meeting. This is the way he does things, caring for what the employee finds important.'

Joshi is impressed by the decisiveness and energy that enables Naik to start new businesses in his seventies. Naik is customer-centric too and keeps the big picture in mind all the time, says Joshi. 'We were once considering a residential project in Bandra-Kurla Complex (BKC). The previous day we had just arrived back from Bengaluru at 11.30 p.m. I had told Mr Naik about the project, which would give us profits of Rs 300 crore in three years. He reached home at 1.00 a.m., and at 7.30 a.m. the next day he was at the site. The plot and location by themselves were fine, but the surroundings were not what L&T would want to offer its customers. Mr Naik looked around and shook his head, refusing to be drawn by the lure of profits. Now, this approach to building a brand will never be taught in any B-school. He is a very intuitive person, both in business and personal dealings. If he feels a project is not quite right, he will not hesitate to exit it.'

9

Decoding the Leader

AROUND THIRTY YEARS ago, Naik and his colleagues were in the Powai workshop working late one night as there was a problem with the machinery. After some anxious moments, they finally cracked the problem. Relieved, Naik and his colleagues left the workshop at 2.00 a.m. The next day, at exactly 8.20 a.m., Naik was standing outside the company office's punch card machine and asking the workers why they were late. They said, we left at two in the morning! He replied, 'Coming to work on time is your duty. Going back home after duty hours is your pleasure.'

Today, as he reflects on the incident, Naik says: 'You can excel in leadership only if you are a role model. You must lead by example.' Virtually throughout his career, Naik was the first to arrive at office and the last to leave. But it is his corporate strategy that intrigues analysts. In an interview with global consultants McKinsey, Naik was forthright. Ramesh Mangaleshwaran and Adil Zainulbhai met him at the Powai complex in 2011. Their analysis of Naik's management strategy was clear-headed and perceptive: 'As chairman, Naik's main agenda was to keep the company independent. His gambit: create value and attract and retain the best employees by restoring a merit-based performance-management system. Naik developed an organizational structure with divisions large enough to offer employees room for growth. He also completely revamped the company's human resources processes, from the shopfloor to the boardroom.'

Vijay Kumar Magapu, the former CEO & managing director of what was then known as L&T Infotech and a former head of the Hazira manufacturing complex, retired in 2016. A man of firm views, he decodes Naik, with whom he worked closely for decades, including as a wholetime director on the L&T Board from 2004: 'There are two categories of outstanding qualities that he has. Category one is that he stands apart as a person who can continuously transform himself. From the day he joined, coming from a Gujarat village, not even able to communicate properly—I have seen him since that day. He is a man of very many abilities. This transformation is not just a normal improvement. Some of us stay as we are through our entire career, some improve, but what Mr Naik has done is far beyond any of this. He started with a skill-set of leadership and a lot of energy. He came from a small town, went to a small village school. That's the starting point. When he came to L&T's Powai workshop, the most remarkable thing he did was to bring law into a lawless place. Workmen were recruited from assorted places. In the second shift, the foremen would put their tools down, go across to Powai lake, catch fish, bring them back to fry and eat them.'

Magapu rocks back in his chair as he speaks. He is precise and articulate. 'That was the culture of the Powai General Workshop (PGW),' he says. 'Literally alone, by himself, Mr Naik sought to break this culture. He used to turn up at odd hours in the evenings and nights to catch these unruly workers, at risk to himself. He was very friendly and at the same time very tough with the union workers. He cleaned up a completely lawless PGW into a reasonably good organization. He had no prior experience of these things, he just took them on. That was the quality, I think, which defines him: his ability to transform a situation.

Magapu continues thoughtfully: 'Second, while most of us erroneously believed that HR can be confined merely to the HR department, HR is actually the chief executive's domain too. And Mr Naik keeps track of everybody who reports to him. Most of it is in his memory and the balance lies in a small pocket book. He would frequently analyse his people while going home or coming to work. Amazingly, he knew all the workmen by name. So that is the second transformation, where he took on the role of an HR-oriented leader. We used to have very tough negotiations with the union. During those negotiations he earned the nickname Henry Kissinger. With vendors too, from whom we used to buy a lot of expensive imported equipment, bargaining and negotiating with these people who have several years of selling experience is not easy. But Mr Naik would get us the best bargains. He is an outstanding negotiator.'

Magapu worked closely with Naik as head of Hazira in the 1980s and 1990s. He says Naik was a successful marketing manager too. 'He built customer relationships, which again was not his domain. But whenever customers came to follow up for their equipment which we had made to order, he would use the opportunity to build a relationship with them. So he managed to move away from a manufacturing orientation to a marketing orientation, even though it was not his job specification.'

It was this multi-dimensional approach that marked Naik out as a leader. He had insatiable curiosity about every aspect of L&T: manufacturing, HR, marketing, technology, finance, globalization. 'I remember we were in Hazira, running that place, and we had a surprise visit from a senior management person,' says Magapu. 'It was like a friendly audit of Hazira. The senior management man was taken aback by the Hazira's development in such a short span of time.'

In the early years, business at Hazira was slack. Magapu recalls those days with dry wit: 'We had a phase when we were all dressed up but had nowhere to go. The workshop was capable of doing various things, but we had no business at all, no orders. So we all sat down with Mr Naik for hours and thought: what is wrong with us, why no orders! We realized that we were not reaching out to the market. So Mr Naik just picked up his bag and broke into the very cold atmosphere of government officials, requesting for proposals. His style was to charm them, show his passion and be very persistent. A manufacturing man selling—and succeeding! He did not go to Harvard or do a marketing course. But from then onwards he began to enjoy the process of sales. He would tell us that manufacturing is tough and hard work, but there is a definition to it and a limit to its boundaries, but sales is tougher because there are no boundaries. In manufacturing you will get some good and some bad results, but in sales you can work very hard and yet end up with zero. From that period, he has been the most outstanding salesman for the L&T group. So I would say the transformation from a village student to a manufacturing professional to a good salesman, both here and abroad, was remarkable.'

Delhi was not part of Naik's beat either. But the business L&T was increasingly bidding for needed interactions with bureaucrats and politicians. In time, Naik became a consummate negotiator in Delhi's labyrinths of power. As Magapu says: 'The change from a sales professional to a man who can successfully interact in a political environment is another major transformation.'

Naik continued to evolve. 'Then came the transformation where he became a director on the board and he implemented visionary ideas, like setting up more factories in Hazira, power plants and launching L&T Infotech,' says Magapu. 'Now two other transformations took place. The first was building a global business in information technology and global infrastructure projects in the Gulf. He poured a lot of his energy into these areas. So, moving from a village school to manufacturing to sales to HR, from the political environment to global business—all these are transformations. Only multi-disciplinary personalities can achieve this. Then comes another test, which other leaders would have failed: the Birla episode. But he took it on as if he was an expert in dealing with these matters. Mr Naik is a most outstanding individual, one who has transformed himself on a continual basis, multiple times. He often gives the impression that only results count. But for him the process counts too. If you achieve results using the wrong process, then you get very low marks from him. If you don't get the right result but follow the correct process, you will be encouraged.'

Those who work with Naik say he is compulsively frank, sometimes brutally so. Naik is equally blunt, but diplomatic too, when necessary, with complete strangers. 'He balances bluntness and diplomacy very correctly,' says Magapu. 'The other trait that has played a big role in his career is his extreme restlessness. He wants progress every two minutes. But when he has to show nerves of steel and patience he has done it every time. In times of critical situations and extreme pressure, he has handled the pressure and managed risk. He is known by many people to be a tough disciplinarian, but he is actually very kind-hearted and sympathetic towards genuine causes. Despite the problems with unions, all the workers admire him. Even if he has issued them chargesheets to straighten them out, they still respect him.'

Naik's achievements have transformed L&T from a stodgy, domestic engineering company in the 1980s into a global technology powerhouse. He is in effect the founder of the 'new L&T'. Naik built Hazira from scratch, expanded the EPC groups in hydrocarbon and power, co-founded financial services, founded the infotech, technology services and realty businesses, and remade ECC into the largest group in L&T. Magapu adds, reflectively: 'I would say that while Mr Holck-Larsen and Mr Toubro were the founders of the company, Mr Naik is the "re-founder" of the company. Earlier, we were very respectable, very sedate. He changed everything. We were rewarded for our entrepreneurship, not hammered for our mistakes. You will find that today L&T is in an extremely unique position with cost written-off facilities of world-class quality.'

Naik had many opportunities to strike out as an entrepreneur, says Magapu. 'But he was very devoted to his father's philosophy, and also to his grandfather's. He uses his father's technique of never giving 10 out of 10. He never says you have reached your goals.

That's the secret of constant growth. And above all, he does a lot of significant things that people don't know about, as they are hidden from public knowledge. He has, for example, done philanthropy very silently.'

—ɷ—

A BON VIVANT who lives next to Amitabh Bachchan's bungalow in suburban Mumbai and whose looks belie his age, Ramnath Mukhija joined L&T the same year—1965—as Naik. 'But we were in totally different areas. I had joined the marketing team in Delhi,' he says. Mukhija graduated from IIT Kharagpur, India's first IIT, with a degree in electrical engineering. He arrived in Mumbai twelve years later. In 1999, when Naik was appointed CEO, Mukhija started reporting to him for the first time.

'My first thirty-four years at L&T, from 1965 to 1999, were not with Mr Naik. My bosses had a different style from Mr Naik's,' says Mukhija, with a smile. 'I was in an environment which was more conservative as compared with what it was when I joined Mr Naik. That was not at all conservative. Things had speed! I joined the board within a year, in 2000, and then became president. I retired from the board a decade later, in October 2010. But Mr Naik asked me to continue in the company till April 2014.'

Mukhija's key responsibility was to look after the electrical and electronics business. In addition, he oversaw general management and HR after CFO Y. M. Deosthalee moved to L&T Finance. HR reported to Mukhija, as did L&T Realty. How different was Naik as a boss from those he'd been used to from 1965 to 1999 in L&T's offices in Delhi and elsewhere?

'The kind of vision he has ... not many people have,' replies Mukhija. 'He has long-term vision. And he has the capability to get into micro-details too. So he is a broad-spectrum leader. Such bosses are unique. He is a rare leader. He comes from a humble background and has risen all the way to the top by dint of sheer merit and hard work.'

Mukhija says L&T gives its employees considerable freedom and encourages a spirit of entrepreneurship and professionalism—two qualities Naik values in himself and imparts to others. Mukhija reveals he's had fifteen bosses in his long career at L&T, and marks out integrity as a defining characteristic of the company. He serves on the board of the Tata company, Voltas, and sees similarities in the culture of integrity and fairness the Tatas are known for with the culture L&T has bred. He also says that value creation for all stakeholders, ESOPs and the L&T Employees Welfare Foundation are Naik's lasting legacies to the company he has devoted his life to.

Managing director and CEO S.N. Subrahmanyan, Naik's successor, points out that 'ESOPs were not commonly issued in engineering or manufacturing companies. When Mr Naik thought them up, I don't know how many dollar millionaires must have been created in L&T: 2,500 to 3,000, at least. Plus more than 5,000 rupee millionaires. It was a phenomenal event for employees. It gave them security, a lot of self-confidence and wealth. It brought respectability to their families. L&T was not a great paymaster. We are in a business where we could not pay the kind of salaries IT services companies pay. ESOPs gave employees a great deal of personal satisfaction.'

SHAILENDRA ROY speaks with the clarity and authority of a man familiar with the corridors of power. He is a wholetime director of L&T. Roy recounts the colourful tale of how he was appointed to L&T's board. On a family holiday in Patna during Holi, he received a cryptic call from Naik asking him to return to Mumbai immediately. The next day, as Naik and he drove down to L&T's Ballard Estate headquarters in south Mumbai, there was still no indication as to why he had been called back on an urgent basis. Roy found out just before he entered the boardroom that he had been appointed a director on the board of L&T.

Roy is a keen raconteur who spent his early career in public sector companies. He joined L&T in 2004. Though he had been managing director in a PSU earlier, Roy accepted the post of general manager in L&T. He knew the company held great promise. He was proved right. After five years as GM, he ascended the L&T hierarchy quickly, first as vice-president, then as senior vice-president, and finally, in 2012, as director. Through his early years at L&T too, Roy had Naik's ear. He accompanied him on business visits to China and elsewhere, and was something of a confidant.

Roy looks after the Delhi corporate office, where his goodwill in government circles is an asset. He is in charge of L&T's power business, among other responsibilities, and spends several days in Vadodara's Knowledge City every week. He says thoughtfully: 'I have worked with Mr Naik for over a decade and have keenly observed him. A tough taskmaster, he knows how to bring out the best in his people. His uncompromising attitude ultimately helps us to give of our best. He has risen to the highest level of the corporate ladder in L&T by working very hard over the years. Quite logically, he demands the best from others. I don't have an iota of doubt in endorsing that what L&T is today is largely because of his business acumen.'

Eyes focusing into the distance, Roy adds quietly: 'On a personal note, I have found him to be extremely caring and humane. Recently, I was down with dengue. I have experienced the concern and care he showed, as if he were an older brother, and how he guided me through my hospitalization and treatment. He has been a constant support to me and my family. Beneath his tough exterior, I have witnessed his softer side. He is empathetic to others in difficult times.'

What does he think of Naik's vision for L&T? 'Mr Naik is ahead of his time,' says Roy. 'When many were uncertain about the prospects for Hazira and Vadodara as business hubs, he went ahead with a missionary zeal to set up a world-class manufacturing complex in Hazira for heavy engineering, defence, nuclear and power equipment, and one of the finest design and engineering centres in Vadodara, catering to power, hydrocarbon and technology services. He was always keen on entering the nuclear, defence and power sectors, and was working very hard for the last three decades to make these happen. We are very much into these businesses now. Thus his initiatives were well thought out. L&T has been associated with ISRO as a strategic partner for a long time. Today, ISRO is thinking of giving a greater share in space technology to private sector companies like L&T. This is another aspect of Mr Naik's mission—to make L&T a company of national importance, commanding respect in the country and abroad.'

But it is Naik's entrepreneurial mind that Roy admires most: 'Mr Naik is not just a professional manager; he is an entrepreneurial leader. He believes strongly that though L&T is a professionally run organization, it cannot take major strides unless its professional managers behave like, and develop the traits of, entrepreneurs. One has to "own" his work and take it to a higher orbit as an owner. Business has grown exponentially since he became chairman, creating huge shareholder value. Two-thirds of the current businesses of L&T have been created by Mr Naik. This has helped him manage them even though he has such a diversified portfolio.'

Roy says that by setting up the L&T Employees Welfare Foundation and ringfencing L&T, Naik showed he could grow the company not only in good times, but also fortify it during bad times, turning adversity into opportunity. 'Mr Naik has spent significant time on the shopfloor, even during the time of heightened trade unionism,' says Roy. 'Trade union leaders and workers have always recognized Mr Naik as a fair person and held him in high regard. This quality helped him negotiate and settle their charter of demands successfully over the years. During all such negotiations, his motto was always to work out a "win-win" situation.'

Roy, who lives close to Naik in suburban Mumbai, reveals a facet of Naik's that's not well known: 'Mr Naik has a penchant for old Hindi movies and songs, and once in a while he joins in impromptu singing and dancing in the company of his family and friends. His favourite song is *'Jeena yahan, marna yahan, iske siva jana kahan'*. This aptly sums up his deep affection for L&T.'

SPEED OF action is a quality that particularly strikes Naik's colleagues and associates as a key reason for his success. Srinivas Rajgopal, a retired IAS officer, served as Union cabinet secretary and was one of L&T's longest serving directors till he retired recently. Sitting in his quiet south Mumbai apartment, he says: 'I remember vividly my first interaction with Mr Naik. In 2001 I was in BSES representing UTI. That is when the share transactions took place between the Ambanis and Kumar Mangalam Birla. Mr Birla purchased those shares sometime in November 2001. At 9.00 p.m. one day, the UTI chairman rang me up and said that they would like me to join the board of L&T. He said the CEO, Mr Naik, will phone you. Within half an hour I got a call from Mr Naik. He said they wanted me to become a director and I would have to sign some documents: "We will send you the documents in half-an-hour." I said it would be a pleasure. Then, after exactly half an hour, he rang me up again asking if the documents had come to me and if I had signed them as the board meeting was the next day at 10.30 a.m. I told him that I needed some time. He said no, and that I should come over to L&T's office the next day. "We will induct you on the board." That was my first telephonic interaction with Mr Naik. I had not met him at that time.'

Rajgopal says he hasn't encountered decision-making so swift and intense as he did during that first interaction with Naik. 'Both Kumar Mangalam Birla and Mrs Rajashree Birla were inducted on the L&T Board along with me the next day. Maybe they wanted somebody strong enough to balance out things, I don't know. Anyway, the next morning we were all there.'

Rajgopal makes an insightful point: 'I have rarely found a person who is a professional and yet behaves like a promoter. This is a unique quality. Here is a man whose money is not involved in the company, yet he works like a promoter and thinks for the betterment of the company twenty-four hours a day.'

Rajgopal was a keen observer on the L&T Board as the demerger of L&T's cement business and its sale to the Birlas unfolded. During his nearly fifteen-year tenure on L&T's board, Rajgopal says that what shone through was Naik's strong sense of nationalism. Analysing the evolution of L&T, Rajgopal says: 'Every major international company passes through three phases in its lifetime. There is a strategy phase when it faces a crisis. There is a growth phase after the crisis is over. And at the end of the cycle is a consolidation phase. But in Larsen & Toubro, all three phases have happened in the last eighteen years or so during the stewardship of the company by Mr Naik. In November 2001, when I joined the board, we were going through a crisis.'

That crisis, when the Ambanis sold their L&T shareholding to the Aditya Birla Group, would test Naik's steel over the next three tense years. As Rajgopal notes, the crisis, once resolved, was followed by growth and consolidation. Naik's peers were full of praise for him. Deepak Parekh, chairman of HDFC, said: 'He is a true patriot. He wants to build the nation. Any complicated building, Larsen & Toubro is in the forefront, and Anil Naik is in the forefront. L&T is a multinational with Indian values, and that is Anil Naik's doing.'

NAROTTAM DESAI, at ninety-three, needs a walker to get around his south Mumbai apartment, but the former chairman of L&T retains a sharp mind and an equally sharp memory. Sitting in his living room with wife Anjani, he recalls: 'Young Anil Naik joined L&T in 1965. As the years went by I came to interact more with him. My association with L&T started from February 1946 when it was converted from a partnership firm into a limited company.'

Desai says, contemplatively: 'One meets many people, colleagues, associates. But in the case of Anil, he was different. In 1999, when he became L&T's managing director and CEO, he decided right away to hire top management consultants. This fits in with the earliest thinking of Holck-Larsen. Toubro's temperament was different from Holck-Larsen's. When L&T decided to move to Powai, Toubro said it was a complete jungle! They had to spend a fortune to clear it all up and make it suitable for production. So they ran out of money again! But Holck-Larsen said, no, they would stay. This was the first step in bold thinking. Holck-Larsen had the quality, like Naik, to inspire confidence in whomever he was dealing with: banks, foreigners, collaborators. My father, who contributed seed capital, also had a similar bold outlook. When Anil took over in 1999 he demonstrated bold, positive thinking that has made L&T what it is today. Anil's management style is most effective: look at the working results since 1999.'

Desai was L&T's chairman from 1979 to 1989. Holck-Larsen had stepped down as managing director in 1977 and as chairman in 1978. 'Previously,' recalls Desai, 'Holck-Larsen would be chairman one year, then Toubro would be chairman the next year, and it went on like that till 1963, by when Toubro had retired. It was exciting seeing the way Holck-Larsen functioned. It was quite unique. He recognized people made mistakes and never believed in running a colleague down.'

During the inter-union rivalry between the Shiv Sena and the Communists in L&T in 1977, Desai received an invitation by post to the wedding of one of Shiv Sena leader Balasaheb Thackeray's sons. The meeting between Thackeray and Desai at the wedding ceremony went off pleasantly, despite the ongoing labour problem at L&T, and helped to resolve the strike that had lasted for three and a half months. 'Since then, for forty years, there hasn't been a day's strike in L&T's Powai facility,' says Desai.

K. VENKATRAMANAN, known affectionately as KV in the company, retired from L&T in September 2015 as managing director and CEO. He spent nearly fifty years at L&T, and was recently appointed to the board of directors of Vedanta Ltd, a global conglomerate. A tall, well-spoken man, KV graduated with a degree in chemical engineering from IIT Delhi. He was recruited directly from campus and joined L&T in June 1966, just fifteen months after Naik. As we sit in one of the capacious rooms in L&T's Powai complex, KV says his final interview group discussion for the L&T job took place, coincidentally, in this very room.

Being near-contemporaries, KV and Naik would rub shoulders in L&T for the better part of half a century. 'We were very close from the beginning,' says KV. 'We were the first boys in the workshop and we had a very strong works manager, Tim Baker. Mr Naik used to have a Vespa scooter. When he came to check on the shifts in Powai we would take a ride back with him. He was very hardworking from day one and most of us followed his example. Our group had a lot of opportunities. I received a scholarship in Manchester and Leeds. Being inspired along the way by people like Mr Naik and Mr M.H. Pherwani made us all grow in L&T. Many of those early batches still remain, and went right up to the top. Mr Naik was in charge of planning when I joined. Later on, he came to the shopfloor. One good thing about him is that he respects merit and he respects hard work. Most of us prospered, though some did not quite fit in.'

When KV joined L&T it was still a small company, but growing fast. KV was selected to go to Denmark for nine months in 1967 to work with L&T's collaborators. KV says L&T gave its young engineers 'tremendous responsibility'. When he returned from Denmark in 1968 he was signing drawings and visiting sites to set up projects. 'And at twenty-five, I used to talk to all the senior managers. Our salaries were really very low. But thanks to Mr Naik and his ESOP scheme, our financials improved in the latter part of our careers.'

In 1973 KV was again sent abroad, to America. This was the period during Holck-Larsen's chairmanship, when Naik's career too was on the fast track with multiple promotions. In 1984, KV went to Hazira as production manager, working closely with Naik's team as the manufacturing complex took shape. In 1987, Magapu took charge at Hazira. KV returned to Mumbai and focused on drumming up business for the new complex.

The team worked hard and played hard. KV recalls with a chuckle: 'Mr Naik was very fond of ice-cream and he used to have a lot of it. We both are fond of movies too, so along with Magapu we would watch the night shows. The secret was, after watching the night show we used to be at the workshop at 7.45 a.m. as Mr Naik would be there at 8 a.m., sharp and did not like anyone coming late. We used to drive from Juhu to Powai in twenty minutes flat to be there on time.'

KV was one of the core team members who helped Naik set up the Vadodara facility in the early 1990s. He recalls: 'I was among the first people to go with him for the set-up in 1992. We had decided that we needed to grow in engineering projects. Mumbai being very expensive, we could go either to Pune or Vadodara. When we went to Vadodara, we hired godowns, refurbished them and used them as offices. Old furniture from Powai was refurbished and sent to Vadodara. Knowledge City came up eight or nine years ago, whereas our Vadodara operations started in 1992-93. L&T Chiyoda Engineering Centre, L&T-Sargent & Lundy, and chemical and hydrocarbon-related projects were set up there. What came in a big way afterwards was engineering services, technology services, power, and finally Knowledge City.'

KV was also involved in setting up the Sohar Modular fabrication yard in Oman. 'It was my baby under Mr Naik in 2005-06,' says KV. 'Then, immediately following Sohar, I helped set up Kattupalli—not the shipyard but the offshore facilities for oil and gas equipment.' L&T made the transition from a fabrication company to a projects company in the mid-1990s. Says KV: 'We got the first ONGC order of $156 million, which was very big at that time. I became GM projects, then vice-president, and then moved on as senior vice-president and joined the board in 1999. That is the year Mr Naik became CEO. One thing about Mr Naik is that when the chips are down he will help you. He is fearless.'

KV adds, thoughtfully: 'He is intelligent, down-to-earth, doesn't get enamoured by frills; he comes from a humble background so he respects all, and most people at L&T are middle class anyway. He is well-meaning, tough but a very good person at heart, knowledgeable, disciplined and a supporter of merit. Above all, he is a humane person, a peoples' man.'

Not many know, though, that Naik was a handy cricketer; a canny leg-spinner. KV laughs: 'We had an R&D team v/s workshop team match once, and Mr Naik used his leg spin to good effect.' To keep fit, Naik, till recently, used to play badminton regularly, something he misses today.

What do his predecessors say about Naik? How do they assess his performance? Remarks S.D. Kulkarni, whom Naik succeeded as managing director in 1999: 'Mr Naik's depth of knowledge is truly extraordinary. He is also a tough taskmaster. Plus he is a hands-on leader – one who will be engaged in every aspect of every operation. He has clear vision, knowing exactly where he wants to go. He also has a global perspective. That leads to benchmarking global standards of quality. Mr Naik is capable of a remarkable degree of focus. He pursues ideas relentlessly and is also very good in execution.'

U.V. Rao, who was managing director of L&T from 1989 to 1994, analyses Naik with perspicacity: 'It is no exaggeration when I call Mr Naik the second visionary after Holck-Larsen. He converted L&T into a super-giant with several new and challenging activities, products, projects and factories in many parts of the world. If Holck-Larsen were alive today, he would have been very proud of Mr Naik. It's a pity he is not here to see this. Mr Naik is not only a visionary, like Holck-Larsen, he is also a great motivator, entrepreneur and leader. On a personal note, when we were under threat of takeover, which lasted for nearly three years, I was under extreme stress. Besides fighting the boardroom battle, I had a fair-sized company to run. I would have probably given up the fight if it were not for the great support I got from Mr Naik! We spent a great deal of time together. He made many good strategic suggestions. I am personally grateful to him for this.'

J.P. NAYAK is a remarkably fit man for his age. Well into his seventies, Nayak says, mischievously, 'I am one up on Mr Naik only on one count: I joined the L&T group before him!' Nayak, a mechanical engineer from Pune College of Engineering, joined the company twelve days before Naik, on 3 May 1965. He was recruited by Tractors Engineers Ltd, a 50:50 joint venture of L&T and Caterpillar of America. He rose rapidly through the ranks, looking after the earthmoving and construction machinery business before briefly heading L&T's cement business in 2001-04 during the taut negotiations with the Aditya Birla Group. Nayak says the most impressive quality about Naik is that he is a fast learner. 'Not only that,' he adds, 'Mr Naik puts that learning into quick action.'

When Naik took charge as CEO, Nayak's cabin was next to his and the two men interacted often. Not given to effusive praise, Nayak purses his lips as he says: 'I have never seen a person who works as hard as Mr Naik. His dynamism is inspiring.'

Naik himself, though, can be refreshingly honest about his own imperfections: 'You have to introspect on your strengths and weaknesses,' he says. 'Weaknesses are something you have to think especially deeply about—and be most worried about. Total elimination of weaknesses is not possible, but you have to reduce them. I have not been able to do it. I am by nature an impatient man, very impatient. When I want something I want it done then and there. I often get irritated, angry at times, but later on when I think about it, I feel I need not have been so upset. I must have thought about this hundreds, even thousands, of times. This is my daily routine. Evenings I go home and think, I may have hurt someone. I am easily prone to hurting others because of this impatience and irritability. That is my single biggest weakness. But if you don't get irritated and instead say the same thing in a nice manner, things may not get done. I do it the other way, so it hurts people. I also know this approach does not give a person credit for the good work he might have done because you have already hurt him. I need to moderate my impatience, be more conscious of the fact that others also have feelings and they could be hurt. But my strengths so overwhelm my weaknesses that I have not fully acknowledged this as a weakness. A soft approach without losing discipline may be a better policy.'

It is a rare admission from a man who has an intimidating exterior. There is more in his *mea culpa*: 'I have many times tried to change my style, but succeeded only 0.1 per cent each time. Cumulatively though, I have probably changed more than 30 per cent. I was too short-tempered earlier. Now I am somewhat better!'

Naik's humane nature is attested to by virtually every employee I met in Mumbai, Surat, Hazira, Vadodara, Chennai and elsewhere—several dozens in all. But, as Naik says, 'My caring part, people forget. The fact that I got angry is always remembered.'

Does Naik, now that he has assumed a new role from 1 October 2017, regret this? He is candid: 'I do, I do. Because people would have remembered me much, much more had I not had this little shortcoming.'

And yet, there are redeeming features to Naik's strong managerial style. 'People have the freedom to lift the phone and speak to me,' he says. 'Because they realize I am considerate, caring. People have realized it doesn't matter that he gets angry but he is a nice man. That is why a lot of people write directly to me, phone me, and sometimes come and stand here and say we only want to shake hands with Naik. Now that would not happen unless there are people who believe that I have some sense of caring. So I do have that quality which makes people feel I am approachable even after they have retired twenty years ago.'

Again, memories of his parents and grandparents come flooding back: 'My father and grandfather motivated me. What they did over a period of over 100 years, between the two of them, was always for the poor. All of this I have seen as a little boy of ten. If my father had wanted to, he could have stayed on in Mumbai in Hansraj Morarji Public School. He could have been principal. But he quit. He said, now a school is coming up in the village, we must go. It was a high school. Today every village worth talking about in south Gujarat has a high school. At that time, among twenty-two villages there was only one such school. So he went to teach in the villages. And I have seen this happening day in and day out—he was not able to give money as he did not have money, but he "gave" with his deeds.'

A colleague of Naik's, who was part of our discussion, recalls: 'Mr Naik's father once asked him to give some money for a cause. He did not have funds as at that time salaries were not so good. But he still gave Rs 4 lakh.'

Naik interjects: 'I had Rs 2.5 lakh in the bank and Rs 1.5 lakh in my provident fund in 1995. The first thing my father asked was: "Where did you get this money from?" He was thinking I would give Rs 25,000. He too gave Rs 25,000 when he retired. He had Rs 32,000 in his account, including his pension. That was everything he had.'

Naik reveals his personal management philosophy: 'Plan optimistically, spend realistically, promise conservatively. Because when you promise, then you will have to take care of all kinds of impediments that may occur along the way. When I went to the United States, I used to fly Delta Airlines till some ten years ago. It flew non-stop to New York. I would reach JFK airport at 7-7.30 in the morning. If the flight reached early and I got out of the airport at 8.00 a.m., I would go to Citibank, just opposite Starbucks. I would sit in Starbucks, wait for the Citibank doors to open, which they did just before 9 a.m. At five minutes to 9.00 a.m., I would be inside the bank, having arrived from Bombay for a meeting. If there is a nine o'clock meeting, it means nine o'clock in the conference room. People are informed or are already waiting or they come within a minute or two. Then comes the next meeting, then the next, then the next. Even in a city like New York, I have four to five meetings a day.'

In full flow now, he continues: 'Observation is the key to success. Different organizations love different characteristics and styles. I would observe why Dhirubhai Ambani is successful and someone else is not. I keep analysing in my mind. My work habits are similar to that of an entrepreneur. You must practise it till it becomes a way of life. So twenty-five years ago, I made a conscious decision that I would do things in a particular way till it became a habit. Everything must be done in the most optimum manner, in the most normal and efficient manner. And now it's part of my DNA.'

Philanthropy is not something Naik likes to dwell on, although he has publicly declared that he will donate 75 per cent of his entire income to charity in his lifetime. 'I enjoy giving,' says Naik, reflectively, his expression softening as he rocks back in his chair. 'I have learnt that from my father.'

WHAT IS Naik's agenda for L&T, going forward? Under Lakshya 3, L&T will target the doubling of its revenue in the five years to 2021 as it focuses on sectors with high potential for growth. That translates into an average annual growth rate of 14 per cent. In the five years to fiscal 2016, L&T's revenue grew at 14.5 per cent annually despite a slowdown in the economy, delayed environment clearances and complex land acquisitions which stalled investment demand.

L&T had begun systematically pruning its portfolio several years ago to focus on its most profitable businesses. It shed non-core businesses that fetched low returns and occupied disproportionate management bandwidth. The company had earlier sold its glass bottles and leather businesses, both clearly non-core. It had divested its cement business to the Aditya Birla Group and ready mix concrete business to LaFarge. It sold its stake

In 1986, Naik was appointed General Manager in charge of a cluster of businesses known then as Group II.

In 1989, Naik was inducted into the Board of Larsen & Toubro.

The high-tech turbine facility in Hazira is an example of the company's commitment to the highest standards of manufacturing excellence.

'Knowledge City', Vadodara, complements L&T's manufacturing capabilities.

At Kattupalli, north of Chennai, L&T has built a major shipbuilding yard to meet the needs of the Indian Navy. Adjacent to the shipyard is a port.

A sculpture commemorating Naik's role in propelling the Vadodara campus from concept to reality.

Naik's ability to strike a chord across ranks is at the heart of his enduring popularity.

When a workman at the Powai campus came up with a lyric extolling the chairman's leadership, Naik responded with an impromptu jig.

As the Group's IT subsidiary adopts a new brand identity, Naik advises young techies on the road ahead.

'L&T is always close to my heart' – Naik at a function to felicitate him on 50 years of service in the company.

Lifelong devotion to L&T finds expression in a soulful rendering of the classic *'Jeena yahan, marna yahan, iske siva jaana kahan'*.

Showing National Security Advisor Ajit Doval around L&T's Hazira campus.

On 2 April 2016, Naik and Subrahmanyan presented a ceremonial sword to the Prime Minister of India, Narendra Modi, when he visited the L&T project site in Riyadh, Saudi Arabia. L&T is a consortium partner in a metro project that will form the backbone of the new public transportation network of Saudi Arabia's capital.

Work on the Riyadh Metro. Modi visited the site on 2 April 2016 and interacted with L&T project personnel. 'India's workforce,' the Prime Minister said, 'will soon meet the world's need for manpower, and through their efforts across the globe, they are enhancing India's prestige and value in the eyes of the world.'

Left: Posing with an end-shield at L&T's Hazira facility. End shields are critical parts of nuclear power plants. India's first indigenous nuclear reactor was manufactured by L&T, and since then the company has remained closely associated with India's nuclear power programme.

Below: Naik passes a ceremonial baton to the CEO & Managing Director designate S.N. Subrahmanyan at a function in Mumbai on 29 June 2017. Having identified Subrahmanyan as his successor, Naik mentored him for over three years in a seamless, well-calibrated transition of leadership.

Naik interacts with Kumar Mangalam Birla at one of L&T's Annual General Meetings. Post the demerger of L&T's cement business in 2004, the Birlas continue to remain valuable customers of L&T.

The reactor building at Kakrapar Atomic Power Project in Gujarat being capped by L&T engineers with a 355-tonne dome.

A BrahMos missile launched from an Indian naval vessel. L&T has supplied a number of launchers and weapons systems for India's defence forces.

L&T won a contract for the supply of howitzers – tracked, self-propelled gun systems – to the Indian Army. This was the largest ever contract placed by the Ministry of Defence with a private Indian company.

The Pinaka, a multi-barrel rocket launcher, adds punch to India's defence forces.

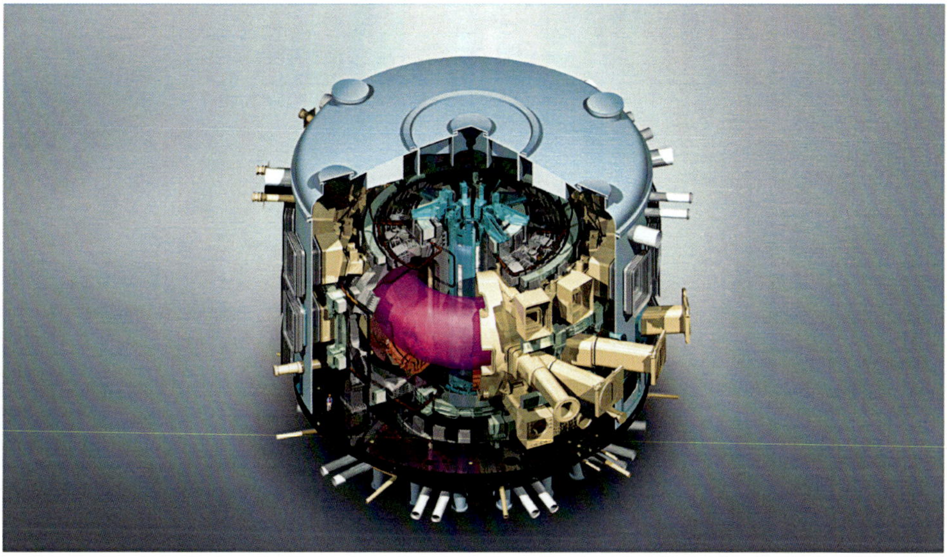

L&T is making the world's largest high-vacuum pressure vessel for ITER, a unique global project that seeks to tap energy through nuclear fusion.

L&T played a major role in building the INS *Arihant*, India's first nuclear-powered submarine.
(Picture for representational purpose only)

Over the last 40 years, L&T has built critical subsystems for all of ISRO's space missions, including India's first moon and Mars space probes – Chandrayaan and Mangalyaan.

A giant process platform complex, India's largest, on Mumbai High executed by L&T on a complete 'EPC' (Engineering Procurement Construction) basis.

A lube base oil project built by L&T in Malaysia.

Terminal 2 of Mumbai airport, built by L&T, provides an impressive new gateway to India.

L&T's 2x700 MW supercritical thermal power plant at Rajpura in Punjab.

The Delhi Metro: L&T has constructed several critical sections of the metro project in India's capital.

Vocational training at the Anil Naik Technical Training Centre has transformed the lives of thousands of village youth around Kharel, Gujarat.

The Nirali Memorial Radiation Centre in Surat is a boon to thousands as it is one of the few advanced radiological centres of its kind between Vadodara and Mumbai.

Mr and Mrs Naik, their children and grandchildren at the inauguration of the healthcare facility in Powai, Mumbai.

in L&T Case Equipment to joint venture partner CNH Global. It divested its medical equipment business to Skanray Healthcare. And in 2016 it sold its general insurance business to HDFC Ergo for Rs 551 crore.

Naik's objective was to leave behind, on relinquishing his executive role, a globally competitive company, profitable and secure from corporate raiders. Naik began planning early. His first task in 2012, as he began his tenth year as chairman, was to simultaneously consolidate L&T's status as an Indian multinational and shed flab at home. He set about both tasks with his trademark vigour. Over the last five years he has divided L&T's complex web of sixty-five businesses into twenty-one independent entities. Naik then shifted his focus to L&T's plethora of joint ventures, around fifty in number. He reviewed the future of some of the manufacturing JVs and selectively exited those in which L&T was not a majority shareholder. As he told the *Financial Express:* 'The company is working on re-looking at the portfolio for the next five years. Every third year, when we undertake a review, what was core earlier, becomes not so core. We are in 65 businesses, and we can't remain in all these businesses. Therefore, if a business is non-core or too small, we need to exit it or close it down."[1]

Plain-vanilla operational assets are expected to be sold in the future. L&T has been divesting assets from its portfolio of twenty-seven infrastructure projects valued at a total of Rs 60,000 crore. Raising external resources is another priority. In 2015, Canada Pension Plan Investment Board bought a minority stake in IDPL through a Singapore subsidiary. Dhamra port, which was losing Rs 300 crore a year, was sold to Adani Ports, while Kattupalli port is to be put on a long-term lease before being sold, after the completion of legal formalities, to the Adanis who are currently managing it. L&T is also in talks to divest its Rajpura power plant and exit the

---

[1] http://www.financialexpress.com/archive/lt-seeks-shareholder-nod-to-hive-off-ea-biz/778395/

power generation business. The company will continue to retain the capability to build and service turbines and boilers.

CONTINUING TO reorganize L&T's businesses, Naik in 2013 hived off its hydrocarbon division into an independent subsidiary named L&T Hydrocarbon Engineering Ltd (LTHE). The idea was to exploit its potential and explore more opportunities globally. The company is organized under several verticals: offshore, onshore, construction services, modular fabrication and engineering services. It offers design-to-build solutions to the oil and gas processing, petroleum refining, chemical, petrochemical, and fertilizer industries. The hydrocarbon business has been one of the leaders in L&T's sustained effort to expand internationally. The company's clients are spread across the Middle East, north Africa, India, south-east Asia, Australia and the Commonwealth of Independent States (CIS). International business constitutes about 50 per cent of the company's revenue, making it an exemplar of L&T's expanding global footprint.

Meanwhile, L&T's Kansbahal plant in Orissa, near Rourkela, is set to get a licence to manufacture alumina, with an investment of $1.2 billion (Rs 7,800 crore). The project is estimated to make an annual profit of Rs 1,500 crore. The strategy is to set it up as joint venture and run it for the next several years. The focus for L&T, however, will now be on areas such as smart cities, water effluent plants, nuclear equipment, defence, aerospace and railways. The full picture that emerges from Naik's strategy is of an L&T of the future that will be a lean, well-structured behemoth straddling high-growth segments in infotech, realty, finance, defence, aerospace and nuclear energy, apart from L&T Construction's traditional strengths in infrastructure.

This is part of Naik's vision for a future-ready L&T. The strategy aims to make the company more focused on high technology and large projects, a significant departure from L&T's old way of doing things. 'L&T had too many businesses, and there is the need to reduce the complexity by rationalizing its portfolio so that it becomes a manageable company with a degree of focus,' says Naik. 'If I can finish this, I will be a happy man when I retire from this wonderful company of ours.'[2]

As far back as in 2011 Naik spoke to *Business Today* in the same vein:

> You have to create a company within a company such that it runs like a listed entity and is ready with a governance structure, with a CEO and a knowledge of how an external board member behaves, how he has to manage the board. So we have three external people in each of the boards and one parent company's non-executive nominee – and each one of them has been told to run this 'virtual' company and bring it to a level of maturity where the parent can trust them to spin it off so that it does not spoil the name of L&T. We are trying to simplify L&T and make it worthwhile to compete with the gorillas of the world. If we don't do proper restructuring a lot can go wrong, therefore we have to make it work. So we have to work day and night, relentlessly, and make sure we do everything, think and reinvent to suit the individual businesses to be run in the best possible manner in the industry and be one up against them. The answer is that it will take five years.[3]

At the heart of the streamlining process is the firm belief that L&T should remain immune to takeovers. The restructuring of businesses into independent but unlisted companies within L&T's fold is meant to make the job of management simpler and prepare the ICs for future listing. Shedding non-core businesses has also freed up management bandwidth. Naik is acutely aware that managing L&T's future will require a distributed leadership model. Delegation and decentralization are the key. Naik acknowledges, though, that the new generation of managers aren't willing to sacrifice a work-life

---

2 *Hindustan Times*, 24 March 2015.

3 *Business Today*, 17 April 2011.

balance. 'It will be tough to expect them to work eighteen hours a day without holidays, like I used to,' says Naik, with a smile.

NAIK HAS been a bold critic of China's dumping policy that hurts India's manufacturing sector. At the sixty-seventh AGM of L&T in August 2012, he thundered: 'China has been dumping around the world and this has raised great concern. Eighty per cent of what is being dumped is from China. Nobody now wants to invest in manufacturing as there is no safety net. Unless the government gives a guarantee, people are not interested to set up units. Recently I had been to Germany and they were very concerned about dumping from China. They fear that they will soon be losing their manufacturing capability. Large-scale imports of power equipment from China by Indian power producers has created a major problem for us. The quality of Chinese equipment is inferior and the lifecycle of such plants is questionable. You, as shareholders of those (power) companies, should question their management as to why they are going in for such equipment.'

When the global economic slowdown in the wake of the sub-prime financial crisis roiled businesses round the world, L&T had displayed an agility rare for a company of its size. In the six years between 2008 and 2014, it invested around Rs 30,000 crore across businesses. The order book grew by over Rs 1,00,000 crore in the space of these six years, from Rs 70,000 crore to Rs 1,89,000 crore in a tough global business environment. Sales doubled, from Rs 40,000 crore to Rs 80,000 crore. Return on capital invested fell to around 11 per cent in 2013-14, from 18 per cent in 2008-09. One reason was the sluggish business environment. Another was that in some cases investments preceded opportunities. Funds thus remained blocked. Shipbuilding and defence are two such examples. Both needed large investment, and gestation periods were long. Returns were adversely affected.

L&T is the only Indian company with capabilities in four

defence segments – warships and submarine building, artillery systems (rocket launchers and guns), naval and land-based weapon launchers (missiles, torpedoes) and engineering systems (bridges, drop platforms, naval equipment and systems) and military communications. These capabilities are in addition to its expertise in nuclear, hydrocarbon and other specialized segments. L&T has a warship design group that can build warships from scratch. The company's Rs 4,500 crore investment in shipbuilding will turn positive in time, Naik asserts. Only six countries in the world can build nuclear-powered submarines, and India is one of them (L&T in collaboration with DRDO). Defence electronics is the next big opportunity as communications and connectedness assume critical importance. L&T is targeting Rs 25,000 crore in defence electronics contracts over the next five years as part of the 'Make' programmes worth Rs 70,000 crore, and over Rs 4,300 crore from the tracked self-propelled howitzer programme, which it won from the Ministry of Defence in May 2017.

The government of India is planning to procure missile systems indigenously. Having pursued a relationship for over five years with MBDA, Naik in February 2017 announced a 51 per cent JV with the European weapon systems major to develop and supply missiles and missile systems to India's armed forces. MBDA is jointly held by Airbus Group, BAE Systems and Leonardo. It is the world's largest missile systems exporter. In the joint venture, L&T will hold 51 per cent, while MBDA the rest of the equity. The JV will develop and supply fifth-generation anti-tank guided missiles, coastal defence systems and high-speed target drones by 2020.

IN AUGUST 2016, Naik had told shareholders that a 'new L&T' is emerging. He said: 'Your company is future-ready. The theme of Technology Leadership is at the heart of the new L&T. Our mission is profitable growth through technology leadership – year after year. The goal is to achieve a revenue of Rs 2 lakh crore by 2021 – without compromising on our margins and by achieving an order inflow in excess of Rs 2.50 lakh crore per annum.'

Naik's forecast is obviously based upon the opening up of the defence sector and the 'Make in India' thrust of the government. Orders the Ministry of Defence could place in the coming decade are estimated at around Rs 13 lakh crore. Stable leadership at the helm of the ministry and a series of reforms have cleared about Rs 4 lakh crore in the order pipeline. The medium-term prospects remain promising. The nuclear power sector could offer opportunities for another Rs 50,000 crore over the same period, once pending fuel-related issues are fully resolved following a better understanding of the Nuclear Liabilities Act—especially by the Americans. Other focus areas, Naik says, are satellite launchers (where L&T is a supplier), smart cities, urban housing and infrastructure—roads, ports, airports and railway corridors.

India's infrastructure pipeline has projects estimated at over Rs 10 lakh crore. Naik points out that L&T has the expertise and track record to make the most of each of these project opportunities: 'Over the years, we have set benchmarks only to surpass them ourselves. Whether it is the longest, tallest, heaviest, first, largest—we have made it.'

Naik's focus on leadership and talent management remains laser-sharp. He has initiated a seven-step leadership programme designed to build a robust pipeline of future leaders. The stages include training at some of the world's leading business schools like IIM-A, Ross, INSEAD, Harvard and, at the final stage, mentoring by Naik himself. By 30 September 2020, when Naik completes his tenure as chairman, L&T will be a finely honed, globally competitive company with a turnover approaching Rs 1.75 lakh crore a year.

At a function to mark Naik's fiftieth year at L&T in March 2015, former President A.P.J. Abdul Kalam was the chief guest. Naik was his usual blunt self. He said: 'L&T has too many businesses and needs to reduce the complexity by rationalizing its portfolio so that it becomes a manageable company with a degree of focus.' Kalam lauded Naik's contribution in making L&T one of India's most admired companies. He endorsed the company's constant endeavour to 'build' the nation, adding: 'We should focus on the manufacturing sector which has been recognized as an engine for economic growth. Biomedical engineering, oil and gas, defence, transportation, aerospace, hardware, information technology and electronics are some areas which we must focus on.'

In an extraordinary show of support and empathy, over 3,000 L&T employees turned up at the function to celebrate Naik's fifty years with the company he regards as his temple. Naik emphasized again to *The Hindu* in March 2015: 'L&T is a firm that builds the nation.' While reaffirming the nationalistic spirit that has driven him through a stellar career, he added that the 'company's prospects are due to timely implementation of infrastructure projects by the government.'

Displaying the outspoken candour he is known for, Naik added: 'In India, things will move at a snail's pace. It will be little faster now because the government has an absolute majority. They are not going to get a majority in Rajya Sabha for some time. By then, their term will be nearing the end and they will start preparing for new elections. I think today government – instead of announcing new programmes and initiatives – must create a very dynamic implementation process.'

L&T in future will function increasingly like a holding company with profitable subsidiaries . Naik had observed this trend as early as in 2015. On 5 March that year he said: 'In time L&T will be 55 per cent of its size as the holding company and the rest will be part of the overall group. All I am saying is seven companies will either be merged or listed, and that it is significant. We need to identify the absolute core. We have sold 14 businesses in the past few years. What is there in L&T now is almost the core. The core keeps getting redeemed every few years.'[4]

---

[4] *Business Standard*, 5 March 2015.

NAIK HAS received global recognition for converting L&T into a world-class Indian multinational. When he received the Order of the Dannebrog, Knight-First Class from Queen Margrethe of Denmark in March 2015 at a function felicitating his fifty years at L&T, Naik gave a rousing speech that walked his audience through fifty years of his life and work:

> I am overwhelmed at the felicitation. As you know, I am not one who is normally at a loss for words. But I truly do not know how to respond to this outpouring of affection and joy. I can only say thank you very much. You expect me to make a speech. But this is not an occasion for speeches. So I will simply go back across my span of 50 years in the company and give you what, in cricket terminology is called 'Highlights'.
>
> Recently, when someone interviewed Mr M.H. Pherwani, former head of Powai and my former boss, he said it was clear from my first day, from day one, that I was cut out to be a leader. I have not consciously set myself to become a leader. There was no Leadership Development Academy in those days! So I learnt leadership the hard way, and what is probably the best way. I set down goals very clearly. I worked out a plan to achieve those goals and I explained them to my team. And I made sure the goals were achieved 100 per cent. Only now, people say these are exactly the principles of good leadership that you will find in management manuals!
>
> A leader cannot guarantee that the organization he leads will only have good times. So is it with L&T. And each time L&T was confronted with a tough situation and no solution seemed to be in sight, we have managed to overcome the challenge and - not just that - we have emerged stronger. I think this is the hallmark of leadership. The company is going through a transformational process which will sharpen its business focus. The process is on-going and we have quite a way to go.
>
> My mantra to work is very simple. It is Passion, Commitment, Devotion. This cannot come from outside. It has to come from deep within you - only then will it be sustainable for months that will become years and years that will become decades, and decades that will become - who knows - half a century! So I say this to you - be

passionate about the tasks given to you. If you are uninterested and half-hearted, you are doing your job and yourself a disservice.

If you have passion, you will want to always be in the thick of the action. Right from my early days, I could never remain a passive spectator. The chair given to me in D4 Building was empty most of the time. My then boss Mr Baker asked someone about me, and was told: 'Mr Naik is always in the workshop'. If I had continued to sit in the chair, and attempted to supervise operations from there, I would not have reached the position I am in today. Wherever I have been in the last 50 years – at the workshops, in the old Group II, as the CEO and later as Chairman – I bring in action with me. And it is action that marks you out as a leader.

People say that in the course of 50 years, I have found innovative solutions, thought out of the box and overcome difficulties. I think it all boils down to one simple but irreplaceable characteristic – courage. I learnt this when I was a child. My father told me – if you are in the right, you have nothing to fear. Courage is the No. 1 trait of leadership. Courage does not mean being abrasive or aggressive. It means that come what may, you refuse to back down. There can be no compromise on your core principles.

We are living in an age of short career spans. Your children probably would not be able to imagine how anyone could spend 50 years in the same organization. People say that long service was more common in the old days because there were no options. I say this is only partially true. I had many options – offered by industry leaders. Let me tell you an anecdote not many would know. The Birlas – both Kumar Mangalam and his father – were after me to join them. So, when the Birlas came on board in 2001, do you know what Kumar said to me? He said: 'You have not come to us so we are coming to you.' The point I am making is that we stuck on – not because of a lack of options but the same three qualities that I talked about earlier – Passion, Commitment, Devotion.

Many people have told me that the Employee Stock Options (ESOPs) changed their lives forever in a manner that they could never have imagined. I am happy to have made that possible. When I look ahead now, we all know that the future is going to be challenging. And we need to ask ourselves today – what kind of leadership will succeed tomorrow. The answer clearly is we need entrepreneurial leaders. I have always said, the professional leader is one who maintains value, the entrepreneurial leader is one who multiplies value. Success in the future belongs to this breed. Let me tell you, I would not have achieved the success that I have got if I had been content remaining a professional leader.

Across the last five decades, I have received many trophies – all of them coveted. They include national honours, regional recognition and awards from media and trade bodies. In fact the rack in my room in C Building is full. If you ask me which is the one trophy I cherish the most, it is the one I carry in my heart – the affection and regard of all of you.

I know that I am very tough and demanding. In fact my wife often tells me to let go and take it easy. But believe me, I have always had your interests at heart. It would have been easy for me to win cheap popularity by saying goody-goody things about each of you. But in my book, that would have been wrong and dishonest. I would not then be doing my duty to the company, to the cause we work for, to the country and most of all, to you as an individual.

Let us resolve to take this great company of ours to even greater heights. By making the company strong, we will be contributing to making the community vibrant and the nation strong. And then, my friends, we will be living our dream, and helping to build the India of our dreams. This function has been called 'The Golden Age'. But I assure you if you resolve to work with passion, dedication and commitment, the Golden Age will continue far into the future.

NAIK HAS known Prime Minister Narendra Modi since his days as chief minister of Gujarat. The two share similar values. On 26 May 2014, when Modi took the oath of office, Naik wrote him a congratulatory letter but made sharp points on the post-UPA economy:

The people of India have reposed faith in your leadership and now look up to you to steer the country through the current economic slowdown which has come in the way of growth and development.

> As a leading driver of infrastructure projects in the country and as an acknowledged nation builder, L&T looks forward to working closely with the new government and partner the responsibilities of meeting new industrial and social goals.
>
> I am sure that India's economic growth will reach greater heights under your able leadership, and this will lead to India achieving its rightful place as a global economic power.

Naik says of the prime minister: 'I have known Modiji since October 2001 when he took over as chief minister of Gujarat and rapidly built a reputation as a leader who could galvanize the state. I envied Shri Modi's energy levels and strength of purpose then, and I admire them even more today when he leads a nation with the same unrelenting passion. As prime minister, he has championed inclusive change in vital sectors. Modiji recognized early that in a world of interdependent nations, it was essential that India's voice was heard in international forums. He has built bridges with distant lands, and his charismatic outreach to countries in the east and west has created a positive global tide in India's favour.'

Like the prime minister, Naik, while a strong disciplinarian, has a softer side. 'Mine is the life story of a boy from a village and how he reached out to the world,' he says with a smile. 'I grew up with boys from scheduled tribes and studied with them. I did not study in a convent school. I could not speak English for even five minutes. I made a lot of grammatical mistakes. I bought English-learning cassettes to hear how words were pronounced. I picked up dictionaries to understand the real meaning of English words and then to understand their spellings, how they are spoken. After all that was done I would stand in front of a mirror and speak to see visually if the expression is correct.'

Naik tries to stay ahead of the curve. He looks ceaselessly for opportunities to upgrade his knowledge and go beyond technological thresholds. Looking back at his key milestones, Naik says: 'When I took over heavy engineering, it was anything but heavy. It was a thin 3 mm dairy shop. The heavy workshop was under construction because we had signed an agreement in 1964-65 to make nuclear reactors. This was for RAPP-1 in Rajasthan, where the main equipment was imported. For RAPP-2 onwards we got the orders to make the equipment. I always say, for L&T the 1960s belonged to nuclear, the 1970s to aerospace, the 1980s to defence research technology and the 1990s onwards to today, to whole projects.'

NAIK'S TRANSFORMATIVE agenda has enabled L&T to synergize and leverage its strengths in heavy engineering, construction, IT and new-economy businesses. An example is the company's debut in the smart cities segment, where L&T is equipped to provide services ranging from design and engineering all the way to project execution, synergizing its capabilities across construction, real estate, IT and related domains. Technology leadership, says Naik, lies at the heart of the new L&T. He describes the path ahead succinctly: 'Profitable growth through technology leadership.' Naik adds that L&T's strategic plan involves re-allocation of resources—talent and capital—to businesses with clearly visible potential for value creation.

Aligning itself with focus areas of the government and absorbing the requisite technology to emerge a leader in specific businesses is a well-established L&T practice. Ranging from the nuclear power industry to aerospace, L&T has been a first-mover. It was closely involved in the earliest satellites launched by India as well as in ISRO's recent moon and Mars missions. It was a pioneer in building India's first nuclear power plant and nuclear-powered submarine. 'As you know, we have always been aligned with the nation's priorities, developing capabilities to meet India's needs,' says Naik. Again, the overriding desire to build a strong nation pervades Naik's thinking. It is manifest in L&T's strategic business initiatives.

Naik is not an easy man to please. He is parsimonious with praise. But for his successor, Subrahmanyan, he makes an exception.

'I mentored Subrahmanyan actively for several years,' Naik says. 'About two and a half years ago he went to the US for four months to review the potential of IT, and then went to Europe for one month. At that time I publicly declared him as my future successor. He is a conscientious and capable person. Many IC heads are a part of the mentoring process. I started a new mentoring team nearly a year ago. The first phase of mentoring is on camera so the person who is being mentored gets a copy; he can see where he did not respond correctly, where he could do better. He can constantly think things over and then, if he wants to, ask questions.'

Naik's single-minded objective: to make L&T future-ready.

10

Future-Ready: India's Era

WHAT DOES THE future hold for L&T? In a column for *Business India* in its 18 June 2016 issue, Naik expounded on the importance of skill-building to India's growth story: 'Today's employees, unlike pervious generations, have a wider menu of career choices and enjoy greater mobility. Hence attracting and retaining the right talent has become increasingly difficult. With our youth, as with many others in society, perception is the new reality. A lot depends on their perceptions of value creation which in turn could hinge on what is currently trending on social media! Since this is the nature of the beast, we cannot but engage with it. Ultimately, organizations and nations are as strong as the ability of its people to generate a sustainable competitive advantage. Given our native skills and the innate soundness of our economical and social systems, I am sure we have within us the seeds of great change. If we do things right and do them in time, the future could well be India's era.'

The idea of treating different verticals as operating companies with a hybrid holding company at the centre was first mooted in 2009. The structure also borrowed generously from the American giant GE, with which L&T is often compared. Two companies, L&T Infotech and L&T Technology Services, had successful public issues in 2016. More public issues could follow, beginning with

L&T Hydrocarbon Engineering. Lakshya 2021's future goals include managing portfolio risks and conducting a portfolio churn to transform L&T into an 'asset-light organization'. As Naik told *Moneylife*: 'A lot has been done in taking L&T to the next level in infrastructure building with the help of engineering, project management and other skills that we are building up, even in the middle of all this turmoil of talent loss.'

The 2021 vision continues to address residual issues such as talent retention even as it provides a roadmap for the future. 'Some 70 per cent of the best Indian talent goes out of India,' says Naik. 'Out of the balance 30 per cent, 25 per cent takes up non-infrastructure, non-manufacturing-oriented jobs. So only 5 per cent of the talent is available to us. L&T grabs the best ones and then, after a year or two, with the golden stamp of L&T, seven out of ten leave. So, within three years, we are back to square one. All I do is training and more training.'

Analysing some of these issues at the Vibrant Gujarat Summit in January 2015, the first with Modi in attendance as prime minister, Naik spoke to an audience of international and Indian business leaders with his usual gusto:

> Let's begin by saying that Larsen &Toubro is proud to have been associated in building this magnificent Mahatma Mandir where you are seated now. We are also proud of our role in the iconic Statue of Unity project. When complete, India's Iron Man, Sardar Vallabhbhai Patel, will tower over every other statue in the world. Our Honourable Prime Minister has repeatedly emphasized the importance of skills and human resources development as the key to sustainable success. L&T is a 'human capital intensive' company. Every year we train over 15,000 people through our training institutes spread across the country. We have also established a unique project management institute in Vadodara and a safety innovation school in Hazira. Our commitment to innovation and technological development is visible around the country. At our Knowledge City in Vadodara, over 4,200 engineers work on cutting-edge technology.

When the Prime Minister launched the Swachh Bharat Abhiyan, L&T was among the first companies to respond with a comprehensive plan that will add traction to the national movement. L&T will build 7,000 to 10,000 toilets at the cost of Rs 60 crore. Of this, 2,000 to 2,500 toilets will be built in Gujarat. I am happy to share how L&T has translated into action our Prime Minister's 'Make in India' campaign. A few months ago we inaugurated India's first fully indigenous supercritical power plant. It was designed in Vadodara, with equipment manufactured in Hazira and installed in Punjab – Made *in* India, Made *by* India, Made *for* India.

OVER 110 million homes are needed to be built by 2020 in urban and rural areas to house India's growing population. The government has initiated several policy reforms in the sector. L&T's Smart World & Communication business vertical is designed to provide end-to-end solutions as a master systems integrator in security solutions for critical infrastructure: ports, airports, metros, IT parks and public buildings. It has built one of the largest surveillance projects comprising 6,000 cameras across over 1,500 locations in Mumbai, and city surveillance and Intelligent Traffic Management Systems in Ahmedabad, Gandhinagar and Vadodara. In Jaipur, India's first smart city, L&T provided smart solutions like wi-fi hotspots, citizen interactive information kiosks, environmental sensors, parking information systems and surveillance cameras. In the pipeline is a surveillance project in Hyderabad which will feature the largest number of cameras in India, and a comprehensive metro telecom package for the Lucknow Metro.

The government has identified L&T as its implementation partner to convert Nagpur into the country's first large-scale integrated Smart City. The project will be executed by L&T Construction's Smart World & Communication Business. Phase 1 of the project involves laying a 1,200 km optical fibre network backbone, creating

136 city wi-fi hotspots at key locations, establishing 100 digital interactive kiosks and developing city surveillance systems with 3,800 IP-based cameras.

A strip of approximately 6 km (from Japanese Garden Square to Orange City Hospital Square) in Nagpur will be developed as a 'smart strip', with state-of-the-art systems powered by smart ICT interventions like smart transport, solid waste management and smart lighting. These can be leveraged in a phased manner to cover the entire city. L&T won another smart city project in 2017: Pune. Here too, wi-fi will be operational at around 200 strategic locations across the city. The project includes establishing emergency call boxes and public address systems, environmental sensors, variable messaging displays, network connectivity and video analytics integration. The project will have a frontline Smart City Operation Centre to integrate all its services and applications on a single platform. This single point interface will be a holistic platform with the potential to accommodate future needs through the integration of various citizen-centric applications. The project includes a revenue monetization model, the country's first in the smart cities domain.

Engineering and construction projects, though, remain L&T's bread and butter. One of the company's most challenging projects was building a new integrated passenger terminal at Chhatrapati Shivaji International Airport. L&T had to carry out its work without disrupting the airport operations. There was no extra land in case expansion was required. The terminal handles over 40 million passengers and 1 million tonnes of cargo per year. The ultra-modern structure has set architectural benchmarks for airports across the world. L&T has helped build the Mumbai, New Delhi, Bengaluru, Kochi and Hyderabad airports. The company has also built an airport in Salalah, Oman.

Mumbai's ambitious metro network has, meanwhile, given L&T new opportunities as the city builds a modern transport infrastructure. L&T's joint venture with STEC won two packages, valued at Rs 5,273 crore, of the total seven awarded by Mumbai Metro Rail Corporation (MMRC) as part of the third phase of the city's metro network. MMRC, a joint venture between the Maharashtra government and the central government, is developing the complex 33.5 km underground corridor with twenty-six metro stations. The project is expected to be completed by 2021.

Among L&T's most prestigious projects, which Naik often speaks about, is designing and constructing the Rs 2,989 crore Statue of Unity, a 182-metre (597 feet) statue of India's first home minister, Sardar Vallabhbhai Patel. The statue is being built on SadhuBet Island, 3.5 km south of Sardar Sarovar Dam at Kevadia in Gujarat's Narmada district. L&T will build the statue, along with an exhibition centre at its base, a memorial garden, a designer bridge connecting Sadhu Island with the mainland along the Narmada river, and an internal 5 km roadway. L&T has been contracted to maintain and manage the project site for fifteen years after completion.

Work on the statue has picked up pace. Workers from the TQ Art Foundry of Jiangxi Tongqing Company will help assemble the bronze cladding of the façade in Kevadia. According to one report,[1] TQ Art Foundry has 'designed about 5,000 bronze panels under the supervision of artist Ram Suthar. These will be assembled in a workshop before being clad to complete the façade in phases. The TQ Art Foundry workshop has completed precasting the feet and the *dhoti* for the first stage. Thousands of high-quality prototypes of the precast façade will be shipped in from abroad and assembled at the site,' said R.G. Kanungo, superintending engineer of Sardar Sarovar Narmada Nigam Ltd (SSNNL). Simultaneously, the steel framework that will give the exterior shape and hold the bronze cladding together will be shipped from Trichy, where it is being manufactured. Close to 100 workers from overseas will arrive and work on the cladding. By then, the height of the statue will be 90

---

[1] *The Indian Express*, 6 June 2017.

metres, almost halfway through. Over 2,400 workers are at the site on day and night shifts to complete the statue on time.'

AS L&T eyes the next business to list, the focus is on L&T Hydrocarbon Engineering, a wholly-owned flagship subsidiary responsible for the high-profile business of providing EPC solutions to the oil and gas sector. L&T Hydrocarbon was spun off as a subsidiary six years ago. Earlier, it was part of parent L&T and, along with the heavy engineering and defence businesses, constituted Group II—the group that Naik piloted to prominence. L&T Realty could be listed one day too. It is one of the fastest growing businesses in the L&T group: its growth over the past few years has been exponential. With a premium attached to the L&T brand, it is likely to emerge as a significant driver of profits for the group.

L&T Realty's focus hasn't been confined to premium real estate. In March 2017, Maharashtra Housing and Area Development Authority (MHADA) chose L&T to redevelop the BDD chawls at Naigaon, Dadar, in Mumbai. Built by the British in the 1920s, the chawls' redevelopment will create much-needed low-cost housing in Mumbai. It fits in perfectly with Naik's own philosophy of caring for the weaker sections of society. S.S. Zende, vice-president and chief executive of MHADA, says: 'Larsen & Toubro was the lowest bidder for the Naigaon site, and Shapoorji Pallonji for the N.M. Joshi Marg site. The work will involve not just redeveloping the chawls and rehabilitating existing tenants, it also involves creation of on-site and off-site infrastructure, such as roads, open spaces, landscaping and so on.'[2]

Unlike other large companies, L&T has mostly maintained a low profile. It does relatively little advertising. Despite this, L&T has over

[2] *Hindustan Times*, 22 March 2017.

the past decade consistently featured in surveys by newspapers and magazines as one of India's ten most admired companies. Naik too ranks in the top ten lists of India's most admired business leaders. L&T was ranked No. 8 by *Business Today* in 2014, ahead of Tata Motors (No. 10) and Bharti Airtel (No. 12), and just behind Infosys (No. 7) in a survey of the best companies to work for. A study done by *Harvard Business Review South Asia* in its January-February 2013 issue ranked Naik No. 4 in a list of India's best-performing CEOs, ahead of HDFC Bank's Aditya Puri (No. 5) and just below Reliance Industries' Mukesh Ambani (No. 3).

When Naik was selected *Business India's* Businessman of the Year in 2015, RPG Group chairman Harsh Goenka observed: 'Naik beats all entrepreneurs in his passion to grow L&T. Contracts for L&T are not given on L1, L2, L3 basis, but on brand L&T basis. That is the trust L&T evokes.'

The rise of L&T's financials and market capitalization over the past twenty-seven years is revelatory. In 1990, L&T's annual turnover was Rs 1,024 crore, and market cap Rs 1,134 crore. In just over twenty-seven years, sales have leapt 100-fold and market cap 130-fold – most of the steep increase coming after 1999 when Naik took charge as CEO. In 1994, when Naik was GM of Group II, L&T's market cap was Rs 5,710 crore.[3] Its pace was glacial until 1999, when he took over as CEO, and its compounded annual growth rate (CAGR) was less than 1 per cent a year. The trajectory then changed dramatically. Between 1999 and 2017, L&T's market cap climbed from Rs 2,000 crore to around Rs 1,60,000 crore in 2017, at a CAGR of nearly 28 per cent. The acceleration in growth tells its own story.

---

[3] *Business India*, March 2015.

NAIK'S STRATEGY of mentoring young leaders has played a key role in keeping the management pipeline full. Mentoring takes place at all levels—junior, middle and senior. S.N. Subrahmanyan's ascent to the top in L&T is an outcome of mentoring at the highest level. Uniquely, though, over the years, Naik has nurtured executive assistants (EAs) in his office. Many have gone on to head independent divisions of L&T in India and globally. Pankaj Chadha, a metallurgical engineer, was chosen as an executive assistant in Naik's office in 2003. Today he heads one of L&T's most important sites for its defence business in Visakhapatnam as GM, Defence. 'I am general manager in the submarine business,' he says. What did he learn from Naik during the time he spent as his EA? Says Chadha: 'Passion and energy. And how you communicate with passion with diverse groups.'

Jayant Kohale joined L&T in 1998. A mechanical engineer with an MBA, Kohale was Naik's EA for two years. He says Naik is methodical, plans his day by the minute and yet has a humane side. After working in Naik's office, Kohale was posted to Munich for ten years to develop L&T Technology Services' business in Europe. On his return to India in 2015, Kohale has been closely involved with L&T's ambitious Smart Cities project as Joint GM, Smart World & Communications.

Sidharth Mohata, a personable young man from an IIT-IIM background, works on the power business and handles corporate affairs in Naik's office. He says: 'The experience of working with Mr Naik ... you won't get that anywhere else. He plans each and every item on his agenda. He is prepared for every venture. He is a tough taskmaster and expects you to be up-to-date about everything going on in the business. I look after power, corporate affairs and CSR, and earlier was handling heavy engineering and defence. Currently there are nine EAs in Mr Naik's office. He starts the career planning for his EAs the day he meets them.'

Rohit Kamal, a mechanical engineer from Pune University, agrees. He has an MBA from the Asian Institute of Management in the Philippines and joined Naik's office as an EA in July 2016. 'I have learnt what determination, perseverance and focus can achieve by working with Mr Naik,' says Kamal. His focus areas are L&T Infotech and L&T Technology Services. R.B.S. Anand, also a mechanical engineer, joined the L&T group in 1992. In a mid-career move, Anand became Naik's EA for two years from 2005 to June 2007. 'He has taught me to see things from a broader perspective,' Anand says. 'I went to Africa to set up L&T in Johannesburg and came back in 2016. I am now a part of the Smart World & Communications project.'

Such calibrated career progression was replicated with Mukesh Ahlawadi, a mechanical engineer who has been with L&T for fourteen years and is currently posted in Paris. 'I have worked in production management in Hazira,' he says,over the phone from the French capital. 'In 2014 I got the opportunity to work with Mr Naik for two years. I was also given a chance to finish my MBA from 2008 to 2010. I moved to Paris in August 2016 as chief representative, Europe, to get new business for heavy engineering, defence and nuclear. It was a great experience working with Mr Naik. He always pushes you to learn, take up challenges. Even if you have made errors, he encourages you to correct them and move forward.'

YOGI SRIRAM heads human resources (HR) at L&T. Given the importance Naik attaches to leadership mentoring, Sriram's role is key to L&T's personnel strategy. An HR veteran who has worked with Taj Hotels and British Petroleum, Sriram has interacted closely with Naik for over a decade. Sriram analyses Naik with the practised air of a man who has seen it all and done it all in a long career where an understanding of human psychology plays an important role in assessing new recruits.

'I report to Mr Naik directly,' he says. 'I meet him every day, sometimes more than once a day. We have 55,000 people in L&T, 20,000 in L&T Infotech, 10,000 in L&T Technology Services, 6,500 in

L&T Finance. That's 91,000 in total. Mr Naik is an interesting mix—extremely empathetic and at the same time a no-nonsense person. Extremely detailed, no fluff, very approachable. He is informal, but not casual. It's easy to have a conversation with him provided you know your facts. His intellect is lightning-fast. He has an interesting perspective on different issues. He himself shows interest in recruiting. For senior level leadership recruitment, I report to him but keep Mr Subrahmanyan fully involved and informed about HR.'

Chetna Patnaik looks after leadership talent acquisition in L&T's bustling HR division under Sriram. Originally from Odisha, Chetna joined L&T in 2012. She says HR has been Naik's priority. He makes sure the team constantly works on leadership hiring. 'It's a machinery he has created here,' she remarks. 'The focus of our HR group is more on leadership and talent building. Mr Naik initiated a process in the organization where leaders are trained internally. He developed a Leadership Academy in Lonavala. The academy is one of its kind in India. It's not only a workshop where programmes take place throughout the year. It also has a development centre, an assessment centre, leadership programmes and global CEO programmes. It's a residential facility and among the best in the country.'

Chetna says Naik is 'just like a coconut, very hard on the outside and extremely soft inside. I have closely interacted with Mr Naik for the last five years. While business is a priority for him, he spends four to five hours on HR every day. This is on various aspects—it could be performance, it could be compensation rewards and recognition, it could be talent acquisition, it could be organizational structure discussions. Mr Naik likes to meet people, interact with them. He likes to learn. Agility and adaptability are alive in him.' Naik's personal secretary, Mario Fernandes, agrees. He says Naik likes people who are humble about their achievements and who let their actions do the talking.

The emphasis on international standards, of getting the best mentors from around the world, is particularly evident at L&T's

Leadership Development Academy at Lonavala. Harvard University and INSEAD Singapore conduct regular programmes here. At every opportunity, Naik tries to motivate the company's young managers.

In a speech at L&T's Powai campus in 2015, Naik had special words of advice for his young colleagues:

> Fifty years ago when I first entered Powai Gate 1, as a junior engineer, I was conscious that I was *living my dream*. L&T had always been my dream company. And so on my first day, I was full of passion, enthusiasm and determination. To this day, when I come to work in the morning, I still do so with the same level of passion and the same level of determination. Many things have changed since that day in March 1965, but my sentiments have not changed. I urge you all to sustain the passion for your career and your company. Never let the flame go dim.
>
> Plan your day, your year and your future. Every day at every level, I used to introspect. I used to ask myself – how did I perform, could I have done better, could I have aimed higher? Never mind what people say. My bosses used to say 'Mr Naik is doing an excellent job.' That is how I became the youngest manager in the history of Larsen & Toubro. But I did not become complacent. You have to be a more stringent critic of yourself than your boss. In 2003, when I was appointed Chairman, I was the first Chairman to actually have come up the ranks. They said I was the 'People's Chairman'. As I rose up the corporate ladder, I did not lose touch with people at all rungs. It is important that we do not let success take us away from those around us.
>
> People say that Mr Naik is an impatient leader who wants to accelerate the pace and reduce deadlines. So how did I not lose patience across fifty years? The answer is that the heart wins over the mind. First put your heart into your career. Then bring in the mind and let it determine how best to do what you are doing.

It is a message Naik has put into practice throughout his life and work. L&T under Naik has constantly sought newer geographies beyond India. At L&T's seventy-first AGM in August 2016, Naik reiterated the company's global agenda: 'As an Indian multinational, your company is strengthening its operations in the Gulf, Africa and South-east Asia. We are competing with the world's best in those markets and ensuring that our projects and services are truly globally benchmarked. Our manufactured products are exported globally and meet the highest international quality standards.'

AT L&T'S corporate office in the bustling Mumbai suburb of Andheri, preparations for a smooth leadership transition began several months ago. It was in the works for years, after Naik publicly announced that his successor would be S.N. Subrahmanyan. Earlier, speculation in the media had been rife, given the sensitive portfolios of defence, nuclear and aerospace that the company handled. In 2007, when Naik turned sixty-five, the board asked him to continue in the absence of a credible successor.

In 2011, Naik explained to *Business Today* the reasons why it was not easy to find a successor: 'L&T is not one company, it is twenty-five companies. Can it be run by a single man? People tell me you have not left a successor. I tell them, you find a man in the world who will kill himself four times a day, has worked for more than a hundred years, started more than 60 per cent of the company himself with devotion and passion, and is not bothered about his own family. The day you find such a man he is my successor. So what should we do? There is no such person. And therefore you cannot run L&T as you ran it before.'[4]

Towards the end of Naik's second tenure as chairman in 2012, L&T went through a phase when most of its key senior management retired or resigned in quick succession. In 2011-12, J.P. Nayak, president of the machinery and industrial products division (MIPD), who was second-in-command in L&T's hierarchy, retired.

---

[4] *Business Today*, 17 April 2011.

K.V. Rangaswami, head of construction, too hung up his boots. Another contemporary, Y.M. Deosthalee, rumoured at one point to be a strong contender for the top job after running a tight ship as CFO, moved to L&T Finance as chairman in 2011. Ravi Kant Uppal, whom Naik brought in from ABB, quit after a year of growing the company's power business to head Jindal Steel & Power Ltd.

At L&T's annual general meeting in July 2003, shareholders demanded that a company of its size should have a full-fledged executive chairman. They argued that things had gone on for far too long without one. The shareholders' demand presented the board with an opportunity. Naik's term as managing director and CEO was coming to an end in April 2004. In December 2003 Naik got the board's nod to be named executive chairman and managing director.

Naik's ascent spawned L&T's golden era. The economy picked up dramatically during this period. L&T began to provide guidance to equity investment firms that its biggest businesses would grow annually at over 25 per cent a year. Sales growth surged. Business margins started improving dramatically. The L&T board was buoyed, as were investors.

Given the background of rising expectations, Naik always knew it wouldn't be easy for a successor to step into his shoes. He made sure Subrahmanyan was not dropped at the deep end of the pool. 'I don't want the criticism that Naik did a great job when he was present, but as soon as he went the company did not do so well,' says Naik. 'I have treated this company as my life, and nobody will be more interested in creating an outstanding successor than me. I have considered it as a temple with priority beyond my wife and children, and I would want the company to be even more prosperous after me.'

Naik's tenure as chairman has already been the longest since founder Henning Holck-Larsen's protracted innings. When Subrahmanyan was appointed to the board of L&T Infotech and L&T Technology Services—two companies overseen by Naik directly, which Subrahmanyan would head well before his succession—Naik had remarked: 'Subrahmanyan is so hardworking and committed that even when he was in the US for four months, he kept track of what was going on here.'

Naik said in a press statement on 7 April 2017: 'I am confident that under Mr Subrahmanyan's high-calibre leadership, the company will accelerate its growth momentum and continue to play a vital role in building the nation.'

L&T's official statement added: 'Taking into account the need for seamless transition of leadership in an organization of the scale and complexity of L&T, the board of directors requested Mr Naik to provide advice, guidance and mentorship to the firm's executive management in the capacity of non-executive chairman. Given Mr Naik's understanding of the complexities of high-tech businesses and his rich experience in the field, the board felt his role as advisor to the next generation of leadership would be essential for sustaining growth and profitability. Mr Naik has acceded to the board's request.'

Subrahmanyan was succinct: 'This is well-thought succession plan worked out by Mr Naik. He identified me twelve years ago and has been grooming me for the past two-three years. Therefore there is full consensus on how we go about the business. It is business as usual, with assured stability.'[5]

SUBRAHMANYAN HAS not worked anywhere else but in L&T. 'This is my first job,' he smiles. 'I am a true-blue L&T-ite. After doing my civil engineering and management, I got this offer and I have been here for over thirty-three years.' His tenure is set to get a lot longer: he is still only fifty-seven, coincidentally the same age as Naik when he was appointed CEO and managing director back in 1999. Subrahmanyan joined the firm in Chennai. 'I started as a

[5] *The Economic Times*, 8 April 2017.

project planning engineer,' he says. 'If you look back at ECC from where I originated and have grown, it was a Rs 95 crore entity when I joined. Today we are budgeting an annual revenue of Rs 70,000 crore. So we've come a long way. It has been a truly remarkable journey.'

Subrahmanyan graduated from NIT in Kurukshetra with a civil engineering degree, followed by a management course at Symbiosis in Pune. SNS, as he is known in L&T, says what really attracts executives and engineers to L&T—and retains them—is that it is a professionally managed company. 'People are empowered,' he says. 'We all feel like owners, you can call us emotional owners, professional owners, involved owners. You feel this is your company. Some of us have ESOPs, thanks to Mr Naik. The key point is that you feel the company is your own, and if anything happens to it you feel hurt. If anything good happens, you feel good, it becomes a part of your life. Every decision and action you take is from that point of view. It's like that from the day you join. The bosses give you freedom to take decisions, it's not top-driven. There are a few principles and strategic ideas which arrive from the top, obviously, because from the top of the pyramid you see the world in a different manner, in a different context. But as a professional you feel totally empowered. As an engineering company our margins are not very high. It's a competitive world out there. We had to struggle to be what we are.'

SNS has a deep understanding of L&T's complex business. He says candidly: 'With our kind of margins we cannot match the pay scales of finance, IT and consumer companies. But that does not deter us from putting in our best. There are many people here who slog eighty-five to ninety hours a week, including on Sundays. It's a great organization to work for, one of the few organizations where the thrust is on speed and scale and completing projects on time and within budget. We put our architects and engineers on the job, struggle along with our workmen and complete it. At the end of the day you feel very proud when a big project is completed.

We may not be called on to the stage. Promoters and political leaders sit on the stage, but when you see the project having taken shape, getting inaugurated, you feel very proud to be an engineer, even prouder to be an L&Tite. And above everything it feels great to be an Indian, that Indians can do some of the world's best projects—from nuclear-powered submarines and space satellites to the Riyadh Metro and Mumbai's international airport. That is what keeps the adrenaline pumping, you just want to come here every day, and keep pushing yourself. I was in the office at 7.00 a.m. today and mostly I work till 8.00 p.m.'

Among the key projects that were given to Subrahmanyan to head was the Hyderabad Metro, considered a difficult assignment. Naik's plan was that before his own retirement, Subrahmanyan should have been running L&T for a few months: 'Obviously, he will become stronger by the day as he gets more and more experience,' said Naik. Subrahmanyan was the beneficiary of Naik's mentoring since 2006. He was present during most of his high-level negotiations and business meetings. Naik describes Subrahmanyan as the 'brightest that we have got.'

HYDERABAD METRO is one of the largest public-private partnership (PPP) metros being developed in the world. A predominantly private partnership, L&T has pumped in both equity and debt. The project received financial assistance, in what is known as a variable grant, from the central government. The total investment in Hyderabad Metro is Rs 19,000 crore. It is the largest investment L&T has made in a single project and ranks among the largest investments by any private sector firm in a standalone infrastructure project in India. L&T has invested over Rs 4,000 crore and borrowed more than Rs 13,000 crore for the Hyderabad Metro. It owns 100 per cent of the metro's equity. The rest of the funding is debt. One 'golden vote' vests with the government of Telangana. It has a say in the project since the concessionaire is the government of Telangana. The project is complex, especially since Hyderabad is a bustling and crowded old city.

'When you do such projects, though the agreement says all licences and clearances would be done on day one, it is not so,' says Subrahmanyan, ruefully. 'There are old electricity lines, there are encumbrances in the form of properties, trees and government of India properties, defence lands, temples, mosques, railway lines to be crossed. And one entity does not control all this, multiple entities are involved. On top of this, you have NGOs and other organizations which have their own agenda or things to look at, and therefore to go through this maze and keep the project moving is not easy. Our team there has done a tremendous job. The government has, in a very visible manner, supported us. But in spite of government support these hurdles take time to sort out. The project is two years behind schedule. It will be completed by September-November 2018. We have 20 km ready so we have requested the Telangana government that if they are okay with it we are willing to inaugurate it. We will be ready with two of the lines. The project is nearly done and by next year it will be totally done from our point of view. From there we need to see how to take it forward. The time extensions and costs have to be dealt with, so we have contacted the authorities, and a good solution should emerge.'

When finished, Hyderabad Metro Rail will have a network of around 72 km across three corridors: Miyapur to LB Nagar, JBS to Falaknuma, and Nagole to Shilparamam. The first bidding process for its construction was won by Maytas Infra in 2008. However, the company could not achieve financial closure within the scheduled time. The contract was cancelled. Subsequently, a re-bidding process was initiated. Six companies were in the running. In 2010, a three-member committee awarded the project to L&T, which arrived at financial closure at Rs 14,920 crore, with the entire debt requirement of Rs 11,480 crore sanctioned by a consortium of banks led by the State Bank of India. The equity component of Rs 3,440 crore was infused primarily by the L&T Group.

Metro stations are located at roughly every kilometre along the route across Hyderabad. The metro rail will be integrated with the existing suburban railway network and bus stops, ensuring seamless travel. The metro is expected to carry the same amount of traffic as seven lanes of bus traffic or twenty-five lanes of private cars, reducing travel time for passengers by 50 to 75 per cent.

The project will earn revenue through fare box collection from ridership, rentals from transit-oriented development space totalling 18.5 million sq. ft, advertising, parking and carbon credits. It is also likely to stimulate economic activity and boost employment in the Hyderabad region. Hyderabad has a rocky strata; hence the decision for an elevated rather than an underground metro. The project is in keeping with L&T's asset-light policy, says Subrahmanyan: 'We don't want to keep an asset for the very long term. Our primary interest is engineering, procurement and construction (EPC). Once that is over, we fulfil certain obligations like minimum liability period, minimum equity holding, etc. But after a period we would like to take our money out and invest in some other project. The Hyderabad Metro would see the same churn as any of our other investments. But when that will happen, I am not able to speculate right now. It will take some time. Right now our immediate focus is on completing the project and running the trains to show that the metro is a quality project.'

L&T's Hyderabad Metro project was especially challenging for Naik. Cost overruns of nearly Rs 2,000 crore took place. There was a delay of two years because the state government could not give L&T the right of way. 'Now we have talked to them, to the Centre,' says Naik. 'We have spoken to the urban development minister and it will hopefully be sorted out quite soon. Thereafter we should possibly come to a point where we don't lose money. After we do a good job of running the Hyderabad Metro for a few years and we think we will get a premium, we could consider selling it. Owning infrastructure of this kind is not our job. It is like running a company itself. In any part of the world, running a metro in a city is a big, big responsibility. Bechtel of the US does not own anything. Doosan of South Korea builds for others. We build, but we own assets too. We took up the Hyderabad Metro project seven years ago, but today if another one comes up for bidding we will not bid. We are not bidding for any new roads or transmission lines either. Owning assets, unless the tenders are reasonable, can be loss-making.'

L&T, meanwhile, continues to systematically divest its non-core businesses. 'The forging business is being sold,' says Subrahmanyan. 'We have come out of excavators, we have come out of the tractor business, out of the shoes business, the packaging business. So slowly we have been moving out of those businesses in which we had got in for some reason but were not able to do very well in.'

Even where profits are high (in the range of Rs 700 crore a year), L&T is negotiating a sale. One example of this is the electrical and automation business, whose enterprise value is around Rs 18,000 crore. Apart from its financials, the business has to fit into the 'new L&T' and its relentless focus on core activities. Naik has long been focused on L&T's bigger businesses which deliver a more robust top line. He had told *Hindu Business Line* as far back as on 9 September 2012: 'I am not interested in small companies, they are distracting me, I want to do big things. Over the next few years we will close (or sell) businesses which don't have revenues of Rs 1,000 crore. I have been saying we have to get out of our smaller businesses. We sold cement, we sold ready-mix, bottles and petrol pumps, we are selling the plastics machinery business now, medical also; we've closed many businesses, they are all tiny. Only bigger projects were making money and smaller ones were eating into the profits.'

So what changes will Subrahmanyan bring about after 1 October 2017? 'When someone hands over such a well-managed business, the task of the successor is to maintain good stewardship,' smiles Subrahmanyan. 'Many things have been put into place and thought through.' Subrahmanyan sees the main drivers of future growth on the services side: L&T Infotech, L&T Technology Services, L&T Realty and L&T Finance. Other core businesses with longer gestation periods like defence, nuclear, aerospace, heavy engineering, water management and Smart World & Communications too hold promise as L&T prepares for the future.

SUBRAHMANYAN WAS first noticed by Naik in the mid-1990s. In the twelve years he had spent in the company at that point, Subrahmanyan had played key roles in projects in India and overseas, including major airports across the country. They were all marquee projects. Says Naik: 'In the last few years, after he joined the board, I took to very active mentoring on a day-to-day basis. In the last six months, knowing that the company is very complex, apart from L&T Construction, which he ran and which accounts for a large portion of the business, he has been involved in many other businesses. I gave him shipbuilding, then I gave him the Hyderabad Metro, I involved him in infotech and technology services.'

Naik recalls that his first impression of Subrahmanyan was that he was 'arrogant'. When Subrahmanyan got to hear of the boss's opinion of him, he went to work on himself. 'I became introspective,' he says. 'Every evening I would stand before the mirror and think about my contributions to the company. This helped me stretch my abilities.'

The first formal move to put the succession plan in place was made in September 2015, when Subrahmanyan was elevated to deputy managing director and president with effect from 1 October 2015. The appointment was made at the same time as then chief executive and managing director K. Venkataramanan's retirement. Speaking at the function commemorating his fifty years at L&T in March 2015, Naik had declared: 'My plan for the next two and a half years is to build a team and complete the succession planning exercise.'[6] He has done exactly that.

---

[6] *Hindustan Times*, 24 March 2015.

As with Naik's execution of other projects, ranging from Hazira to Kattupalli, Subrahmanyan's succession was executed with clockwork precision.

—w—

MEANWHILE, L&T's makeover is moving ahead steadily. Says Naik: 'Not many people understand L&T today. They think L&T makes tall buildings and bridges. That is only one part of our activity. We make "super high-tech" – not even "high-tech" – plants and products. For example, in the International Thermonuclear Experimental Reactor (ITER) Cryostat project in France, a programme by a few chosen nations, L&T represents India, as some key components of the Cryostat are being manufactured in our Hazira complex.'

Naik says L&T's gross profit margins have historically been around 11.5-12 per cent, but are down to 10 per cent today. The fall in margins is mainly because of stalled hydrocarbon projects in the Middle East, the loss-making nuclear forging workshop in Hazira and the investment-heavy shipyards. 'I think these problems will be over and we will have very robust profits by 2018-19,' says Naik.

That appears well within reach. 'The aim is to increase Return on Capital Employed (RoCE) to the pre-2010 level of around 30 per cent,' observes L&T's chief financial officer (CFO), Shankar Raman. Even if we achieve 20 per cent RoCE from the present 12 per cent, it will substantially increase profitability. By 2018-19, we expect an economic boom, and it will help us reach the target.'

L&T's RoCE has been a concern for a number of years. In 2008-09, it was 18.48 per cent but slipped gradually to 16.71 per cent in 2009-10; it was 14.58 per cent in 2010-11, 13.52 per cent in 2011-12, 12.11 per cent in 2012-13 and 10.88 per cent in 2013-14. Naik would like it back at over 15 per cent by 2018-19. Much of the current restructuring is aimed at achieving that objective.

The audited results for 2016-17 bear this out. L&T's sales revenue in 2016-17 rose 8 per cent over the previous year's, to Rs 1,10,011 crore. Profit after tax (PAT) grew 43 per cent, to Rs 6,041 crore. The order book rose by 5 per cent, to Rs 2,61,341 crore. International projects comprised 34 per cent of total sales, while global orders constituted 27 per cent of the order book.

An analysts' report said: 'L&T's Return on Equity (RoE) improved and its working capital needs reduced in fiscal 2017. RoE rose to 12.8 per cent in 2016-17, compared with 9.9 per cent in the previous year. Similarly, net working capital amount used in day-to-day operations as a percentage of sales dropped by 19 per cent in 2016-17. Higher RoE and lower working capital feature among major variables that dominate L&T's five-year strategic vision from 2016 to 2021. Analysts expect RoE to reach 14 per cent in the next two fiscals. A sizeable improvement in L&T's RoE will lend more credence to the management guidance on profitability of operations.'[7]

Naik's move into new-economy businesses too has paid off. In 2016-17, L&T Infotech recorded an audited revenue of Rs 6,501 crore and net profit of Rs 970.90 crore. L&T Technology Services did equally well: revenue in 2016-17 clocked Rs 3,248 crore and net profit a robust Rs 425 crore. L&T Finance Holdings registered consolidated profit after tax of Rs 1,042 crore and return on equity (RoE) of 12.31 per cent—both sharply up from the previous year. While L&T Construction accounts for the largest slice of the L&T group's top line, the infotech, technology services and finance subsidiaries now contribute significantly to the group's bottom line.

INFRASTRUCTURE DEVELOPMENT Projects Ltd (IDPL) was L&T's original vehicle for concession projects. It invested in Bengaluru airport. The company held equity in the project, but once the engineering, procurement and construction (EPC) was done an opportunity arose to sell its shares. L&T divested its equity in the Bengaluru airport project. 'We are not an airport holding

[7] ET Markets, May 30, 2017.

company or airport operating company, that was not our interest,' says Subrahmanyan. 'The same philosophy applies to ports like Kattupalli. We are not long-term port players. In IDPL we have nineteen roads with us. Roads continue to be held by us under the L&T IDPL umbrella. We have a Canadian fund partner. But we need to look at it long term. Under L&T IDPL, we have a transmission line that is now completed, and we will have to examine how to take it forward. We have been investing and doing infrastructure projects. But as a prudent business house we have to look at the returns. If we are not able to do well, but someone else is able to do better, then it makes better business sense to sell.'

After India's airport sector was opened up to private companies, L&T played a significant role in setting up airports in Hyderabad, Delhi, Mumbai, Bengaluru and Kochi. 'These airport projects make us proud,' says Subrahmanyan. 'I was personally involved in many of the projects. They were very challenging, very huge projects. It was satisfying to deal with new and different kinds of clients. To conceive these projects and to execute them within schedule and budget was tremendously challenging. They all have state-of-the-art infrastructure. Mumbai and Delhi airports have been rated as the best in their categories. What it shows is that L&T is capable of taking on $2 to $3 billion projects. We have the people, the ability, the calibre.'

How does Subrahmanyan assess his predecessor who has set a high bar for performance? 'Mr Naik is a full-blooded L&T person,' says Subrahmanyan. 'His mind, heart and everything is in L&T. He breathes, walks, eats, sleeps L&T. He is a true nationalist, a believer in the fact that you can do anything if you set your mind to it. It's about the application of your mind, getting into the details and putting your heart and soul into it to make it happen. He calls it devotion, commitment, passion, conviction towards work. That is how he has built many parts of L&T: through true grit and determination and the belief that we can do it. He is a visionary. He is able to think out of the box and ahead of the times. For example, several years ago he realized that the Indian economy will see a downturn. So he placed some challenges in front of a few managers, including me. Develop another geography, he said. He kept pushing us into the Middle East. We ended up with projects valued at nearly $9 billion there. It wasn't easy, but it sustained the company for several years when the Indian economy slowed in 2009-12.'

As Subrahmanyan settles into the corner office at L&T's Mumbai corporate headquarters, a raft of issues awaits him. He, though, is as sanguine about the future as he is about the past. 'L&T is a part of a $6.1 billion consortium for the Riyadh Metro. We won the Doha Metro contract as well. It's a $4 billion job. We have many road contracts in Oman, and airports and stadiums in Qatar, Oman and Saudi Arabia. In hydrocarbons we bid against the best in the world. For a couple of years I was travelling back and forth without a break, often on one of the L&T jets. In the morning I would to fly to Salalah, the next day to Muscat, then to Riyadh, then Doha, Abu Dhabi, Kuwait, then back to India. And I kept doing that for two years.'

Besides visionary thinking and a forward outlook, Naik developed many ideas which were important from a purely business point of view. He developed filters for business. He rejected certain geographies and projects. A good manager, he maintains, is one who learns to say no. Subrahmanyan confesses he learnt this from Naik. 'A project looks tempting, everybody justifies everything, but sometimes you just have to stand up and say no,' he shrugs. 'Later you find it was a good decision—a competitor took the job and got entangled in all kinds of issues.'

Though he stepped back from executive responsibilities on 30 September 2017, Naik's appointment as chairman till 30 September 2020 will ensure he wields influence over L&T. He will chair board meetings and his diary and work schedule will remain full well into the future, including philanthropic activities in healthcare, education and community service.

Subrahmanyan concedes that L&T has not done leadership and succession planning very well: 'I think all of us have failed. As an organization we are not developing that many leaders, we are not talent-rich, it's a fight for talent, leadership.' Naik's antidote to that has been to mentor leaders at different levels—from young executive assistants to middle-level managers. This will build a seamless leadership pipeline. Today's thirty-year-old EAs may well be ready for a top leadership position after twenty years when L&T approaches its centenary.

Subrahmanyan, at fifty-seven, has more than a decade ahead of him to sculpt L&T in his own mould. He says: 'With the world going digital, a world which is IT-enabled—that is the future. If the services business today comprises 10 per cent of L&T's revenue, our strategic plan is to make it 20 per cent. I think that's a key contribution that Mr Naik has made: the gradual shift to services, in line with India's new economy where services account for 60 per cent of total GDP. Defence is another very important area for us, but it's a difficult area because decision-making is very slow and complicated. There is a procurement process involved, testing of equipment involved. We are already the largest defence player today. We are doing work for the army, the navy and to some extent the strategic forces, and we would like to keep it that way.'

For Naik, defence manufacturing lies at the heart of his national vision.

11

In Defence of the Nation

DEFENCE OCCUPIES THE gravitational centre of L&T's past, present and future. The company has been involved with India's nuclear-powered submarine programme for decades. But it's the future that could be compelling. Jayant D. Patil heads L&T's defence and aerospace business. On 29 May 2017, Patil was elevated to the board of directors of L&T as wholetime director and senior executive vice-president – defence business. The induction signalled the company's increased engagement in defence-related businesses and reflected the importance that the sector plays in L&T's strategic plans. Speaking to the media about the appointment, Naik had said: 'L&T is well positioned to capitalize on the government's plan to increasingly indigenize defence production, and we are confident that under the leadership of Mr Patil, L&T will be able to grow its defence business substantially.'

A top-ranker MTech. in mechanical engineering from IIT Bombay, Patil is a gregarious man who exudes confidence and bonhomie. In May 2017, L&T received an order from the Ministry of Defence (MoD) for 100 high-tech howitzers, valued at over Rs 4,366 crore. The howitzers will be mounted and integrated into a tank. 'They can move at 72 km per hour, they can also go on sand,' says Patil. 'Their shelling range is 43 km.'

The 100 self-propelled, tracked K-9 Vajra T-howitzers, to be made by L&T in collaboration with its South Korean partner, Hanwha Techwin, will be delivered in forty-two months, Patil confirms. They are likely to be deployed on the LoC with Pakistan. Because of their range, firepower, accuracy and mobility, they could prove a gamechanger as India battles infiltration and terrorism on the border. The guns will be manufactured in a new factory at the Hazira complex, says Patil. He is full of praise for the former defence minister, Manohar Parikkar. 'Mr Parrikar, being a top-class engineer himself, could get into the basics of defence equipment and question people,' says Patil.

Patil joined L&T in 1978. Like other old-timers, he lauds the vision and direction Naik has given L&T. He laments, though, that India's entire defence sector is PSU-driven. 'Rs 60,000 crore of defence equipment is ordered from PSUs every year,' he says. 'Of this Rs 60,000 crore, Rs 30,000 crore is imported by the PSUs. Overall, 65 per cent of our arms are imported. We are the second largest importer of weapons in the world. We used to be the largest, but right now it's Saudi Arabia. In 2006, we were only the sixth largest arms importer and China was the largest. By 2012, during the former defence minister A.K. Antony's time, we swapped positions with China and began importing more and more. When this government came in 2014, things started changing.'

The government's Strategic Partnership (SP) policy is a significant boost for the 'Make in India' initiative in the defence sector, says Patil. 'It will provide opportunities valued at about Rs 2 lakh crore in defence manufacturing over the next ten years to L&T,' he reckons. India's defence budget (2017-18) is Rs 2.74 lakh crore (excluding Rs 85,740 crore for defence pensions). India is now the world's fifth largest military spender (after the United States, China, Russia and Saudi Arabia), with a capital spend of Rs 13 to 14 lakh crore likely over the decade. It is expected to order Rs 6 to 7 lakh crore worth of military equipment in domains in which L&T will operate over the next decade. Much of it will be sourced domestically as part of the government's Make in India thrust. L&T aims to garner a significant share of this business.

Patil's bullishness was evident even last year, when he declared: 'We have a Rs 1.5 lakh crore opportunity in defence within the next four to five years. This is in the naval sector where submarines and ships are to be ordered by 2020. The opportunity in weapon systems, where we already produce airframes, launchers, fire controls and sensors and deliver to the armed forces, is also very large. We are looking at a Rs 85,000 crore market.'[1]

He added that the company delivers major components and systems for the Akash surface-to-air missile system, the BrahMos land attack and anti-ship missile system, as well as upgrades of Russian BM 21 Grad BM21 rocket launchers and Pinaka systems. India's defence equipment manufacturing potential could finally justify Naik's prescient investment in Hazira, Talegaon, Coimbatore and Kattupalli.

Consider India's long-term military requirement:[2]

- 1,000 helicopters, valued at $16 billion over the next ten years;
- 2,000 armoured combat vehicles worth $10 billion to replace the old T-72 battle tanks;
- 100 single-engined multi-role fighter jets for $10 billion;
- Six conventional submarines, valued at $8 billion.

Add nuclear-powered submarines, howitzers, guns, air defence systems and warships, and the potential is clearly vast. Patil is optimistic that the defence order pipeline will become robust and start flowing more quickly in the next fiscal.

'Mr Naik has the unique ability to negotiate without breaking negotiations,' says Patil. 'It is easy to break down a dialogue. He will not let anything get completely cut off or broken. He is absolutely fearless and blunt. He is very supportive too. He has been my

---

[1] *The Economic Times*, 15 February 2016.

[2] *India Today*, 8 June 2017.

mentor. He has a unique insight on what to focus on and what not to and possesses clear long-term vision.'

—∞—

NAIK'S FORESIGHT in investing heavily in L&T's defence facilities could pay rich dividends in the future. India now accounts for 14 per cent of total global defence imports. With nearly two-thirds of India's own defence requirement met by imports, Modi has laid increasing emphasis on domestic manufacturing. In defence, the potential for indigenous production of weapon systems for the navy and army— L&T's strong points—therefore has significant upside.

Addressing a press conference at Aero India in February 2017, then Defence Minister Manohar Parrikar said the Indian armed forces require at least 400 fighter jets and 800 to 1,000 helicopters over the next decade. He added: 'Our helicopter engine requirement in ten years is 5,000 and we will need over 400 LCA (light combat aircraft) as well … All these aspects open up huge potential.'

In an interview with *India Today* on 6 March 2016, a year before he returned to Goa as chief minister, Parrikar said: 'There are two aspects to indigenization. One is total indigenous content. The other is when a supplier manufactures equipment, but uses imported components, such as chips and basic electronic circuits. When we (the NDA government) started, only 30-35 per cent content was indigenous; we are slowly working to increase this. 'Buy global' or direct imports is the least favoured option. The preference is for indigenously Designed Developed and Manufactured (IDDM) systems. Next is "Buy Indian", with 40 per cent indigenous content, then 'Make in India' projects, and the third is "Buy and Make" certain systems in India with 40 per cent indigenous component. About 70-80 per cent, or Rs 99,000 crore, of the Acceptance of Necessity (AoN), which is the first step in a contract, granted this year are for IDDMs.'

In an insightful article, Naik dealt specifically with India's strategy to enhance its domestic defence manufacturing sector and at the same time boost defence exports:

The government's recent decision to deregulate the manufacture of a number of items used by the defence forces will result in new players and SMEs entering the sector. Easy entry will result in an increase in the number of manufacturers, with the benefit of competition that will improve both quality and cost-effectiveness. This will also encourage them to seek export markets for their products. A small country like Israel, which gained independence at almost the same time as India and with a population less than 1 per cent of India's, today accounts for 10 per cent of total global defence exports. China which until 2006 was the largest importer of defence goods is today the fifth largest defence equipment exporter. Paradoxically India, with its huge pool of technically qualified, globally competitive manpower, in dire need for employment for its population, has emerged as the largest defence importer.

India's approach to defence exports will be guided by changes in the geopolitical situation as we build stronger diplomatic ties, particularly with nations in the Indian Ocean Region. If the government and national defence industry embrace the challenge, India can not only effectively meet domestic needs but also emerge as a major exporter of defence products. We need a major thrust – a national mission on defence equipment exports.

THE GOVERNMENT of India has chosen defence as a flagship sector for the Make in India programme and has taken a number of initiatives to achieve greater indigenization. These include preferential acquisition of future programmes from Indian companies, either for indigenously designed and developed products or through collaboration with foreign OEMs or by developing them *ab initio* with 90:10 government: industry funding. The policy initiatives include creating a level playing field for the private sector, entering into strategic partnerships for mega-platform programmes, enhancing FDI for setting up defence units and providing preferential market access through defence PSUs, besides inversion of the acquisition categorization to favour Indian companies. Programmes worth Rs 4 lakh crore have been cleared for acquisition over the coming years, with nearly 80 per cent to be ordered from Indian industry, whether public or private.

L&T's defence and aerospace businesses operate across military platforms, with the ability to build complete platforms in naval and land systems domains. The company collaborates with DRDO and ISRO to develop indigenous technology for defence and space launch programmes. It also partners with public sector defence undertakings such as Bharat Electronics Ltd (BEL), Bharat Dynamics Ltd (BDL), Mazagon Dock Shipbuilders Ltd (MDSL), Garden Reach Shipbuilders & Engineers Ltd (GRSE) and others for the production of various systems and critical sub-systems as well as warships and submarines. It makes sizeable investments for developing in-house capabilities across the value chain—from technology and product development to manufacturing technology, systems integration and obsolescence management during life cycle support.

Dedicated product and technology development centres create niche products and solutions for internal projects as well as collaborate in joint development programmes with global majors on even-keel basis. Young teams, under the watchful eyes of their seniors, are tweaking their own Futuristic Infantry Combat Vehicle (FICV) solution, a gen-next light tank-cum-armoured personnel carrier, and positioning it at the forefront of the race for the next 'Make' programme worth Rs 50,000 crore. These could become the mainstay of India's mechanized forces for 2050 and beyond. Meanwhile, another team is busy developing an unmanned underwater vehicle and getting it ready to go into the water for trials. A third team is working on adapting their UGV (Unmanned Ground Vehicle) solution to the army's BMP upgrade programme.

With the simplified Defence Procurement Procedure (DPP) 2016 coming into effect, defence procurement is set to gain traction. Military programmes worth Rs 3 lakh crore are expected to get converted into orders for Indian industry. Over the next few years, significant opportunities will present themselves in programmes for new-build naval platforms (warships and submarines), refit of conventional submarines, artillery and air defence systems (guns and missiles), close-in weapons systems, military bridging systems, missile programmes, communications and fire control systems, and sub-systems for space launch vehicles.

The sheer breadth of its manufacturing facilities and its eclectic range of products place L&T at the cutting edge of Indian industry. Naik's strong nationalistic zeal has moulded L&T over the past two decades into a company with a sharp focus on developing new defence technologies. The Strategic Systems Complex in L&T's Talegaon facility is a state-of-the-art manufacturing unit for fabrication, modular assembly, integration and testing of weapon systems, sensors and military engineering systems. Having won the largest-ever armoured gun system programme in collaboration with its foreign technology partner, Hanwha Techwin, L&T is setting up a greenfield Armoured Systems Complex at Hazira. This is a first for an Indian private sector company. The complex will produce fully built armoured systems (tanks). This is where the K9 VAJRA-T, 155 mm/52 Cal self-propelled tracked guns will be made and supplied to the Indian Army. Except for gun firing, they will also be completely tested at Hazira.

Further afield, in the south, L&T's Precision Machining and Systems Complex in Coimbatore produces airframes, sub-systems and complex assemblies for missiles and space vehicles. The Strategic Electronics Centre in Bengaluru is a design, engineering and manufacturing facility for defence electronics systems for military communications, avionics, electronic warfare and special sensors. The centre has built the entire back-up-secured wireless communication network for the Indian Navy, with installations across thirty-two locations. The Technology Centre is making gen-next communication systems, building blocks such as high-capacity radio relays and field wireless systems. Also under development are Chemical Agent Monitors (CAM), co-developed in 50:50 participation with DRDO to warn infantry and armoured columns of chemical attacks. In competitive trials conducted recently, these monitors emerged as the best performing global CAMs. The centre is also developing stealth radar technology and a family of products in the form of Ground-Wall Penetrating Radars. The feeder facility co-located at government-designated sites builds special structures for integration into strategic submarines under the GOCO (Government Owned/Contractor Operated) model.

—∾—

THE TECHNOLOGICAL bandwidth of L&T's capabilities in defence equipment is unmatched in India. Spectrum Infotech, for example, is a wholly-owned subsidiary that undertakes technology development and manufactures avionics Line Replacement Units (LRUs) for military applications. It focuses on embedded solutions, control systems and signal-processing as well as the manufacture of defence avionics LRUs. Certified by the Centre for Military Airworthiness and Certification (CEMILAC) of the Ministry of Defence, it has played a key role in designing and developing integrated life support systems for the indigenously-built light combat aircraft (LCA) Tejas and ALH.

Since taking office in 2014, the NDA government has stressed that defence manufacturing is crucial to revitalizing the manufacturing sector and making India self-reliant in defence equipment. Naik estimates that defence will contribute Rs 10,000 crore to L&T's annual revenue by 2021.

The key products in L&T's arsenal are naval and land platforms, and weapon systems across naval platforms. The indigenous ASW Rocket Launcher (IRL), a ship-based anti-submarine rocket launcher system capable of firing twelve radially arranged, depth-charge rockets at submerged targets in both single and salvo mode and torpedo launch systems integrated with a sonar and fire control system, is an L&T offering that has drawn international attention.

—∾—

FOR LONG under-reported by the media, L&T has built landmark projects overseas. It has constructed hotels in Uzbekistan, infrastructure in Russia, a power plant in Sri Lanka, airports and metro networks in the Gulf, hospitals in Saudi Arabia and a bridge in Jordan, among a host of international projects. In 1976, L&T-ECC had made a strong global debut by winning the contract to build the new Abu Dhabi International Airport, which was designed by Aeroport de Paris. The project was awarded by the prime contractors—a joint venture of Takenaka Komuten Co. Ltd and Kumagai Gumi Co. Ltd. It was L&T-ECC's first major overseas project. It certainly wouldn't be its last. At 121 million dirhams (Rs 28 crore at the time), it was the single largest order the company had won till then. The project was completed successfully, and on time, giving the company an early international reputation for reliability.

In India, L&T's reputation for constructing compelling structures had already been established. One of the most architecturally innovative buildings in Mumbai is the Bombay Stock Exchange (BSE). The BSE building, a towering edifice, was constructed by L&T-ECC in phases. In March 1993, the city was hit by serial terror attacks. The BSE building suffered significant damage in one of the bomb blasts. The tower block of the building, however, was not harmed structurally because of its core strength. The responsibility of repairing the damaged portions was given to L&T-ECC.

The company has built several other landmark edifices over the decades. It constructed the Jawaharlal Nehru Stadium in Chennai, which accommodates 40,000 spectators. The structure was inaugurated in 1993. L&T won the Rs 400 crore project on a turnkey basis and completed it in 260 days. In 1994, the stadium was adjudged the 'Most Outstanding Concrete Structure in India' by the American Concrete Institute (Maharashtra–India Chapter). One of L&T's most evocative assignments was the Baha'i House of Worship in New Delhi. It is the seventh in a series of temples constructed around the world and has been designated the Mother Temple of the Indian subcontinent. The house of worship, which is in the form of a half-open lotus, attracts thousands of visitors every day. The structure's architect and project manager was Fariborz Sahba, an Iranian-American who shuttles between Canada and the US. L&T-ECC took up the project in 1980. The construction of this stunning temple, one of L&T's most complex projects, was completed in 1986.

Reliance Petroleum's refinery in Jamnagar, Gujarat, was another challenging assignment. The refinery is the largest single-stream grassroots refinery in the world, with a capacity of 1.24 million barrels per day. L&T's engineering and construction skills in multiple domains played a part in transforming Dhirubhai's audacious dream into reality. Civil projects too commanded L&T's interest. The Mumbai-Pune Expressway, India's first six-lane concrete, high-speed, access-controlled tolled expressway, was designed to ensure rapid traffic movement. The expressway was fully operationalized in 2002, reducing travel time between the two cities by an hour and a half.

In December 2016, the Gujarat Cricket Association (GCA) handed L&T the task of redeveloping the Sardar Patel Cricket Stadium in Ahmedabad. Strongly backed by Prime Minister Narendra Modi, the project involves the construction of the biggest stadium in the world at Motera, located in the city's Sabarmati area. Global architecture firm Populus, which designed the Melbourne Cricket Stadium, is the Motera stadium's principal architect and designer. The previous structure, with a capacity for 54,000 spectators, has been demolished. L&T has begun work on the new stadium, which will accommodate 110,000 spectators, surpassing the capacity of the Melbourne Cricket Ground (MCG), which can hold 100,024 spectators.

Naik is especially proud of L&T's fifty-year association with the Indian Space Research Organization (ISRO). On 15 February 2017, India became the only country to launch 104 satellites into space on a single rocket. This is the highest number of satellites launched in a single mission globally. It drew immediate comment in the US Congress and praise from around the world. ISRO's Polar Satellite

Launch Vehicle (PSLV) launched the satellites from the Satish Dhawan Space Centre in Sriharikota. L&T played a crucial role in this historic achievement. The company's aerospace business unit manufactured the S139 motor casings (middle segments) that were used for launching the PSLV-C37 into orbit.

L&T SHARPENED its focus on international markets, especially the Gulf, from 2010. Since then, from under one-tenth, international business now contributes around one-third to both order inflow and revenue. L&T has set up a full range of operations in the Middle East catering to the Gulf and North Africa. Many of the projects are being undertaken through joint ventures with leading companies based in the Gulf. Projects in the pipeline include hospitals, institutional spaces and commercial buildings. L&T has emerged as one of the leading builders of metro systems in the Gulf. It is building part of the Riyadh Metro and is working on phase one of the Doha Metro in Qatar.

L&T has carved a track record across geographies. It built the world's heaviest tubular reactor—1500 MT—in Hazira and shipped it to Kuwait, an order valued at $421 million. For Malaysia it has built the world's biggest multi-wall ammonia converter. L&T provides turnkey solutions across key regions: the Middle East (UAE, Qatar, Kuwait, Oman, Saudi Arabia and Bahrain), Africa (Algeria, Kenya, Ethiopia and Malawi) and ASEAN (Malaysia and Thailand). The range of work is wide and varied: high-voltage substations, power transmission lines, extra-high-voltage cabling, and instrumentation and control systems.

L&T's tower manufacturing facilities, with a capacity of 1,00,000 metric tonnes per annum, at Puducherry, Pithampur and Kancheepuram, service an order book that includes design and construction of substations for utilities in Qatar and Saudi Arabia and for private sector customers in the UAE. Africa is a promising growth area. Ethiopian Electric Power in Addis Ababa and substations in Malawi, funded by the US government from the Millennium Challenge Account, are already delivering results in East Africa.

The Power Transmission & Distribution business has erected more than 2,60,400 circuit kilometres of overhead transmission lines on an EPC basis, with voltage levels of up to 800 kV. Though water management is a comparatively new thrust area for the company, L&T has won prestigious orders in the Gulf. These range from a 375 MLD (million litres per day) sewage treatment plant at Jebel Ali, Dubai for the Dubai Municipality, to a water transmission line from Bawsheer to Seeb in Oman for the Sultanate's Public Authority for Electricity & Water.

Sohar in Oman is L&T's major manufacturing base in the Gulf Cooperation Council (GCC). This joint venture with The Zubair Corporation Oman manufactures equipment for the hydrocarbon and power sectors. The facility focuses on equipment for refineries, petrochemicals, fertilizer projects and other process industries. It has one of the largest open fabrication yards in the country.

The number of projects under way in the Gulf is impressive. L&T Hydrocarbon Engineering is executing Saudi Aramco's offshore facilities on an EPC basis in a consortium with EMAS AMC, Singapore. L&T Chiyoda and L&T-GULF provide engineering and consultancy services for onshore hydrocarbon plants and pipeline projects. L&T Arabia LLC in Al-Khobar, Saudi Arabia, undertakes Saudi Aramco's in-kingdom EPC projects. The company has executed projects for oil and gas majors, including Saudi Aramco, Petroleum Development Oman (PDO), Kuwait Oil Company and SABIC, among others.

L&T's relationship with Abu Dhabi has, meanwhile, grown stronger over the years. In 2013, L&T won a $320.16 million contract from Abu Dhabi Airports Company (ADAC). The scope of the project includes construction of taxiways, aircraft parking concrete hard stands at remote aprons and contact stands around the new midfield terminal building, a traffic tunnel within the airport infrastructure, an automated people-mover tunnel and various utility services, including a jet fuel network.

Continuing its run in the Gulf, L&T and its joint venture partner in Qatar, Al Balagh Trading & Contracting, won a $360 million contract for construction of a stadium that is part of Qatar's preparation for the 2022 Football World Cup—the first World Cup to be hosted in the Middle East. GCC countries now account for a significant portion of L&T's revenue.

As the domestic infrastructure project pipeline ebbs and flows, L&T continues to prosper, despite low oil prices, in the Gulf. L&T also built the new Salalah International Airport, alongside joint venture partner Galfar Engineering & Contracting under a $764 million contract. The airport opened in mid-2015; it can handle two million passengers a year. This could eventually be upgraded to six million passengers a year. L&T Oman has also won a $94 million contract to build an airport of a similar size as Sohar in Duqm city.

In a major breakthrough, L&T secured a $740 million order from Qatar Railways Company for design and construction of the Doha Metro project's Gold Line in Qatar. L&T won the order along with its joint venture partners Aktor-Greece, Yapi Merkezi Insaat-Turkey, STFA Group-Turkey and Al Jaber Engineering-Qatar. The total value of the order for the joint venture is $3.3 billion. The contract includes design and construction of twin tunnels and nine underground metro stations. Scheduled to be completed in fifty-four months, ahead of the football World Cup in Qatar in 2022, the project has been named among the key infrastructure projects in the Qatar National Vision 2030.

The largest overseas order won by L&T is in Saudi Arabia for a 41-km-long rail line that will involve driverless operation. The total value of the project, won in a consortium, is Rs 35,000 crore. The other companies in the consortium are Ansaldo STS, Italy, Bombardier Transportation, Impregilo, Italy, and Nesma & Partners, Saudi Arabia. L&T is involved in the design, construction and commissioning of the 41 km Line 3 of the metro project. L&T has also won a Rs 3,375 crore order for an integrated light rail system in the tropical island of Mauritius.

In India, meanwhile, L&T's new track construction machine has set a benchmark in high-speed rail building on the Western Dedicated Freight Corridor project. The machine can lay 2 km of track per day. L&T is executing a number of prestigious railway projects, both in India and the GCC region. It designs and constructs above-ground corridors, piers and complex superstructures, including underground corridors using sophisticated tunnelling techniques. L&T first ventured into metro rail construction in 2001 with the Delhi Metro project. Since 2001 it has emerged as the leading builder of metro systems in the country, executing nineteen ongoing projects, including the Hyderabad Metro.

Speed of execution defines L&T. In a short span, L&T has channelized a water and waste water network of 50,000 km and constructed and commissioned 4,000 mld of water and waste water treatment plants in India. L&T's water business is built on leveraging its construction and engineering capabilities. It deals with water and effluent treatment, water supply, distribution, conservation and re-use.

THOUGH HE was so very busy with his corporate responsibilities, Naik managed to find time to interact with students, something he greatly enjoyed. A two-time chairman of the Indian Institute of Management (IIM) Ahmedabad himself, Naik spoke eloquently at the forty-eighth annual convocation of India's leading business school on 23 March 2013:

> As I stand here at the first convocation as a Chairman of the IIM-A Board and Society, I feel proud and happy to be in front of some of the brightest young minds of India, graduating from a school that is at the leading edge of management learning in the

country. It is a special honour to have with us this evening the 'man of steel', Mr L.N. Mittal. As we know, we are facing a difficult economic environment, and all of us will need Mr Mittal's resolve of 'steel' to surmount the many challenges. Our chief guest is a true global Indian. If someone were to ask how successful Indian entrepreneurship can become in an international setting, we have only to look at Mr Mittal's rise to the helm of the world's largest steel and mining conglomerate. He is a multiple role model – as pioneer, leader and gamechanger. I thank you, Mr Mittal, for the interest you showed right from our first dialogue on this convocation. I am certain that our young minds will derive immense benefit and encouragement from your thoughts.

We are all aware that the world is passing through one of the most turbulent phases in history. These uncertainties are also reflected in the recruitment levels of IIM students in the current year. However, our own story is more heartening. The successful recruitment cycle of PGP, PGP-ABM students of our institute demonstrates the high calibre of our students and the impressive brand equity of IIM-Ahmedabad. But it is precisely in this negative environment that we need to stand firm against cynicism and despair. While we agree that the Indian economy is not decoupled from the world, choppy economic trends need not necessarily cause an adverse impact on India. There is a need to harness our inherent strengths in times of global uncertainty and capitalize on them. In fact, I have on several occasions spoken openly that if we only had our house in order, India would have been the largest beneficiary in the current global economic scenario as our country could have been the preferred destination for global investors.

It was Naikspeak at its bluntest. He delivered an upbeat message to the students about avoiding cynicism while upbraiding the government of the time for not putting India's 'house in order'.

A year later, in March 2014, Naik again spoke at the IIM-A convocation, this time with Anand Mahindra, chairman of the Mahindra group, as chief guest. He was optimistic about the global economy on the eve of what would prove a pivotal Lok

Sabha election that propelled Narendra Modi two months later to power. Naik said to IIM's graduating class of 2014: 'Looking at the world outside, the global economy has started showing signs of improvement. The latest indicators for the world economy suggest that after several years of extreme weakness, high-income economies appear to be finally turning the corner, contributing to a projected acceleration in global growth from 2.4 per cent in 2013 to 3.2 per cent this year. It is further expected to increase to 3.4 per cent in 2015, and 3.5 per cent in 2016.'

Underscoring further his reputation for farsightedness laced with earthiness, Naik shared his vision at L&T's annual general meeting on 26 August 2016. 'Building on our inherent strengths of engineering excellence, professionalism and financial prudence, a new L&T is emerging—one that is innovation-driven, agile and asset-light,' he declared.

Prime Minister Modi had kickstarted a slew of reforms in July 2014. The cap on foreign direct investment (FDI) in the insurance sector was raised from 26 per cent to 49 per cent. Within months, the government raised the FDI cap in the defence sector from 26 per cent to 49 per cent, albeit with a rider, that in joint ventures involved in manufacturing defence equipment, control will remain in the hands of the Indian partner. Through this move the government aimed to give a fillip to the domestic defence industry and reduce India's reliance on imports.

In addition, the Modi cabinet opened up railway infrastructure and permitted 100 per cent FDI in high-speed trains, suburban corridor projects through public-private partnership (PPP), rolling stock (including train sets and locomotives and coaches and their manufacturing and maintenance facilities), dedicated freight lines, railway electrification, signalling systems, and freight and passenger terminals. FDI was barred only in train operations.

These initiatives were part of the prime minister's broader 'Make in India' campaign. The objective was to encourage multinational and domestic companies to manufacture their products in India, spurring job creation. Twenty-five key sectors were identified, including automobiles, chemicals, information technology, pharmaceuticals, textiles, ports, aviation, leather, tourism and railways.

Naik was delighted with these moves. His mission to transform L&T into an Indian multinational dovetailed with the prime minister's own economic philosophy: India First. Modi's reform initiatives paid off. They helped the country attract record levels of foreign direct investment. In 2015, India replaced China as the world's leading destination for FDI. The majority of investments, though, went into services—computer software and hardware, trading, telecommunications, hospitality and e-commerce start-ups—rather than in the manufacturing sector. Consequently, the Department of Industrial Policy and Promotion (DIPP) decided to focus on a few crucial industries from the original list of twenty-five sectors in order to catalyse FDI in manufacturing.

The Modi government, in the fourth year of its five-year tenure, is keen to unlock more shackles. Among a slew of policy changes, several stand out. The Foreign Investment Promotion Board (FIPB) had clearly outlived its usefulness. In May 2017 it was abolished. Just as the Planning Commission had given way to NITI Aayog in the first year of Modi's prime ministership, the FIPB's abolition pointed to the Modi government's determination to remove hurdles in the way of doing business.

'Non-strategic sectors should be on automatic clearance,' said a senior government official to the *Economic Times*.[3] 'The multiple layers in clearance often lead to unnecessary delays.' The government official justified the decision to put more sectors on the automatic approval route, saying it would boost the larger economy. He added: 'Most sectors have automatic approval for investments up to 49 per cent. Government approval is required for investments in sectors such as telecom services, food products retailing, mining and minerals, multi-brand retail and private security agencies.'

---

[3] *The Economic Times*, 20 April 2017.

Meanwhile, India's biggest reform in decades, the Goods and Services Tax (GST), is set to impact nearly every aspect of business—logistics, pricing margins and working capital. It is expected to attract investments, lessen instances of tax evasion and trigger a new period of growth for the economy. While the extent of GST's success in India will depend on its efficient implementation, the new unified tax is a gamechanger. Economists estimate that GST will increase baseline GDP growth by 1-2 per cent a year in the medium term.

L&T, A CORPORATE proxy for the broader economy, is today India's largest engineering and technology firm and Asia's most valuable construction company. In 2015, the company was ranked amongst the top ten most valued brands in India by *Brand Finance*, an independent intangible asset valuation consultancy. L&T was the only player from the engineering and construction sector that made it to the list.

To improve its bottom line, however, L&T is attempting to cut costs in several areas. It has cut staff and overheads to tackle an increasingly competitive environment. Nevertheless, the company's enormous strengths in technologically complex project implementation across geographies remains unmatched. It was, after all, this capability in engineering and technology that had made it such an attractive target for India's two largest business houses led by the Ambanis and the Birlas.

In an interview with a business publication, Naik reflected on his corporate 'journey' with customary candour:

> I have always relished a challenge, right from my days on the shopfloor where I made a name for myself as a leader who could change things around, infuse vigour and galvanise the system. That reputation has stayed with me for more than five decades – so obviously, there must be some truth in it. I am impatient with the status quo. It doesn't get the adrenaline going. Transformation has been my mantra. When I took over as CEO in 1999, I drew up

> a roadmap for transforming L&T into a world-class conglomerate. The milestones along that journey were clear – I had to formulate a new vision for the organization, energise the team, engineer a strategic shift in business direction, rev up the innovation engines, drive internationalization and re-mould mindsets. And all this to be accomplished within an inelastic timetable!
>
> Disruptive thinking is a recent buzz word but I feel I have been a disruptor of the conventional long before the term entered the business lexicon. It is evident in almost everything I do and it is obvious in the company's current business mix. Today, a significant percentage of L&T's portfolio and a large share of its revenue come from new businesses – businesses that I identified, incubated and built to their potential. We are re-inventing ourselves on a virtually ongoing basis. My corporate journey has also involved hard work. My rigorous work schedule has remained virtually unchanged since the days when I was a twenty-year-old. People ask me what drives me to sustain this level of commitment at this stage, and the answer is simple: passion and devotion.

Naik relates a story of how his disciplinarian ways worked out well for his employees eventually: 'One day I went to Dubai, after some twenty years, and a lot of L&T people from faraway places drove to a town hall in Dubai for a get-together to honour me. There I met two workers. They both said, "You remember you sacked us. But had you not sacked us, we would not be where we are. Here if we do a little mischief or don't work for one hour, we are deported. Out! You taught us discipline and even when we lost our jobs we knew we were going to the Middle East so we didn't have hard feelings, but the fact that we are till today doing well here is due to the grounding you gave us."'

Naik is justly proud of his record at L&T over nearly fifty-three years. 'L&T has traditionally had four levels of leadership,' he says. 'Mine is the first level, which has now passed to Subrahmanyan. Directors form the second level. ICs are the third level. And SBUs are the fourth level. Four levels of diversity: they are not aligned to one another. This structure does not exist anywhere else in the world, and I am saying that without exaggeration. It can be independently checked with McKinsey, BCG, Bain—all the top consultancy firms worldwide. I once asked them, you show me one example of such a structure worldwide. But not one of them has!'

Naik adds quietly: 'I am very proud of being an Indian. I go around with my Indian flag all over the world. That reminds me of my duty to the nation at every moment. You build your company strong, you build your nation strong. At the same time, the satisfaction you will get by doing that—you will have a great sense of individual fulfilment that money cannot buy. That, I think, has been my life. And I will cherish every moment of that till the end of my life.'

In April 2017, *Outlook* magazine placed Naik among India's fifty 'greatest CEOs'. It wrote: 'An engineering graduate of Birla Vishwakarma Mahavidyalaya, Gujarat, Naik is an exemplar of vision and confidence. He was determined to push ahead with indigenization of the manufacture of critical equipment for the defence sector and process industries.'

The passion to build a strong India has driven Naik through a remarkable career, with its share of triumphs as well as trials and tribulations. But even as he contemplates a lighter workload after October 2017, Naik's mind ticks over with ideas for L&T: 'In future, we should get out of small businesses. They take away a lot of attention. Profits are not high so we would not be losing much. It does not make a significant impact on the overall profitability of the company but does divert attention which should be focused on our bigger businesses that make more money. Around nine-ten businesses will have to go. So a few companies will go from the twenty-one we have today. We would like to have ten companies in all, but that will be in Lakshya 4—2021 onwards. What businesses we are planning now should become big enough for us to be able to remove (from the L&T fold) not only a Rs 2,000 crore business, but even a Rs 5,000 crore business.'

In an interview with *Business Standard,* Naik took stock of his fifty-three transformative years at L&T, analysing both gains and losses: 'The biggest gain is that from zero we (employees) became owners of the company. There is no precedent to this and perhaps there would not be any. This would be my biggest legacy.' He was candid, though: 'We over-indulged in development projects like roads and power which are highly capital intensive and possibly, if I was to rethink, I may not do it today.'

As he moves to a new phase in his extraordinary career in L&T, Naik will also spend more time on what he possibly cherishes the most: family and philanthropy.

12

The Silent Philanthropist

NAIK TAKES PRIDE in his humble beginnings. When peers ask him, 'So, are you from Wharton or Harvard?', Naik's answer is an unequivocal 'no'. If they assume he must be from one of the IITs, he is at pains to correct them and speaks with pride of his modest learning ground—the Gujarati-medium school in a village where he learnt valuable life lessons, sitting on an untiled earthen floor. His school in Kharel village was among the first schools opened in a south Gujarat village after Independence.

Mahatma Gandhi said: 'When you invest in education, you invest in the country's future.' That philosophy has guided three generations of the Naik family: Nichchhabhai, Manibhai, and now, Anil Naik. Naik's charitable contributions to education, healthcare and community service, especially in rural south Gujarat, have been among the largest philanthropic endeavours in the region. He has over the past decade donated generously from his personal funds to building schools, hospitals and advanced diagnostic centres in the region. Additionally, Naik has donated fund to various trusts, institutions, local village *mandals* and temples before he created his own family trusts. He says you cannot put a price tag to philanthropy.

Jayantilal Bavabhai (J.B.) Desai is an L&T veteran. Just past seventy, Desai looks after Naik's trusts and enjoys the chairman's confidence. 'He is my guru, my *gurudev*,' says Desai. 'I have not only learnt from him in the past, but even today I learn from him. So I am his *shishya* and at the same time I am his *bhakta* too.'

Desai joined L&T in July 1970 as a twenty-three-year-old junior engineer. Naik, twenty-eight, then a rising engineer himself, selected him from the same college he had attended. Desai recalls: 'I completed my mechanical engineering and I was to go to the US. I got admission there but after I spoke to Mr Naik I opted to stay back and join L&T. No regrets. There's so much that I've learnt from L&T and Naik *saab*; I am happy I stayed back.'

He knew Naik's father, Manibhai, or Bapujee, as Desai refers to him, well. After Bapujee passed away in March 1997, Desai began looking after the family's trusts and its widening range of philanthropic activity: 'I was encouraged by whatever Bapujee had done for the villagers and for his students, so I decided to write a book about it – *Prapanch No Padkar* – with the help of Dr Lalitaben Shah, Bapujee's sister. The book covers the life of Bapujee, the great work he did, and how he helped village schools bring about a social transformation in the rural districts of south Gujarat. It was published on the first *punya tithi* – death anniversary – of Bapujee – at the hand of Maniba.' The book was well received and it led to more such publications and articles in leading Gujarati magazines.

Naik has two personal trusts: the Naik Charitable Trust, which looks after education, community service and development, and the Nirali Memorial Medical Trust, which is engaged in healthcare. He is also the chairman and managing trustee of the Kharel Education Trust and the Kharel Vibhag Samaj Seva Trust.

Desai looks after Naik's personal trusts. 'Nirali Memorial Medical Trust caters to the needs of society. It was started in 2009,' says Desai. 'Naik Charitable Trust's activities are focused, as I said, on education, skill development and social upliftment.' Naik also looks after the L&T Employees Welfare Foundation, besides his own trusts, and the company's own trusts and CSR activities too.

The A.M. Naik Charitable Healthcare Facility in Powai, inaugurated on 9 June 2017—his seventy-fifth birthday—is an impressive structure with state-of-the art medical equipment. It was built under the aegis of the Nirali Memorial Medical Trust. When Naik laid the healthcare facility's foundation stone, he said: 'I consider myself fortunate to be in a position to give back to society in general, and particularly to my *karmabhoomi* – Powai. If I can, in some measure, help to relieve pain, alleviate suffering and provide care to those most in need, my efforts would be richly rewarded.'

The facility at Powai is easily accessible from the western and eastern suburbs in Mumbai, and_caters specifically to the underprivileged. It has three operation theatres for general surgery, gynaecology, obstetrics, orthopaedics and ENT. It also has ophthalmology and dialysis units, and pathological and investigative diagnostics, along with systems for sonography and ECG/EED/TMT. A crèche and vocational training facility for the youth, a library for senior citizens, a meditation centre and a ladies club at the facility underscore the attention to detail that is the hallmark of Naik's initiatives—whether in corporate projects or charity.

NAIK WAS an early proponent of philanthropy. In 1995, he donated funds to Kharel hospital to construct an additional floor in grandfather Nichchhabhai's name. Apart from the hospital's expansion, a colony was built for the staff. It was named Geeta Gram after Naik's wife, Geetaben. The Nichchhabhai Ratanji Naik Wing of Kharel hospital belongs to the Kharel Vibhag Samaj Seva Trust. It is managed by the Gram Seva Trust—an operating trust comprising doctors and professionals.

Later, Naik developed a 25-acre area around Kharel and set up a clutch of schools, hostels, a housing complex and a vocational training complex. Naik says he continued giving charitable donations on an ad hoc basis until 2009. After that his personal funds were routed through the private family trusts. 'I wanted everything given through my trusts,' says Naik. 'Otherwise I was donating to someone else's trusts, organizations and village *mandals*.'

Naik is today one of corporate India's most generous philanthropists. Few have given as much of their personal wealth to charity as he has. He has publicly pledged to donate 75 per cent of his income in his lifetime. Fostering a culture of giving, he has prompted senior executives to fund the L&T Public Charitable Trust. L&T's own CSR activities are also widespread, and amount to around 2 per cent of its net profit—a figure few other companies have attained.

For all his ceaseless global travel, Naik remains firmly rooted in the soil of south Gujarat that moulded his character. Among his first phone calls after being appointed managing director and CEO of L&T were those to J.B. Desai, a confidant of over forty years who has managed the school and hospital Naik built in Endhal village, to his maternal uncle at Samarawadi and to the village elders of Kharel village.

Over the years, Naik has helped develop the Chikhli-Gandevi-Kharel areas on NH8, where his father had lived and worked for years. His father remains the biggest influence on Naik. Education lies at the heart of Naik's philanthropy. Like his father, Naik plans to immerse himself even more deeply in educational and healthcare philanthropy in the future. Naik has built a primary school in Endhal, a higher secondary school and junior college in Kharel, and a vocational training institute for school dropouts. He developed the village dispensary into a multi-disciplinary hospital with modern equipment.

Father Manibhai's attachment to Kharel has rubbed off on Naik. Manibhai would often implore Anil to do something about the state of the village hospital. He said if Anil could arrange funds from various people or institutions it would be an important contribution to the villagers' welfare. The hospital had a shortage of space for beds. The major part of the building was used to house doctors.

Naik, despite his limited resources at the time, donated Rs 4 lakh, which amounted to his entire bank balance plus his Provident Fund. Principled as ever, Manibhai sought to know how his son had come by the money for, even in matters of charity, everything had to be above board. Young Anil had to produce bank passbooks to prove to his father that the money was indeed legitimately earned. It was only then that Manibhai smiled, and said, 'Son, I am proud of you.'

In 1997, when the Kharel Education Trust, led by the late Haribhai Bhimbhai Naik, approached Naik to join the society that had been revived by his father, he could not refuse. With his mother's active consent, Naik became president of the society. Not a man to remain passive for long, he took up the challenge of giving the society new direction. Among the first tasks he undertook was revamping the higher secondary school in Kharel and adding a girls' hostel.

The higher secondary school and junior college building—Manibhai Nichchhabhai Naik Uchchtar Madhyamik School—named after Anil Naik's father, and a girls' hostel, Kashibaa Bhuvan, named after his grandmother, were completed in 2000. They have some of the best facilities in the form of biology, chemistry and physics labs, a special IT computer room, a commodious staff room, a library and a new office for the principal and staff. Within a couple of years, a girls' hostel and another for boys—Maniba Bhuvan—and accommodation for doctors and paramedical staff, Geeta Gram, were completed and handed over to the society.

SURAT, NAIK'S birthplace, holds a special place in his heart. Says Desai: 'There was no radiation centre between Vadodara and Mumbai. That's how the local trustees came together and said they wanted to build a radiation centre in Surat. Mr Naik generously agreed. Then it came down to locating the land and developing it. Mr Naik took care of everything—including approvals from municipal authorities and other government bodies like the PWD, water department, etc. He took it up as a project, and whatever was needed to be done was done. The machines were expensive. Add to that the CT scan, the Brachy Therapy unit and laboratory equipment, and the oncology department, and the total cost rises even higher. To install the machine we needed a two-and-a-half-metre-width RCC wall to protect the surroundings from radiation hazards. The radiation results have to be approved by the Bhabha Atomic Research Centre (BARC), then comes the civil work, the building, the beautification and interiors.'

The Nirali Memorial Radiation Centre in Surat was set up by the Nirali Memorial Medical Trust jointly with Bharat Cancer Hospital & Research Centre. The centre is managed by Bharatimaiya Memorial Foundation. At Nirali Memorial Medical Centre, an average of 100 treatments are conducted every month. The doctors work in multiple shifts. A waiting list of 30-35 patients (occasionally going up to 50-60) has reinforced the need for a second radiation machine. Internal accruals from the existing centre will fund over half the cost of the new state-of-the-art machine.

The radiation centre in Surat, the only one of its kind in the Valsad region, will also help patients from south Gujarat and even parts of north Gujarat and Maharashtra. The Surat centre already treats people from contiguous states. Recruiting doctors for work in Valsad and other areas, though, is not easy. 'We are working on creating one more set of doctors and nurses for Valsad,' says Naik. 'We will give them quarters, senior doctors will get a bungalow, the chief medical officer will get a four-bedroom bungalow. Everything will be there.'

The centre in Surat is equipped with state-of-art systems, including an advanced radiation machine. Actual measurement readings of radiation levels are far below the acceptable limits set by BARC and the Atomic Energy Regulatory Board (AERB). Since many patients come from outside Surat, the centre offers accommodation for family members. Naik wants to set up a fully equipped cancer cure centre in either Valsad or further north, in Navsari. Search for land in these areas is on. Naik, meanwhile, hasn't forgotten his roots.

He is building an old age home in Kharel. Set to be ready in 2018, the old age home will be built on three acres of land.

More is being done on the education front. As the Naik Charitable Trust puts it, 'The Geeta Vaidik Gram at Magod in the Valsad district of Gujarat is a major step towards facilitating value-based education and revitalizing India's cultural heritage. It flows from the belief of the Trust that strong roots are vital for a vibrant, progressive and wholesome society. The Trust sees merit and value in the educational objectives of the Shree Muktananda Sanskrit Mahavidyalaya (SMSV), that is:

- Make educational accessible to India's economically challenged.
- Establish institutions for education and research that will interpret the profound knowledge of vedic scriptures to contemporary needs and contexts.
- Promote the use of such knowledge to create a society in which the values implicit in 'Satyam Shivam Sundaram' (that which is true is auspicious and is beautiful) remain foremost in thought and action.

Gurukul schools lie at the centre of Naik's vision for preserving India's rich traditions of vedic teaching. The Naik Charitable Trust has helped Shri Muktananda Sanskrit Mahavidyalaya, a traditional Vedic school, to expand its facilities at Magod, Gujarat. The Trust has built apartments to accommodate teachers (*acharyas*) and a hostel for students (*chhatralayas*).

According to the Trust, the Kharel Education Society has also set up a number of institutes to promote education in three talukas of south Gujarat—Navsari, Chikhli and Gandevi. In addition to modern educational facilities, the Maninagar Campus provides accommodation to girl students. It is one of the few campuses in the region offering accommodation to girls in the secondary and higher secondary sections. This facility motivates parents to allow their daughters to pursue education.

Both the Naik family trusts, under the direction of Naik, have raised education levels in the interior villages. Around forty-one schools in many villages around Kharel have been adopted to provide them better and improved facilities. A mobile van donated by the Naik family and operated by the Agastya Foundation, Bengaluru, adopts innovative methods for teaching subjects like physics, chemistry, biology, math and geography to help disadvantaged village students. Structured 'health check-up' programmes are also a boon for the villagers. A new dimension has been added at Kharel with the Urmi Science Centre.

When it came to choosing marriage alliances for his children too, it was the educational background of the families that weighed with the Naiks, who are both open-minded, progressive individuals. His daughter and son are married to children of educationists.

NAIK, AT seventy-five, shows little signs of slowing down. His schedule may no longer be as punishing as it used to be for over fifty years when he routinely worked sixteen-hour days, seven days a week, with no Sundays off and no vacations. The tempo has moderated, but Naik still wakes up at 6.45 a.m. He's in office by 9.00 a.m. He still puts in nine hours of work a day. And he still works on Saturdays up to 3.00 p.m. and on some Sundays too.

'There were days in the 1960s when I did not sleep at all,' he says, laconically. 'I was staying in Andheri West in a one-room kitchen flat and used to reach L&T's Powai office by bus. That bus would start from Andheri East and head towards Powai. I used to cross the railway bridge from west to east. From my house to the bus stop on foot took me fifteen minutes, then again around fifteen, maximum twenty, minutes by bus to reach Powai. So the total time taken would be around thirty-five minutes. This went on for two years, after which I got a Vespa scooter. Then, after another one and a half years, I was given an Ambassador car by the company.'

Naik suffers from sleep apnea and uses a machine to aid breathing. 'I sleep for four hours, then wake up, then again sleep for another three to four hours.' That hasn't dampened his spirits or his love for life. Naik's favourite foods hark back to his native Gujarat: dhokla and khakra. He loves sweets too: 'That is how I got diabetes,' he laments. He continues to take three insulin injections a day. Naik has a stent and a pacemaker, signposts of a life led in the corporate fast lane.

Wife Geetaben, a calm presence in the Naik home, says: 'He spent sixteen hours in office, so there wasn't much time at home! But when it came to admission for the children in school or college, he was always present. He would treat that also as a project, so it had to be fulfilled!'

Naik interjects with a smile: 'The first project was my son, Jignesh, when the Nav Nirman agitation in Gujarat took place. He was studying at Vallabh Vidyanagar. Jignesh began studying electronics engineering, but he studied only up to two years. There was again a major agitation over the Mandal Commission and the college was closed for five months.'

Naik's famed bull-terrier approach took over. 'We collected all of Jignesh's certificates and applied to 130 US colleges, shortlisted five good ones and finally got him into a top-ten college, GeorgiaTech. It gave him 150 credit hours instead of 100 because I managed to get the credit hours presented in a way that the college gave credits even for Gujarati! GeorgiaTech sent the papers back to us, saying we cannot understand these papers so we cannot give the credit hours. I went to the American university's offices and talked to them and sorted it out, helping my son gain credit hours for his studies in India. Jignesh joined GeorgiaTech in 1990. He was there for three years, two years for his BS degree, one year for his MS. He went to the US at the age of nineteen, and at twenty-two he was through with his studies. Jignesh then joined Arthur Andersen Consulting and later started his own company, along with others. It was the dot-com era, and things did not work out so they shut it down. Jignesh then joined Google, and ever since he's been in its infrastructure department.'

Geetaben adds: 'My daughter, Pratiksha, was born in 1966. She is five years older than Jignesh. Pratiksha got her MD from Ahmedabad. In 1997 she went to America when she was around twenty-nine, and later married Mukulbhai Shah.' Geetaben says Naik is a loving father and has a kind heart. Whenever required he would help the children patiently and advise them. 'He would always remember his father,' she says. 'The children have also seen and been with their grandparents as they were living with us for twelve years. My daughter was nine and my son four years old at that time.'

NAIK PERFORMS puja every morning before work. At the temple in his spacious house, he prays for ten minutes in front of a framed photograph of his father and mother. Geetaben smiles as she recalls how they got married: 'We were married on 14 May 1964. Ours is both a love and arranged marriage. He is related to my *mama*'s family so we knew each other. My *mama* sent a proposal to my father for him. My *mama*'s son and he came along to meet me. My father also liked him. He was twenty-one years and eleven months old when we got married. I was seventeen years and four months old! We got married in Haria village in Valsad. It was a simple wedding. For quite a long time we had no house, so after getting married we went to the Kandivali sanatorium. Then for a month he stayed in my house in Malad. So for six months we stayed outside, and then finally our house got ready. We were in our Andheri flat from 1964 to 1968. We then shifted to Vile Parle, stayed there till 1975, and then came to live in this bungalow in Bandra over forty years ago.'

Naik chips in, precise as ever and setting the record straight. 'In Mumbai, before marriage, I had three homes. To begin with, I came from the village and stayed with my sister for one month, then got a job. Meanwhile, someone from our village staying in suburban

Matunga had a locked house, so I approached him and he gave me the key and I stayed alone in that house. Before that I stayed for a month and a half in Grant Road at the house of the sister of a very close friend. There were four of us, and we all stayed together like college students.'

Naik's home since 1975 has been a bungalow, High Trees, surrounded by greenery. As we walk into the large, aesthetically but simply furnished home, Naik changes from his formal office suit and tie into a T-shirt. Geetaben is a quiet but smiling presence. There is an affectionate bond between the couple, now married for over fifty-three years.

The Gujarati publication *Ujas* dwelt at length on the Naiks' close family bonds:

> During the final days of his father, Manibhai, Anilbhai had brought both his parents to Mumbai. He had made all arrangements for their comfortable stay, with modern facilities, including a chauffeur-driven car. It was obvious that Anilbhai could not meet them on a daily basis because of his busy schedule. In such circumstances Geetaben proved to be a strong link between Anilbhai and his parents. She used to take complete care of Manibhai and Manibaa. When they wished to go to their village during vacations, Geetaben would oversee all arrangements of opening up the village home, getting it cleaned up, purchasing the necessary provisions and making travel arrangements. Vacations used to provide Manibhai an opportunity to refresh his village memories. He and his wife used to spend summer in their native place and return to Mumbai with the onset of the monsoon. This trend continued for some years. During his stay at Endhal village, Manibhai also looked after the management and arrangements of the family's farm and its produce.
>
> Right from her childhood, Anilbhai's daughter, Pratiksha, was greatly influenced by her aunt who was the first doctor in the Anavil community and had settled in Ahmedabad. Thus Pratiksha had always dreamt of becoming a doctor and realized her dream by becoming a child specialist from Mumbai University. Anilbhai's

guidance, *samskaras* of the grandparents and Geetaben's support proved very helpful in achieving this success.

The Naiks celebrated their fiftieth wedding anniversary with family and friends in May 2014 at functions in India and Kentucky in the US. On the occasion, Jignesh's wife Rucha, a gifted artist, surprised her in-laws with a warm portrait. Naik's family is spread globally. A nephew, the son of his second sister, the late Pushpaben, lives with his family in Kuwait and another nephew lives in Australia. His oldest sister, Urmilaben, and her husband live with their son in Florida, USA, and their three daughters are settled in the US. Daughter Pratiksha visits India twice a year and the Naiks visit their son and daughter in the US twice as well.

TRAGEDY STRUCK the Naik family in 2006. The memories of those traumatic days bring the couple to tears. Geetaben is the first to speak: 'The cancer was detected when our granddaughter, Nirali, was one year and nine months old.'

As she turns emotional, Naik steps in: 'Everyone said my granddaughter, Nirali, took after me.' He struggles to narrate a story that is the worst nightmare of every parent or grandparent: the tragic death of a child.

Nirali was born on 3 February 2005. She was Jignesh's first child, but the Naiks' third grandchild after daughter Pratiksha's two children. Nirali was a seemingly healthy and cheerful baby. But when she was sixteen months old, her parents noticed a red rash on her legs. Doctors said it was an allergy and there was nothing to worry about. But the rash persisted. When a fresh diagnosis came, it was devastating: little Nirali had a rare form of blood cancer.

Naik remembers the day he received a call from son Jignesh as if it were yesterday. With the diagnosis of a rare form of cancer confirmed, Naik flew to America. There he began a campaign to search for a matching bone marrow transplant that could have saved

Nirali's life. The Swaminarayan Sampraday swung into action. Over 6,000 people volunteered. Not one bone marrow, though, matched Nirali's. Tragically, just a month before she died, one donor's bone marrow turned out to be a perfect match. It was too late. The cancer had spread too far, too fast.

The Naiks tried every treatment, including chemotherapy. Nirali's condition, however, worsened. At times the pain she suffered was unbearable. Nirali died on 27 April 2007. She was just two years and two months old.

Geetaben fights back her tears as she says: 'Nirali was not even identifiable at the time of her death. She was a very beautiful baby and very intelligent too. It was very painful for her. For us to watch her suffering was unbearable. We did chemotherapy, a bone marrow transplant, everything.'

Eyes moist, Naik adds: 'I did a worldwide campaign for her. Thousands of people enrolled to help. There was a volunteer from each centre of Pramukh Swaminath. Everyone used to say she is just like me, her grandfather, and she will look after her grandfather's properties. No one in our family has been able to recover from this tragedy. My son decided not to have a second child. In my room there are two photos: one of my granddaughter, Nirali, and the other of my father sitting in a chair and I standing behind him.'

NIRALI'S DEATH changed the Naik family in an undefinable way. Naik himself redoubled his work in medical philanthropy, setting up a world-class radiation diagnostic centre and hospital. Jignesh, though, withdrew into a shell from which, a decade later, he has only now begun to emerge.

Naik's daughter, Pratiksha, has two daughters—Riya and Sharini—and is close to her brother Jignesh. 'My son always wanted to come back,' says Naik. 'But then came a period after Nirali's passing when he decided he did not want to come back to India. My daughter and son-in-law, Mukul, a senior paediatric specialist, have decided they never want to come back to India. But my son, I feel, may one day come back. When I am no more, he will not leave his mother alone. My son has changed dramatically in recent years. Previously I was so busy, I hardly talked to him. Now I talk to him often, and he too asks me about my health. The last time when he came to India some months ago, he said he will come thrice a year in future and so will his wife, and each time stay for ten days.'

Despite his 24x7 schedule, Naik manages to take out time for the family. His niece, Preeti, says with a smile: 'We all know how busy he is, but he still squeezes out time for all of us. He always attends each and every family function because he loves to spend time with the family and tries not to miss any get-together. He inquires about our well-being, guides us, talks on current topics, politics, etc., and makes us feel cheerful.'

IF NAIK had to choose his life and career again, what changes would he like to make? 'In the early days I did not take even one day's leave,' he says. 'I feel that was not right. Taking at least fifteen days off every year would have made me fresher, given time to me and my family. My health would have been better. I should have been more attached to my son, my daughter, my wife. I gave all my devotion to L&T. It is like my temple, and I forgot that there is another part of my life. You have to be devoted but also create a balance with your family. I could have done much better in that respect.'

Was Naik a caring husband? Geetaben smiles shyly. Naik chuckles: 'Once I was in Germany and she was passing through Paris. The Air India flight had a technical problem and she was stuck. So I was constantly calling her till I could track her down as there were no mobile phones at that time. I went through a one-day torture to ensure she was safe!'

Geetaben laughs: 'When he shows his love and care, he does not even look at the time. These small gestures show his genuine caring.'

Geetaben recalls Naik's standing instructions early in his career: if he was not home by midnight, he would come home only in the morning. She says that from the first day of her marriage to Anil in 1964, she understood that L&T was his first love and that she would have to make room for his professional ambitions to make a success of her marriage. She quickly learnt the art of spending quality time with Anil, taking over the running of the house and supervising the children's school and extra-curricular activities.

Geetaben is deeply involved with the family charities. 'Whatever we do, we do together,' she says. Naik chips in: 'If the trusts are there today, a big part of the credit goes to her. There are some who would say, why are you giving so much of your time and money to charity. But she has never said a word about it and in fact has been very supportive.'

And then, with a twinkle in his eye, Naik adds: 'When she was young she was very good looking, like wow!'

Geetaben smiles indulgently. For all his achievements, Anil Naik retains the affection, kindness, humour and humility he absorbed from the man he reveres above all else: his father, Manibhai Nichchhabhai Naik.

Index

Acknowledgements

WRITING A BOOK on a company of the complexity of Larsen & Toubro—led by a chairman of Anil Naik's vision—would not have been possible without the unstinting support of a large number of individuals.

Mr Naik himself was a storehouse of information. Articulate, clear-headed and precise, he led me expertly through the extraordinary, and often tumultuous, seventy-five years of his life and work. During the nearly dozen conversations we had at his office and home, he displayed flashes of humour that belied his reputation of being an intimidating boss. Beneath the tough exterior resides a warm, good-hearted man, without any trace of pretension or hubris, despite possessing a formidable intellect.

My thanks too to his wife, Geetaben Naik, whose quiet and smiling presence has been a source of strength to her husband for over half-a-century. Geetaben provided me a unique insight into Anilbhai's personality that few outside his family are fully aware of.

I'm especially grateful to the directors and senior executives at L&T, past and present, for their time and the valuable perspectives they provided on Mr Naik's management style. In particular, I enjoyed my interactions with Mr Srinivas Rajgopal, Vijay Kumar Magapu, K. Venkataramanan, N.M. Desai, Shailendra Roy,

Shrikant Joshi, Ramnath Mukhija, Pathik Kothari, J.B. Desai, J.D. Patil, J.P. Nayak and Yogi Sriram and many others. They helped me decode a multi-dimensional personality.

A special note of thanks to S.N. Subrahmanyan who succeeded Mr Naik as CEO and managing director. He gave generously of his time in Chennai and Mumbai to speak about his vision for L&T's future even as he is still settling into the corner office at the company's Mumbai headquarters.

Visiting L&T's high-technology manufacturing complex at Hazira near Surat, I was impressed by the boundless enthusiasm of Y.S. Trivedi and his team and, in Vadodara's Knowledge City, by K. Ravindranath, Ashok Monga and (in Ranoli) Mukesh Makwana, all of whom provided important information and context.

I must express my gratitude to the indefatigable Vinod Chacko in Chennai and to Admiral B. Kannan, Admiral J.S. Mann and Rajendran Urikouth at the sprawling Kattupalli shipyard, an hour's drive from Chennai, for their time and insights.

In Chennai, S. Gurumurthy too provided an outsider's perspective of Mr Naik, especially about his innovative financial engineering that gave the L&T's Employees Welfare Foundation a 15 per cent shareholding in the company to protect it from future hostile takeovers.

Last but certainly not the least is the cooperation I received during this complex assignment from Manish Kalghatgi, L&T's brand and marketing head, and Jairam Menon, the company's longtime wordsmith. My thanks to both for their invaluable help.

My gratitude as well to members of my research team for the exceptional work they did to collate the wealth of information on L&T, to Rukshana Kumar for her professionalism and diligence and, above all, to my editor Krishan Chopra at HarperCollins India for his patience and guidance.

Finally, my grateful thanks to my family, especially to my wife, Kahini, for being a pillar of support during the long hours, days and months that I spent researching and writing this book.

About the Author

MINHAZ MERCHANT is the biographer of former Prime Minister Rajiv Gandhi and the late industrialist Aditya Birla. He founded the pioneering media firm Sterling Newspapers Pvt. Ltd, which was later acquired by the *Indian Express* group.

A widely published newspaper columnist, Minhaz's book, *The New Clash of Civilizations: How the Contest between America, China, India and Islam Will Shape Our Century*, was published in 2014.

Recipient of the Lady Jeejeebhoy scholarship for physics, Minhaz lives in Mumbai with his wife Kahini. The couple have two children, Suhail and Tehzeeb.